Institutions and Monetary Policy

To my parents

Institutions and Monetary Policy

Credibility, Flexibility and Central Bank Independence

Eric Schaling

Bank of England
UK

Edward Elgar

Published by
Edward Elgar Publishing Limited
Gower House
Croft Road
Aldershot
Hants GU11 3HR
UK

Edward Elgar Publishing Company
Old Post Road
Brookfield
Vermont 05036
US

British Library Cataloguing in Publication Data
Schaling, Eric
Institutions and Monetary Policy:
Credibility, Flexibility and Central
Bank Independence
I. Title
332.46

Library of Congress Cataloguing in Publication Data
Schaling, Eric, 1962–
Institutions and monetary policy: credibility, flexibility, and central bank independence / Eric Schaling.
Includes bibliographical references.
1. Monetary policy—Case studies. 2. Financial institutions—Case studies. 3. Banks and banking, Central—Case studies. 4. Banks and banking, Central—Law and legislation—Case studies. I. Title.
HG230.3.S3 1995
332.4'6—dc20 95–10757
CIP

ISBN 1 85898 162 X

Printed and bound in Great Britain by
Hartnolls Limited, Bodmin, Cornwall

Contents

Figures

Tables

Acknowledgements

This book is the result of the Ph.D. research project 'Rules versus Discretion in the Conduct of Short-term Macroeconomic Stabilisation Policies under Uncertainty'. It was carried out at Tilburg University and CentER with financial support from the Netherlands Organization for Scientific Research (NWO).

At the cradle of this project stood Theo van de Klundert, who conceived the subject of this study. I am very grateful to him for supervising my thesis and for his trust in my abilities. His views on macroeconomics and model building have influenced me considerably. Together with his humour and wit made working with him a time I will cherish.

Fairly soon research began to develop in the direction of central bank independence. At this stage Sylvester Eijffinger joined the project as a supervisor. Together we developed a taste for the application of ideas to practical policy. Sylvester co-authored the papers underlying Chapters 3 and 4. I am very grateful for his never ending support and persistent interest, but most of all for his friendship.

Tilburg University proved an excellent research environment. George Alogoskoufis' visit to CentER inspired me to write Chapter 5. Lans Bovenberg, Matthew Canzoneri, Rob de Groof, Rick van der Ploeg and Martin van Tuijl made detailed comments on this chapter. Harry Huizinga commented on Chapter 4. Work with David Smyth at CentER underlies Chapter 6. Valuable comments on this chapter were made by Andrew Mountford. Discussions with Norbert Funke improved Chapter 7. Alex Cukierman made some suggestions regarding Chapters 2 and 7. Comments by Kevin Dowd influenced the organisation of the book.

The results of this study were presented at several seminars and conferences. I have benefitted from the insights of seminar participants at the Bank of England and attendants at the seventeenth SUERF Colloquium. Useful comments were made by delegates at the 1991, 1993 and 1994 Annual Conference of the European Economic Association, the 1993 European Meeting of the Econometric Society and the 1994 Annual Conference of the Royal Economic Society. Of course, the views expressed in the book are those of the author and not necessarily those of the Bank of England.

Some of the material appearing in Chapters 3 and 4 has been adapted from articles that originally appeared in *Banca Nazionale del Lavoro Quarterly Review* and *Kredit und Kapital*.

Tilburg University provided ample secretarial assistance. I am particularly grateful to Nicole Hultermans for doing a splendid desk top publishing job. Bas van Aarle and Marco Hoeberichts helped me with the figures. Geert Almekinders proved a great colleague.

Finally, I should like to express my special gratitude to Nico van Dam; my brother, my sister and Francien Buylinckx for their support.

1. Introduction

Recently, in many countries both political and monetary authorities have shown an increasing interest in the objective of monetary stability and the position of the central bank.[1] As pointed out by Persson and Tabellini (1993) recent policy reform, as well as historical experience, suggests two different routes to price stability.

The first route is the *legislative* approach, namely to create by law a very independent central bank with an unequivocal mandate to focus on price stability. Interest in this approach is motivated by the success of the Deutsche Bundesbank in maintaining one of the lowest rates of inflation for several decades. The accepted statutes of the European Central Bank are strongly influenced by the German central bank law. Broadly speaking, they guarantee a central bank as independent from national and European political institutions as the Bundesbank. Moreover, France and Spain reformed their central bank laws in order to make the Banque de France and the Banco de España more independent of government. Furthermore, countries in Central and Eastern Europe, such as the Czech republic, Hungary and Poland increased the independence of their central banks.[2] Finally, in Latin America there are tendencies toward granting more independence to the central banks in countries like Argentina, Chile, Mexico and Venezuela.

The second route is the *targeting* approach, namely to let the political principal of the central bank impose an explicit inflation target for monetary policy, and make the central bank governor explicitly accountable for his success in meeting this target. Recently New Zealand, Canada, and the United Kingdom have made some progress on this route. Along these lines New Zealand enacted legislation that increased the independence of its Reserve Bank, while in the United Kingdom there is now a lively discussion of the desirability of making the Bank of England more independent.[3]

The theoretical rationale for central bank independence finds its origin in the ongoing 'rules versus discretion' debate; especially in the monetary policy credibility literature. This literature argues that governments and central banks are tempted to impart an inflationary bias to the economy thereby sacrificing long-term welfare to short-run political gains. The associated time-consistency problem can be overcome by setting up politically independent central banks.[4]

About five years ago Persson and Tabellini made some speculations on where this literature would be headed:

> 'The future research agenda ought to give high priority to modeling the details of political institutions. Adding institutional content is necessary to sharpen the empirical predictions of the theory. It is also necessary to generate interesting normative prescriptions'[5]

This book takes up the gauntlet. It deals with two items currently appearing on the research agenda on positive models of political economy. The first is on how observed differences in institutions affect political and economic outcomes in various social, economic and political systems. Important work in this area is on central bank independence and its relationship with several macroeconomic variables such as output and inflation. The second item is on how the institutions themselves change and develop in response to individual and collective beliefs, preferences and strategies.[6] Here recent research deals with the normative issue of how independent a central bank should be; that is with the optimal degree of central bank independence.[7]

The book starts with an introductory chapter on the rules versus discretion debate in monetary policy. In Chapter 2 we survey this debate. We show that there are basically two major theoretical issues in the controversy. First, policymakers not bound by a rule would be tempted into *excess activism*, destabilizing rather than stabilizing the economy. The second argument finds its origin in the introduction of the notion of *dynamic inconsistency*. According to this literature, the inflationary bias of discretionary monetary policy makes the case for a monetary rule or an independent central bank. However, the dynamic inconsistency literature does not dispute the possibility of stabilizing activist feedback policy. Hence there is a trade-off between the *credibility* gains of avoiding the inflationary bias of discretionary policy and the loss of *flexibility* due to a distorted response to output shocks. We show that this trade-off plays an important part in the literature on optimal institutional design.[8]

Part I of the book (Chapters 3, 4 and 5) investigates the *positive* relationship between domestic monetary institutions and macroeconomic performance. In doing so we focus on the legislative approach to price stability. In Chapter 3 we quantify central bank independence using a number of legal attributes from central bank laws. Twelve industrial countries are examined: Australia, Belgium, Canada, France, Germany, Italy, Japan, the Netherlands, the United Kingdom, the United States, Sweden and Switzerland. First we compare the measures (indices) of central bank independence as presented in the literature. After a critical examination of the existing indices we construct a new index of central bank independence, called the Eijffinger-Schaling (ES) index. According to this index, for example, central banks in which the only or main objective of monetary policy (as specified in the law) is price stability, are classified as being more independent than central banks with a number of objectives in addition to price stability, or banks in whose law price stability is not mentioned as an objective at all. In Chapter 4 on the basis of a monetary policy game with private information about the economy, we derive several propositions concerning the relationship between central bank independence and (the variance of) inflation and output growth. These propositions are tested for the same set of countries for the post-Bretton-Woods period (1972-1991). In testing the model we use the indices of central bank independence discussed in Chapter 3. Chapter 5 analyses central bank independence in the coordination of monetary and fiscal policies. We show that greater economic independence of the central bank - i.e. lower monetary accommodation of government budget deficits - reduces inflation persistence. Thus lower inflation persistence may not only be caused by the *exchange-rate regime* - as shown by recent empirical research - but also by the way monetary and fiscal policy are coordinated, i.e. by the *domestic monetary regime.*

Part II of the book (Chapters 6 and 7) investigates the *normative* issue how central banks and monetary regimes themselves change and develop in response to individual and collective beliefs, preferences and strategies. Both chapters are extensions of Chapter 4; the central or workhorse model of the book. Chapter 6 allows for an inflation sensitive natural rate of growth, while Chapter 7 features an endogenous natural rate of unemployment. Table 1.1 summarizes the extensions discussed above.

Table 1.1 Classification of chapters

Natural rate of growth	Natural rate of unemployment	
	Endogenous	Exogenous
Endogenous	-	Ch. 6
Exogenous	Ch. 7	Ch. 4

Chapter 6 extends Chapter 4 to allow for an inflation sensitive natural rate of growth. Hence, we integrate the longer-term relationship between inflation and growth into the literature on central bank independence. As the evidence points strongly to a predominantly inverse long-term relationship, we assume that the supply-side effect of inflation is negative. We find that this effect reduces the inflationary bias of discretionary monetary policy and mitigates society's credibility problem. As society's optimal framework for monetary stability depends on the balance between credibility and flexibility we show that the higher the supply side effect of inflation, the *lower* the optimal degree of central bank independence. Hence the inflation growth nexus weakens the case for central bank independence.

In Chapter 7 we combine the model of Chapter 4 with labour union behaviour along the lines of New-Keynesian bargaining theories of unemployment. This in order to integrate the study of monetary institutions with that of labour market institutions.[9] We characterize wage setting in a totally unionized economy under a constant money supply rule, GNP targeting, full commitment to a simple zero inflation rule, a discretionary regime and an independent central bank. The wage formation strategy of the union can be either cooperative or aggressive.[10] We show that the natural rate of unemployment becomes proportional to the aggression of the union. Since the natural rate of unemployment corresponds with the labour market distortion, we find that the more aggressive the union the higher the inflationary bias of discretionary monetary policy and the bigger society's credibility problem. With society's optimal framework for monetary stability depending on the balance between credibility and flexibility, we show that the more aggressive the union, the *higher* the optimal degree of central bank independence. Finally Chapter 8 summarizes and concludes.

NOTES

1. For a concise review of recent theoretical, empirical and institutional issues of monetary policy and central banking in America, Canada, Europe, Latin America and Russia see Eijffinger (1994).
2. For an interesting survey of central banking in emerging market-oriented economies see Federal Reserve Bank of Kansas City (1990).
3. For a recent discussion about the independence of the Bank of England and the associated inflation targeting framework see CEPR (1993).
4. The monetary policy credibility literature starts from Kydland and Prescott (1977); see most recently Persson and Tabellini (1993) and Walsh (1993). The literature on central bank independence is summarized in Cukierman (1992).
5. See Persson and Tabellini (1990, p. 177).
6. This research agenda is supported by the Harvard University/MIT Research Training Group in Positive Political Economy.
7. For interesting work in this area see Raith (1993), Cukierman (1994), Debelle and Fischer (1994) and Eijffinger and Schaling (1995).
8. Walsh (1993) and Persson and Tabellini (1993) claim that incentive contracts for central bankers, along the lines of the contract of the Governor of the Reserve Bank of New Zealand, may eliminate this trade-off altogether. We survey their contributions in Chapter 2.

9. For recent work see Levine and Pearlman (1994).
10. This terminology follows Funke (1994).

2. A History of the Rules versus Discretion Debate

I INTRODUCTION

The proper conduct of macroeconomic stabilization policy poses a number of interesting questions. An important and time-honoured issue, particularly relevant for monetary policy, is the rules versus discretion debate. As pointed out by Capie, Goodhart and Schnadt (1994, p. 112) this debate has continued to echo, though continuously revived and discussed in the current setting of its time, mutatis mutandis, through the history of central banking.

In case of discretionary policy making central banks optimize their policy instruments on a period-by-period (or case by case) basis. Policy-making according to a rule exists when the central bank chooses to implement in each period (or case) a formula for setting its instrument. Of course, this formula or rule is then to be applied to periods in general, not just the one currently at hand.[1] Next, if central banks follow rules should those rules be activist or nonactivist?[2] Hence, the rules versus discretion debate overlaps the argument about fixed and feedback policy rules.

Originating in the first half of the 19th century with the British monetary debate between the Currency and Banking Schools, the rules versus discretion debate is now over 150 years old. However, empirical and theoretical issues have not yet been settled.

According to Fischer (1994b, pp. 34-35) there are two major theoretical issues in the controversy. That is, those who favour rules have employed two kinds of arguments in order to demonstrate the undesirability of governmental discretion in monetary policy. First, Friedman's (1959) view is that policymakers not bound by a constant money growth rate rule would be tempted into *excess activism*, destabilizing rather than stabilizing the economy. The second class of arguments finds its origin in the introduction of the notion of *dynamic inconsistency*, which importantly changed the rules versus discretion debate. Kydland and Prescott (1977) and Barro and Gordon (1983a) saw their demonstration of the inflationary bias of discretionary monetary policy as making the case for a monetary rule. Alternatively the time consistency problem may be overcome by setting up independent central banks. Recent work in this area is Cukierman (1992) and Eijffinger and Schaling (1993a, 1993b).

However, as pointed out by Fischer (1994b, p. 35) the dynamic inconsistency literature does not dispute the possibility of stabilizing activist feedback policy. There is then a trade-off between the *credibility* gains of avoiding the inflationary bias of discretionary policy and the loss of *flexibility* due to a distorted response to output shocks.

This Chapter surveys the theoretical literature on rules versus discretion both from historical and analytical perspectives. The major difference with previous surveys like Argy (1988) and Fischer (1990) is that we follow a more analytic line of approach. Throughout we employ variations of a single log-linear model. This has the advantage of both clarifying disagreements between different schools of thought and at the same time identifying common ground. Also we pay more attention to a central relation in the debate viz the Phillips curve.

The plan of this Chapter is as follows. In Section II we discuss the origin of the debate in the first half of the 19th Century and the operation of the gold standard. Next, we turn to the issues raised by the Chicago school. Sections IV-VI address the first class of arguments against discretion. The simple Keynesian framework for stabilisation and Friedman's attack is the subject of Section IV, whilst Sections V and VI feature the intellectual history of the Phillips curve. In Section VII we discuss the basic Phillips curve monetary policy game as introduced by Kydland and Prescott (1977) and Barro and Gordon. The Backus and Driffill (1985) and Cukierman and Meltzer (1986) models of reputation and credibility are the subject of Section VIII. In Section IX we focus on central bank independence and on the trade-off between credibility and flexibility as emphasized by Canzoneri (1985), Rogoff (1985) and Lohmann (1992). The recent contracting approach to monetary policy as pioneered by Walsh (1993) and Persson and Tabellini (1993) is the subject of Section X. Section XI summarizes and concludes. The appendix discusses the short-run leverage of monetary policy in the presence of rational expectations due to the presence of overlapping wage contracts.

II THE GOLD STANDARD

The rules versus discretion debate in monetary policy finds its origin in the country where the practice of central banking developed i.e. the United Kingdom. It dates back to the debate between the Currency and Banking Schools preceding Peel's Act (The Bank Act) of 1844 that bolstered the Bank's monopoly privileges and enhanced its status as an incipient control bank (White (1984)).

A key leader of the Currency School was the leading economist of his day, David Ricardo. However, Ricardo died in 1823, before the Currency School became fully established in the 1830s. This school did not view bank deposits as money. They argued that the quantity of currency should vary precisely as it would if all money were gold, meaning that the balance of payments should determine changes in the quantity of currency. Thus the Currency School favoured the introduction of appropriate controls on monetary growth rather than discretionary authority for the BOE. In this context Capie, Goodhart and Schnadt (1994, p. 115) point out that Ricardo's comment was that

> 'the House [of Commons] did not withdraw its confidence from the Bank from any doubt of its wealth or integrity, but from a conviction of its total ignorance of political economy, a thrust that was greeted with hear, hear, and a laugh.'

The Currency School tended to think that its programme would only be carried out, by the central bankers, if the latter were firmly tied down by clear, transparent, statutory rules.

The Banking School thought it a mistake to treat only currency as money. They criticized the gold standard rule since the appropriate behaviour of the money stock depended on whether movements in the BOE's reserves were caused by domestic or foreign disturbances, and on whether the disturbances were permanent or temporary. Thus the Banking School favoured discretionary authority.

However, an informal rule for BOE operations was suggested by the Banking School's real bills doctrine. The real bills doctrine states that credit should only be issued upon the discount of bills drawn to finance real goods in the process of production and distribution. If the real bills doctrine is followed money can never be excessive, i.e. inflationary, since it purports to match money creation with real output (Sijben (1990, p.8) and Humphrey (1988, p.5)).

The Act of 1844 separated the BOE into an Issue Department and a Banking Department. The Banking Department was to function like any other private bank. Reflecting Currency School views, the Issue Department was to issue Bank of England notes convertible into bars of gold (bullion) or money in coins (specie) according to a prescribed rule. The rule was that there was to be a fiduciary issue of about 18 million pounds above that, at the margin there was to be 100% gold reserve for notes. Thus the debate between the Currency and Banking Schools was won[3] by the Currency School and monetary policy by the BOE was supposed to follow a simple rule: vary the money supply with the gold reserves of the central authorities.

The latter were supposed to vary according to the classical specie-flow mechanism.[4] In case of a British balance of payments deficit, say, adjustment comes through wealth effects (the outflow of gold (specie) from England reduces British spending) and through adjustments in relative prices (British spending is shifted towards home goods).

However because international capital flows responding to interest rate differentials moved gold far more rapidly than the classical specie-flow mechanism, in the period from the Bank Act until 1914, the BOE actively adjusted the rate of discount in response to threatened changes in the gold stock. For instance, in case of a current account deficit, the BOE raised the discount rate thereby protecting the gold reserve and gold convertibility by reducing both capital outflows and domestic demand.

Thus, although the historical gold standard is frequently cited as a precise simple rule for monetary policy the functioning of the system involved the British monetary authorities in a high degree of discretion.[5]

III THE CHICAGO VIEW

In the 1920s the rules vs discretion debate resurfaced in the United States. It figured prominently in the 1926-1927 debates between Congress and the Federal Reserve System (Fed) concerning the proper conduct of US monetary policy.

Congressman Strong thought it wise to constrain the Fed's actions by means of a money-stock-rule aimed at price stability, whilst Fed administrator Miller favoured discretionary authority following the real bills doctrine.[6] The debate was won by the Fed.

As a matter of fact in the 1920s actual US monetary policy was characterized by a high degree of discretion. This was made possible by the Federal Reserve Act of 1913 and the non-functioning of the gold standard during World War I.

The Act of 1913 made price-stability the main objective of the Fed. However, as pointed out by Carlson (1988), it did not specify how:

> 'While the bill instructed that the Federal Reserve's discount rate policy was to be determined with the view of promoting price stability, no formula [i.e. rule ES] was specified. It left open the role for discretion in determining how much the discount rate should be altered when the price level deviates from its objective of price stability.'[7]

At the time of its establishment the Fed was supposed to operate within a gold standard setting. However, in 1914-1918 many countries at war were effectively not on the gold standard. Therefore during the war discount rate changes were neither limited by the Federal Reserve Act, nor did they face the external constraint of protecting US gold reserves.

As long as it was succesful, the discretionary character of US monetary policy in the 1920s was not much argued against. However, after the debacle of monetary policy in the Great Depression[8] - when bank runs reduced the money stock - a group of Chicago economists proposed a system in which banks would hold 100% reserves against checkable deposits. Thus specific arguments for rules in US monetary policy were first developed in the context of a proposal for monetary reform called the 'Chicago Plan'. Proponents of the Plan included Irving Fisher (1945) and Milton Friedman's teacher Henry Simons (1936). Fisher proposed various rules such as a constant money stock, a constant per capita nominal money stock and a price stabilization rule. Simons also considered a constant money stock rule, but because of the danger of changes on the velocity side preferred a price stabilization rule.

Simons made a more general case for rules in his classic paper 'Rules versus Authorities in Monetary Policy'. In this paper Simons compared two polar monetary regimes. On the one hand he set the authority-regime. In this regime the monetary policymaker could have several monetary instruments like the discount rate, reserve requirements and open market operations at their discretion, and be given the objective of economic well-being. Therefore following Sijben (1990, p. 9) the authority regime is constrained by the final-goals of monetary policy. At the other extreme we have the rules-regime. In the latter regime the policymaker could be directed to expand the supply of high-powered money at say, $x\%$ per year. Therefore the rules-regime is constrained by the instruments ('intermediate targets')[9] of monetary policy. To rephrase this taxonomy using the terminology of Fischer (1994b, p. 41), under the authority regime the central bank has *goal independence* (its goals are imprecisely defined) whilst under the rules regime it would not have *instrument independence* (full discretion and power to deploy monetary policy to attain its goals).

Being a liberal economist Simons preferred the rules-regime:

> 'The liberal creed demands the organization of our economic life largely through individual participation in a game with definite rules...[D]efinite, stable, legislative rules of the game as to money are of paramount importance to the survival of a system based on freedom of enterprise.'[10]

Carlson (1988, p. 3) points out that here the essential notion is that government is necessary for establishing laws that would define the rules for a 'game' in which competitive free enterprise could flourish, but that government should not be a player in the game. The idea that government would manage the currency to manipulate aggregate economic outcomes meant that government would be a player and thus violated the liberal creed. The views of Simons and the Chicago School were later elaborated by Milton Friedman.

IV THE KEYNESIAN REVOLUTION AND FRIEDMAN'S ATTACK

After World War II the Keynesian revolution shifted the focus of economic policy from the choice of monetary regimes — i.e. the proper design of institutions — towards the more specific problem of how to achieve full employment by appropriately timed and quantified government action.[11] Therefore Keynesians wanted to set the instruments of economic policy on a period-by-period basis thus favouring discretion.

Typically they saw the economy's structure as deterministic, i.e. policymakers conduct monetary and fiscal policy in full knowledge of the structure of the model. Given sufficient information and the theoretical basis for multi targets and multi instruments provided by Tinbergen (1966), policymakers were able to choose the appropriate policy mix.[12]

According to Argy (1988, pp. 147—148) the analytical base for discretionary stabilisation policy in the early post war short run Keynesian framework can be summarized by the following three propositions: (1) up to full employment nominal wages were rigid, (2) the private sector was very unstable due to animal spirits in investment or to insufficient investment (secular stagnation) and (3) an adverse demand shock could place the economy below its full employment level, where, in principle, it could remain for an indefinite period.

With rigid nominal wages there was no automatic adjustment mechanism. Therefore in case of an adverse demand shock policymakers should increase aggregate demand, increase the price level, reduce real wages and thus restore full employment. The choice between monetary and fiscal policies typically depended on the structural coefficients of the Keynesian system. The steeper (flatter) the IS schedule the stronger the case for the use of fiscal (monetary) policy.

These ideas are captured by the following simple log-linear model. Capital will be assumed fixed in the short run and output is given by a short-run production function of the following type

$$y_t = \beta\, l_t \qquad 0 < \beta < 1 \qquad (2.1)$$

where y is the log of output and l is the log of employment.

For simplicity we do not take account of productivity shocks.[13] Firms determine employment by equalizing the marginal product of labour to the real wage $w_t - p_t$. This yields the following employment function

$$l_t = -\frac{1}{1-\beta}(w_t - p_t) \tag{2.2}$$

where w is the log of the nominal wage and p is the log of the price level.

Following the standard specification of the Keynesian framework we assume that nominal wages are rigid.

$$w_t = 0 \tag{2.3}$$

Substituting (2.3) in the labour demand function (2.2), and the resulting equation in the production function, we get the following relation between output and the price level.

$$y_t = \frac{\beta}{1-\beta} p_t \tag{2.4}$$

A rise in prices reduces the real wage, and causes firms to employ more labour. Thus, (2.4) is the aggregate supply curve.

Aggregate demand is described by a standard IS — LM framework

$$y_t = g_t - \alpha_1 r_t + v_t \qquad \alpha_1 > 0 \tag{2.5}$$

$$m_t - p_t = y_t - \alpha_2 r_t \qquad \alpha_2 > 0 \tag{2.6}$$

where r is the real interest rate, g is real government expenditure m is the nominal money stock and v is a demand shock. Thus, (2.5) and (2.6) are the IS and LM schedules.

Eliminating the real interest rate from (2.5) and (2.6), equating the resulting equation with (2.4) we obtain the following solution for output

$$y_t = \frac{\sigma_1 \beta}{\beta + \sigma_1(1-\beta)} m_t + \frac{\sigma_2 \beta}{\beta + \sigma_1(1-\beta)} (g_t + v_t) \tag{2.7}$$

where $\sigma_1 \equiv \alpha_1 / \alpha_1 + \alpha_2$ and $\sigma_2 \equiv \alpha_2 / \alpha_1 + \alpha_2$
From (2.7) it can be seen that the relative efficacy of monetary and fiscal policy depends on the ratio α_1/α_2.[14]

As pointed out by Capie, Goodhart and Schnadt (1994, p. 34) in the UK the received view in the late 1950s - as presented in the Radcliffe Report 1959 - was that monetary management was often regarded a somewhat subsidiary part of overall demand management. The reason for this was that α_1 was thought to be rather low, while α_2 was felt to be comparatively higher. For ease of argument in what follows we set m_t = 0, that is we focus on fiscal policy.

By setting y_t equal to its target value y^* we obtain the optimal value of the fiscal instrument

$$g_t = \frac{\beta + \sigma_1(1 - \beta)}{\sigma_2 \beta} y^* - v_t \tag{2.8}$$

From (2.8) it follows that the optimal period by period - that is discretionary - setting of the fiscal policy variable must be such as to exactly offset instantaneous demand shocks. Thus Keynesian fine-taning requires correct and complete information about contemporaneous demand shocks.

It is precisely this point which is questioned by Milton Friedman who beginning in the early 1950s vigorously attacked Keynesian stabilisation policies.

Friedman (1951) introduces the problem of information and its relevance for the choice between rules and discretion. A policymaker intent on stabilizing the economy will destabilize if he is misled by incomplete or incorrect information.

Moreover, Friedman (1948, 1953) also emphasized the problem of lags in the effects of policy. Friedman considered various lags. The data lag is the time it takes for policymakers to obtain data about the economy. The recognition lag is the time it takes for policymakers to be sure of what the data are signalling about the future course of the economy. The legislative lag represents the time it takes to pass legislation to implement a particular policy. The implementation lag is the time it takes for policymakers to change policy instruments once they have decided on the new policy. Finally, the effectuation lag is the time it takes for the policy to actually have an impact on the economy.

Because of these lags and the inability of policymakers to predict the behavior of the economic system active stabilization policy is likely to destabilize rather than to stabilize the economy. At a more conceptual level, Friedman tried to show that for government policies to be countercyclical the correlation coefficient between government actions and (demand) shocks would have to be significantly negative.

Now following Argy (1988, pp. 130—131) we can demonstrate Friedman's case against discretion on the basis of our model. Consider equation (2.7). Setting $m_t = 0$, this equation says that the actual level of activity y_t is the algebraic sum of the level of output without the effects of policy v_t and the addition to the level of output due to the effects of fiscal policy g_t. Taking variances of (2.7) we have[15]

$$\text{Var } y_t = \frac{\sigma_2^2 \beta^2}{[\beta + \sigma_1(1-\beta)]^2} (\text{var } g_t + \sigma_v^2) + \frac{2\sigma_2^2\beta^2}{[\beta + \sigma_1(1-\beta)]^2} \rho_{gv}\sigma_g\sigma_v \qquad (2.9)$$

where σ_v^2 is the variance of v_t and ρ_{gv} stands for the correlation coefficient between fiscal policy and the demand shock.

To demonstrate Friedman's case against discretion let us suppose for simplicity that $\sigma_g = \sigma_v$; that is the standard deviation of these two series is the same. We can then rewrite (2.9) as

$$\frac{\text{Var } y_t}{\sigma_v^2} = \frac{2\sigma_2^2\beta^2 (1 + \rho_{gv})}{[\beta + \sigma_1(1-\beta)]^2} \qquad (2.10)$$

For fiscal policy to be stabilizing one should have $\text{Var } y_t < \sigma_v^2$, that is $\text{Var } y_t/\sigma_v^2 < 1$. Imposing the latter condition on (2.10) requires

$$\rho_{gv} < \frac{[\beta + \sigma_1(1-\beta)]^2 - 2\sigma_2^2\beta^2}{2\sigma_2^2\beta^2}$$

To give a numerical example, with σ_1 equal to zero and β being about 0.7[16] for policy to be stabilizing the correlation coefficient between fiscal policy and the demand shock has to be smaller than -0.5. Otherwise ($\rho_{gv} > -0.5$) fiscal policy is destabilizing, while if we require 100% of the initial variance of output to be removed we must have $\rho_{gv} = -1$. These results are summarized in Table 2.1

Applying this line of reasoning to monetary policy it is plausible that because of lags in the effects of policy a constant money rule (Friedman (1959)) is likely to be superior to discretion in stabilizing the economy. Of course the truth about the value of ρ_{gv} is an empirical matter.[17]

Table 2.1 Lags and the effects of policy

ρ_{gv}	>0.5	$-1 < \rho_{gv} < -0.5$	-1
Policy	Destabilizing	Stabilizing	Perfect Stabilization

However on the basis of severaly empirical studies (Friedman and Schwartz (1963) and Friedman (1969)) Friedman concluded that actual policy, especially monetary policy, had been destabilizing.

V PHILLIPS CURVE ANALYSIS

V.1 Keynesianism and the Phillips Curve

In the simple Keynesian framework nominal wages were rigid. Therefore typical Keynesian models — like the one in Section IV — were unable to explain inflation. This was apparently resolved by the discovery of Phillips (1958) of an inverse non-linear relation between the level of unemployment and the rate of growth of money wages for the United Kingdom over the period 1861 — 1957. This relationsip became known as the 'Phillips curve', and suggested a trade-off between wage inflation and unemployment.[18] It was not long before a price change version of the Phillips' relation was developed. Samuelson and Solow (1960) brought the inflation - unemployment version of the Phillips curve to the United States.[19]

Initially presented by Phillips as an empirical relationship without theoretical foundations, it was reformulated as a labour market adjustment process by Lipsey (1960):

$$\Delta w_t = -\theta(l_t^s - l_t) \qquad \theta > 0 \qquad (2.11)$$

Equation (2.11) states that the rate of growth in money wages reflects the degree of excess demand in the labour market as proxied by the level of unemployment ($u \equiv l^s - l$).[20] Of course, θ represents the speed of adjustment to labour market equilibrium.

Now we incorporate the Phillips curve into the macroeconomic model of Section IV.

Setting $\sigma_2 = g_t = v_t = 0$ in equation (2.7), aggregate demand is determined by a simple Cambridge equation[21]

$$y_t = m_t - p_t \tag{2.12}$$

Substituting the employment function (2.2) in the production function (2.1), and the resulting equation into the aggregate demand curve (2.12), we get the following relation between the price level, the nominal wage and the money stock

$$p_t = \beta\, w_t + (1 - \beta)\, m_t \tag{2.13}$$

Substituting (2.13) in the labour demand function (2.2) and the resulting relation in the Phillips curve (2.11) yields

$$\Delta w_t = -\theta\, (l_t^s + w_t - m_t) \tag{2.14}$$

Taking first differences of (2.14) and normalising l_t^s at zero highlights an interesting feature of the model

$$\Delta^2 w_t = \theta\, (\Delta m_t - \Delta w_t) \tag{2.15}$$

From equation (2.15) it can be seen that, if the system is stable,[22] wage inflation converges to an equilibrium where $\Delta^2 w_t = 0$, and hence $\Delta m_t = \Delta w_t$. Substituting the latter result in equation (2.11), it follows that in inflationary equilibruim

$$\bar{l} = 1/\theta\, \overline{\Delta m} \tag{2.16}$$

That is, $l_t > l_t^s$ even in the long run. Therefore, in terms of the Phillips curve (2.11), the monetary authorities can choose a rate of monetary growth so as to achieve the desired level of employment, and trade this off against the resulting wage and price inflation.

Since $\overline{\Delta w} = \overline{\Delta m} = \overline{\Delta p}$ in the long run the rate of growth of real wages is zero. However, this is not true for the *level* of the real wage.

Substituting steady-state employment (2.16) in the labour demand func- tion (2.2) gives the following expression for the long run level of the real wage

$$\overline{w} - \overline{p} = \frac{-(1 - \beta)}{\theta} \overline{\Delta m} \tag{2.17}$$

Therefore, our inflationary equilibrium involves money illusion on the part of trade unions even in the long run.

V.2 The Vertical Phillips Curve

It is precisely this implication of the model that came under serious attack by Friedman (1968) and Phelps (1968).

According to Friedman, the Phillips curve was fundamentally misspecified, and should be cast in terms of the rate of growth of the *real* wage rather than the nominal wage. However, in practice unions negotiate their wages in money terms on the basis of the expected inflation rate. Therefore Friedman specified the Phillips curve in terms of the expected real wage, called the 'expectations augmented' Phillips curve. In order to compare Friedman's findings with the early Phillips curve we now model wage setting on the basis of expected inflation.[23] The nominal wage is set at the end of period t — 1 for period t. In subsequent periods this process is repeated.

Thus, we have one period wage contracts. Suppose the objective of wage setters is to stabilize expected employment during the period of the contract around a target employment level l^*. Then wages in each period are set to minimize

$$E_{t-1} (l_t - l^*)^2 \tag{2.18}$$

where E_{t-1} (.) denotes expectations formed at time t — 1. The minimization of (2.18) is subject to the labour demand function (2.2). From the first-order conditions for a minimum of (2.18) subject to (2.2), the nominal wage is given by,

$$w_t = E_{t-1} p_t - (1 - \beta) l^* \tag{2.19}$$

Equation (2.19) states that wages are set at the end of period t — 1 for period t based on unions' expectations of the price level in period t.

Substituting (2.19) in the labour demand function we get the following relation between employment and unanticipated shocks

$$l_t = l^* + \frac{1}{1 - \beta} (p_t - E_{t-1} p_t) \tag{2.20}$$

An unanticipated rise in prices reduces the real wage, and causes firms to employ more labour thereby raising employment above its target level. Subtracting (2.20) from the labour force l_t^s, using that $u_t \equiv l_t^s - l_t$, and adding and subtracting $p_{t-1}/(1-\beta)$, we get the following expression for the short—run determination of unemployment

$$u_t = \tilde{u} - \frac{1}{1-\beta}(\Delta p_t - E_{t-1}\Delta p_t) \tag{2.21}$$

where $\tilde{u}$ is the equilibrium or natural rate of unemployment $(l_t^s - l^*)$. Thus (2.21) is the famous expectations augmented Phillips curve. Unemployment deviates from its equilibrium rate only to the extent that there are unanticipated shocks to inflation. Next, consider expectations formation. Friedman assumed that unions calculate expected inflation on the basis of past inflation. Suppose expectations of the inflation rate are adaptive and are governed by

$$E_{t-1}\,\Delta p_t = E_{t-2}\,\Delta p_{t-1} + a\,(\Delta p_{t-1} - E_{t-2}\,\Delta p_{t-1}) \tag{2.22}$$

where $\Delta p_{t-1} - E_{t-2}\,\Delta p_{t-1}$ is the forecast error.

By setting $a = 1$ in (2.22) we get

$$E_{t-1}\,\Delta p_t = \Delta p_{t-1} \tag{2.23}$$

Equation (2.23) states that unions use the inflation rate at the time of the wage settlement as a proxy for expected inflation during the period of the contract. Substituting (2.23) in (2.21) we get

$$u_t = \tilde{u} - \frac{1}{1-\beta}\,\Delta^2 p_t \tag{2.24}$$

Equation (2.24) is the accelerationist hypothesis which says that, to keep the rate of unemployment below the natural rate of unemployment the rate of inflation would need to continually accelerate. Substitution of (2.20) in (2.1), equating the result with (2.12) taking first differences, using (2.23), again taking first differences and normalising l^* at zero yields

$$\Delta^2 p_t = \beta\,\Delta^2 p_{t-1} + (1-\beta)\,\Delta^2 m \tag{2.25}$$

From equation (2.25) it can be seen that in the absence of accelerating monetary growth the rate of inflation converges to steady state equilibrium where $\overline{\Delta^2 p} = 0$ and $\overline{\Delta p} = \overline{\Delta m}$.[24] Moreover, if $\overline{\Delta^2 p} = 0$ from equation (2.24) it follows that $\bar{u} = \tilde{u}$, i.e. in steady state unemployment is equal to the natural rate of unemployment. The latter equilibrium became known as the NAIRU, the non accelerating inflation rate of unemployment.[25]

Note that since $\bar{u} = \tilde{u}$, in the Friedman-Phelps analysis the long-run Phillips curve is vertical: there is no long-run trade-off between inflation and unemployment. There is however a short-run trade-off. Following a once and for all monetary expansion, there will be an increase in prices and nominal wages. However, because unions have adaptive expectations they deflate wages not by the current price level but by past inflation. Hence they initially perceive the rise in nominal wages to be an increase in real wages. Therefore the supply of labour will increase to accommodate the increased demand for labour, thus decreasing unemployment. As unions gradually adjust their inflationary expectations eventually money illusion will decrease and real effects will be eroded. Next consider the effects of activist policy in the context of the expectations augmented Phillips curve.[26]

Suppose monetary policy is governed by the integral policy rule

$$\Delta m_t = -d_1 (y - y^*) \qquad d_1 > 0 \tag{2.26}$$

This rule was introduced by Phillips (1954, 1957) to analyse the performance of stabilization policy in achieving a particular policy objective and in achieving a rapid convergense to steady state equilibrium. Accordingly monetary policy is determined by the (integral) sum of past deviations in output from its target. The name of this policy rule derives from the fact that (2.26) may also be written as

$$m_t = -d_1 \sum_{i=0}^{\infty} L^i (y - y^*) \tag{2.27}$$

where L is the backward-shift (lag) operator. Normalizing y^* at zero the dynamics of output when the policy (2.25) is introduced in the model[27] is given by

$$y_t - \frac{\beta(2 + d_1)}{1 + d_1\beta} y_{t-1} + \frac{\beta}{1 + d_1\beta} y_{t-2} = \frac{1 - \beta}{1 + d_1\beta} \tilde{y} \tag{2.28}$$

where $\tilde{y} \equiv \beta \ell^*$.

The characteristic equation of (2.28) is

$$\lambda^2 + \alpha_1 \lambda + \alpha_2 = 0 \tag{2.29}$$

where $\alpha_2 \equiv \dfrac{\beta}{1 + d_1\beta}$ and $\alpha_1 \equiv -(2 + d_1)\,\alpha_2$

The following inequalities (Gandolfo (1983), p. 59))

$$\begin{aligned} 1 + \alpha_1 + \alpha_2 &> 0 \\ 1 - \alpha_2 &> 0 \\ 1 - \alpha_1 + \alpha_2 &> 0 \end{aligned} \tag{2.30}$$

Constitute a set of necessary and sufficient conditions in order that the roots — be they real or complex — of the characteristic equation (2.29) be less than unity in absolute value. It can easily be shown that if $\beta < 1$ (2.28) exhibits global stability.

Now we consider the influence of the monetary policy rule on the adjustment to steady-state equilibrium. The discriminant (D) is given by

$$D = \alpha_1^2 - 4\alpha_2 \tag{2.31}$$

The sign of D depends on d_1. More precisely,

$$D \gtreqless 0 \text{ according to } d_1 \gtreqless \sqrt{4(1-\beta)/\beta} \tag{2.32}$$

Hence, if $d_1 = 0$ — which in terms of equation (2.26) implies the adoption of a fixed money supply rule — $D < 0$. Therefore, adoption of a fixed money supply rule introduces instability in the model by causing the variation $y - \tilde{y}$ being described by a sinusoidal function (conjugate complex roots). This problem can be overcome by activist policy. If d_1 exceeds a lower bound ($d_1 > \sqrt{4(1-\beta)/\beta}$), the integral policy rule removes the coscillations and causes the adjustment path to be monotonically convergent. Moreover, the above example fits into a more general pattern for Argy (1988, p.160) notes that:

> '(As concerns) activist policy in the context of a model of an expectations augmented Phillips Curve (The) principal conclusion is that some activist policy can potentially improve on the performance of a (constant money growth rate) rule.'

VI RATIONAL EXPECTATIONS AND NEW CLASSICAL MACROECONOMICS

The New Classical view of aggregate supply as embodied in the work of Lucas (1973), Sargent (1973), and Sargent and Wallace (1975) may be highlighted by the following 'typical' New Classical model.

We begin by recalling the short-run production function, and labour demand function used in Section IV.

$$y_t = \beta\, l_t + \mu_t \qquad \mu \sim N(0, \sigma_\mu^2) \tag{2.33}$$

$$l_t = \frac{-1}{1-\beta}(w_t - p_t - \mu_t) \tag{2.34}$$

Note that (2.33) and (2.34) are identical to equations (2.1) and (2.2) except for the inclusion of a white-noise productivity disturbance with zero mean and finite variance.

We close the model by adopting the familiar aggregate demand and wage-setting relations introduced in Section V

$$y_t = m_t - p_t \tag{2.12}$$

$$w_t = E_{t-1}\, p_t - (1 - \beta)\, l^* \tag{2.19}$$

We may obtain the aggregate supply function by first of all substituting for w from (2.19) into (2.34). This yields the following expression for employment

$$l_t = \frac{1}{1-\beta}(p_t - E_{t-1}\, p_t + \mu_t) + l^* \tag{2.35}$$

Substituting (2.35) into (2.33) yields the famous Lucas (1973) 'surprise' supply function

$$y = \tilde{y} + \frac{\beta}{1-\beta}(p_t - E_{t-1}\, p_t) + \frac{1}{1-\beta}\mu_t \tag{2.36}$$

where $\tilde{y} \equiv \beta\, l^*$

Equation (2.36) implies that if expectations are fulfilled, actual output will equal the natural rate of output $\tilde{y}$. Moreover, when p_t exceeds its expectation $E_{t-1}\,p_t$, and hence real wages $w_t - p_t$ are lower than their expectation $w_t - E_{t-1}\,p_t$ at the time wages were set, output will increase relative to the natural rate by an amount $\beta/(1 - \beta)\,(p_t - E_{t-1}\,p_t)$.

Equating (2.36) and (2.12) we obtain the following equation for the price level

$$p_t = \beta\, E_{t-1}\, p_t + (1 - \beta)\,(m - \tilde{y}) - \mu \qquad (2.37)$$

To solve for the behaviour of p, we must specify how unions form expectations. New Classical Macroeconomists following Muth (1961)[28] typically assume that unions have rational expectations, that is, expectations equal the mathematical expectation of p_t based on information at time $t - 1$. In defining this rational expectation it is assumed that unions know the model, namely equation (2.37) and the parameters β and 1^*.

Therefore $E_{t-1}\,p_t = E(p_t \mid I_{t-1})$, where $I_{t-1} = \{p_{t-i}, m_{t-i}, \mu_{t-i}, i = 1,\ldots,\infty\}$. $E_{t-1}\,p_t$ is equal to the mathematical expectation of p_t based on the information set I_{t-1}. The information set contains current and lagged values of exogenous and endogenous variables.

Note that the rational expectations hypothesis (REH) assumes that unions exploit all available information i.e. they refrain from making systematic forecast errors concommitant with backward looking or adaptive expectations. Taking expectations of both sides of (2.37) conditional on information at time $t - 1$ we get

$$E_{t-1}\, p_t = E_{t-1}\, m_t - \beta\, 1^* \qquad (2.38)$$

Substituting (2.38) in (2.37) yields

$$p_t = \beta E_{t-1}\, m_t + m_t - (\tilde{y} + \mu) \qquad (2.39)$$

Substracting (2.38) from (2.39) we get the following relation between the forecast error $p_t - E_{t-1}\,p_t$ and unanticipated shocks

$$p_t - E_{t-1}\, p_t = (1 - \beta)\,(m_t - E_{t-1}\, m_t) - \mu_t \qquad (2.40)$$

Equation (2.40) states that rational expectations forecast errors arise because of unforeseeable deviations of random disturbances at t from their mean values of zero and from unforeseeable monetary policy. We assume that the governement wishes to stabilize unemployment around the natural rate of unemployment $\tilde{u}$ in the face of the exogenous aggregate supply shock μ_t, and that it seeks to do this by adopting the state-contingent (feedback) reaction function

$$m_t = d_1 \mu_{t-1} + \omega_t \qquad \omega_t \sim N(0, \sigma_\omega^2) \tag{2.41}$$

where d_1 is the degree of activism and ω_t is a random disturbance with mean zero and no serial correlation, describing the extent to which the actual money supply deviates unpredictably from its systematic component $d_1 \mu_{t-1}$.

Taking expectations of both sides of (2.41) conditional on information at time t — 1 we get

$$E_{t-1} m_t = d_1 \mu_{t-1} \tag{2.42}$$

Subtracting (2.42) from (2.41) we get the following expression for unforeseeable monetary policy

$$m_t - E_{t-1} m_t = \omega_t \tag{2.43}$$

Substituting (2.43) in (2.40) and the resulting equation in (2.36) yields

$$y_t - \tilde{y} = \beta \omega_t + \mu_t \tag{2.44}$$

From (2.44) it follows that, by adopting the REH, y_t and $\tilde{y}$ diverge by a purely random term: output never systematically deviates from its natural rate.

Hence (2.44) highlights the famous Sargent and Wallace (1975) *policy invariance* or *policy neutrality* result. Since the policy parameter d_1 does not appear in (2.44) systematic monetary policy cannot affect real output.

Next we link the Sargent-Wallace result to the Phillips curve debate of the previous section. Subtracting (2.35) from the labour force l^s, using that $u \equiv l^s - l$, we get the expectations augmented Phillips curve

$$u = \tilde{u} - \frac{1}{1-\beta}(p_t - E_{t-1} p_t + \mu_t) \tag{2.45}$$

Substituting (2.43) in (2.40) and the resulting equation in (2.45) we get the following expression for unemployment

$$\tilde{u} - u_t = \omega_t \tag{2.46}$$

Thus unemployment deviates from its natural rate only to the extent that there are random deviations of the money supply from its systematic component.

Equation (2.46) highlights the Sargent-Wallace invariance result in terms of what we might call the rational expectations augmented Phillips curve. In the presence of rational expectations there is no trade-off between inflation and unemployment.[29] Since unions know the monetary policy rule the Phillips curve is vertical even in the short run.

The objective of the central bank was to stabilize unemployment around its natural rate. If the monetary authorities seek to minimise the variance of unemployment around its natural rate the optimal policy problem faced by the central bank is to find that value of d_1 in (2.41) that minimizes

$$\mathrm{Var}\,(u - \tilde{u}) = \sigma^2_{\omega} \tag{2.47}$$

Where Var(.) denotes the variance of a variable and (2.47) is obtained by taking variances of (2.46). It can be easily seen that the variance of unemployment is independent of the degree of activism d_1. Hence it appears that any value of d_1 will yield the same result in terms of carrying out the governments' optimal policy. Therefore the (fixed) rule $d_1 = 0$ is as good as the discretion ($d_1 \neq 0$) in this instance.

Next consider the consequences of purely stochastic changes in policy. Suppose the variability of monetary policy is increased. Thus the mean of ω_t remains zero but its variance σ^2_{ϖ} will be larger. From equation (2.47) it can be seen that more random policies increase the ex post variation of unemployment u_t around its mean level $\tilde{u}$, the natural rate of unemployment. Therefore Sargent and Wallace (1975) have argued that policy rules should be as predictable as possible. Also their analysis may be used to criticize fine tuning and to justify Friedman's (1959) presciption of a constant money growth rule.

VII THE BASIC PHILLIPS CURVE MONETARY POLICY GAME

As noted by Fischer (1990, p. 1169) the nature of the rules vs discretion debate was importantly changed by the introduction of the notion of time-inconsistency by Kydland and Prescott (1977). In the post Kydland and Prescott rules vs discretion debate the case for rules became much stronger as a policy rule can be a means of overcoming the time- or dynamic inconsistency problem.

Following Blanchard and Fischer (1989, p. 592) we define a policy to be time inconsistent when a future policy decision that forms part of an optimal plan formulated at an initial date is no longer optimal from the viewpoint of a later date, even though no new relevant information has appeared in the meantime. In this section we develop the best-known example of dynamic inconsistency viz the single stage (one shot) Phillips curve monetary policy game introduced by Kydland and Prescott (1977). We start with a one period game, then move on to a multiperiod extension.

VII.1 The Inflationary Bias of Time Consistent Monetary Policy

We begin by recalling the Phillips curve used in Section V

$$u_t = \tilde{u} - \frac{1}{1-\beta}(\Delta p_t - E_{t-1}\Delta p_t) \qquad (2.21)$$

In Section V the model was closed by the aggregate demand curve (Cambridge equation)

$$y_t = m_t - p_t \qquad (2.12)$$

In this section unemployment and inflation are determined as in the Barro and Gordon (1983a) model. That is, time-consistent monetary policy is analysed where the central bank minimizes the social loss function

$$L_t = \tfrac{1}{2}(\Delta p_t - \Delta p^*)^2 + \varepsilon(u_t - u^*) \qquad \varepsilon > 0 \qquad (2.48)$$

Hence the central bank is concerned with both price stability and low unemployment.[30] Δp^* and u^* are the inflation and unemployment targets of the central bank. The parameter ε measures the weight of unemployment relative to inflation stabilization in the preferences of the central bank.

The central bank chooses Δp and wage setters 'choose' $E_{t-1}\Delta p_t$. Normalizing Δp^* and u^* at zero yields

$$L_t = \tfrac{1}{2}(\Delta p_t)^2 + \varepsilon\, u_t \qquad (2.49)$$

Hence the model consists of equations (2.20) and (2.49). Substituting the Phillips curve into the loss function yields

$$L_t = \tfrac{1}{2}(\Delta p_t)^2 + \varepsilon(\tilde{u} - \frac{1}{1-\beta}\Delta p_t + \frac{1}{1-\beta}E_{t-1}\Delta p_t) \qquad (2.49)$$

From the first order conditions for a minimum of (2.50), that is $\partial L_t/\partial \Delta p_t = 0$, we obtain the central bank's reaction function given wage setter's expectations

$$\Delta p_t^D = \frac{\varepsilon}{1-\beta} \qquad (2.51)$$ [31]

where superscript D denotes discretion. Assuming rational expectations, wage setters predict inflation by solving out the central bank's optimization problem and forecasting the solution for Δp_t^D as well as possible. In the present case they can calculate exactly the choice of inflation from equation (2.51).

Taking expectations conditional on information at t—1 of (2.51) gives

$$E_{t-1}\, \Delta p_t^D = \frac{\varepsilon}{1-\beta} \qquad (2.51)$$

Since actual and expected inflation are identical unanticipated inflation is zero implying that

$$u_t^D = \tilde{u} \qquad (2.53)$$

Equations (2.51) and (2.53) highlight the time consistency problem. The monetary policy strategy of the central bank, that is equation (2.51) is time consistent in the sense that at each point in time the inflation rate selected is best, given the current situation.

However, as can be seen from equations (2.51) and (2.53),the resulting policy is socially sub-optimal. It is sub-optimal since it results in an excessive level of inflation ($\Delta p_t^D > \Delta p^*$), that is it produces an *inflationary bias* with no gains in the form of systematic lower unemployment ($u_t^D > u^*$).

Note that the greater the slope of the Phillips curve $1/(1—\beta)$ (that is, the greater the reduction in unemployment from unanticipated inflation) and the greater ε (the less costly the inflation) the higher the inflation rate.

Substituting (2.51) and (2.53) into (2.49) and taking expectations, the implied expected loss at time t—1 under the discretionary regime is

$$E_{t-1} L_t^D = \varepsilon \left[\tilde{u} + \frac{\varepsilon}{2(1-\beta)^2} \right] \qquad (2.54)$$

Following Barro and Gordon (1983a, p. 106) suppose now that at time t—1 the central bank announces a rule for determining inflation.

Suppose the rule is

$$_{t-1}\Delta p_t^R = 0 \tag{2.55}$$

where superscript R denotes rules. Equation (2.55) amounts to a constant-growth-rate rule, where the rate of growth of the money supply happens to be zero.[32] If wage setters believe that the central bank will stick to its announcement at time t expected inflation is

$$E_{t-1}\,\Delta p_t = 0 \tag{2.56}$$

Suppose also that the central bank in fact sticks to its announcement that is

$$\Delta p_t^R = 0 \tag{2.57}$$

Since actual and expected inflation are identical unantipated inflation is zero implying that

$$u_t^R = \tilde{u} \tag{2.58}$$

Equations (2.57) and (2.58) highlight the time-inconsistency of socially optimal monetary policy. As can be seen from equations (2.57) and (2.58) inflation is at its target value $\Delta p_t^R = \Delta p^*$ and unemployment at the natural rate.[33] However, this policy is time inconsistent. It is time inconsistent since the rule (2.55) is no longer optimal at time t, even though no new relevant information has appeared in the meantime. This is because once wage setters have 'chosen' expected inflation and wage contracts have been signed at time t—1 — in order to minimize its loss function at time t — the central bank has an incentive to deviate ex post from its announced plan. Thus the plan is time—inconsistent.

Hence the dilemma described by Kydland and Prescott (1977) is that the socially optimal monetary policy strategy (zero inflation) is time-inconsistent, while the time-consistent policy (discretion) is socially sub--optimal. The implied expected value of the loss function under the rules regime is

$$E_{t-1}L_t^R = \varepsilon\tilde{u} \tag{2.59}$$

The welfare losses are obviously higher under the discretionary regime as

$$E_{t-1}(L_t^D - L_t^R) = \frac{\varepsilon^2}{2(1-\beta)^2} > 0 \qquad (2.60)$$

The intuition behind this result is straightforward. Under the rules regime unemployment is still at the natural level but inflation is lower. Hence, the central bank would clearly like to find ways to credibly precommit to lower inflation, as this could reduce her welfare losses. Precommitment and the associated issues of cheating and temptation are the subject of the following sub—section.

VII.2 Cheating, Non-Credible Precommitments and Macroeconomic Performance across Monetary Regimes

As noted by Barro and Gordon (1983a, p. 107) the central bank is tempted to renege on commitments. In particular if wage setters expect zero inflation — as occurs under the rule — then the central bank would like to implement a positive inflation rate in order to drive down unemployment from an inflation shock. Now we will analyse how much the central bank can gain by cheating. Assume that wage setters have the expectation

$$E_{t-1}\, \Delta p_t = 0 \qquad (2.56)$$

If the central bank treats this expectation as given, the choice of Δp_t that minimizes L_t is the one that we found under discretion

$$\Delta p_t^{CH} = \frac{\varepsilon}{1-\beta} \qquad (2.61)$$ [34]

where superscript CH denotes the cheating regime. Subtracting (2.56) from (2.61) unanticipated inflation is $\varepsilon/(1-\beta)$. Hence unemployment under the cheating regime is

$$u_t^{CH} = \tilde{u} - \frac{\varepsilon}{(1-\beta)^2} < \tilde{u} \qquad (2.62)$$

Thus because of the inflation shock unemployment is lower than the natural rate. Substituting (2.61) and (2.62) in (2.49) the implied expected value of the loss function is

$$E_{t-1} L_t^{CH} = \varepsilon[\tilde{u} - \frac{\varepsilon}{2(1-\beta)^2}] \qquad (2.63)$$

The point is that this expected loss is *lower* than that, $E_{t-1}L_t^R$, the rules regime. Following Barro and Gordon we refer to the difference between these expected losses as the temptation to renege on the rule — or simply as the *temptation*. In the present case we have

$$E_{t-1}[L_t^R - L_t^{CH}] = \frac{\varepsilon^2}{2(1-\beta)^2} > 0 \tag{2.64}$$

Note that there is still one more type of outcome. Suppose that the central bank announces the rule

$$_{t-1}\Delta p_t^R = 0 \tag{2.55}$$

but that the private sector expects the cheating inflation rate

$$E_{t-1}\,\Delta p_t = \Delta p_t^{CH} \tag{2.65}$$

Suppose also that the central bank in fact sticks to its accouncement that is

$$\Delta p_t^R = 0 \tag{2.57}$$

Subtracting (2.65) from (2.57) and taking account of (2.61) unanticipated inflation is $-\varepsilon/(1-\beta)$. Hence unemployment is

$$u_t^{RN} = \tilde{u} + \frac{\varepsilon}{(1-\beta)^2} > \tilde{u} \tag{2.66}$$

where superscript RN denotes the non-credible rules regime.[35] Because of a *negative* inflation shock — that is *deflationary* monetary policy — unemployment is *higher* than the natural rate.

Substituting (2.57) and (2.66) in the loss function (2.49) and taking expectations we get

$$E_{t-1}L_t^{RN} = \varepsilon\tilde{u} + \frac{\varepsilon}{(1-\beta)^2} \tag{2.67}$$

The important thing to note is that this outcome is even worse than under the discretionary regime for

$$E_{t-1}[L_t^{RN} - L_t^{D}] = \frac{\varepsilon^2}{2(1-\beta)^2} > 0 \tag{2.68}$$

Therefore at the present stage we have four type of outcomes. Ranging from low losses to high these are

$$E_{t-1}\, L_t^{CH} < E_{t-1}\, L_t^{R} < E_{t-1}\, L_t^{D} < E_{t-1}\, L_t^{RN} \tag{2.69}$$

Rules with people expecting the cheating rate is worse than discretion because the central bank creates excessive unemployment (even higher than the natural rate) which is not worth the lower inflation. Next, discretion is worse than the rule because no inflation shocks arise in either case, but the commitment under the rule avoids excessive inflation. Cheating - when wage setters anticipate the rule — delivers the best results. This is because the inflation shock eliminates part of the unemployment problem which is worth the extra inflation.[36] The foregoing discussion can be summarized in Table 2.2.[37]

Table 2.2 Macroeconomic performance across policy regimes

Actual policy	Expectations of wage-setters $E_{t-1}\Delta p_t = 0$	$E_{t-1}\Delta p_t = \frac{\varepsilon}{1-\beta}$
Rule $\Delta p_t = 0$	Pareto equilibrium $u_t^{R} = \tilde{u}$ $\Delta p_t^{R} = 0$	$u_t^{RN} > \tilde{u}$ $\Delta p_t^{RN} = 0$
Discretion $\Delta p_t = \frac{\varepsilon}{1-\beta}$	$u_t^{CH} < \tilde{u}$ $\Delta p_t^{CH} = \frac{\varepsilon}{1-\beta}$	Nash equilibrium $u_t^{D} = \tilde{u}$ $\Delta p_t^{D} = \frac{\varepsilon}{1-\beta}$

Note that the cheating outcome is feasible only when people can be systematically deceived into maintaining low inflationary expectations. This completes the description of the one period Phillips curve monetary policy game.

We now move on to a multiperiod extension and the associated issues of reputation and credibility.

VII.3 Repeated Games, Trigger Strategies and Reputation

In this section we consider a repeated or super game. Following Barro and Gordon (1983a) we show that repeated interaction between the policymaker and wage setters may give rise to reputational forces that can substitute for formal rules. In the following example of a reputational equilibrium the outcome turns out to be weighted averages of those from discretion and those from precommitment.

The central bank's objective at date t entails the minimization of the present value of the loss function (2.49) that is

$$\sum_{t=0}^{\infty} q^t [\frac{1}{2}(\Delta p_t)^2 + \varepsilon\, u_t] \qquad 0 < q \leq 1 \qquad (2.70)$$

where q is the discount factor that applies between periods t and t+1, that is $q \equiv 1/(1+\rho)$ and ρ is the discount rate. Note that if $q = 1$ equation (2.70) reduces to equation (2.49). Thus (2.70) is a multiperiod extension of (2.49).

Suppose now that the central bank announces the inflation rate.

$$_{t-1}\Delta p_t^R = \Delta p \qquad (2.71)$$

That is, the rule specifies constant inflation (a constant-growth-rate rule). Wage setters choose their inflationary expectations for period t as follows.

$$E_{t-1}\Delta p_t = \begin{cases} _{t-1}\Delta p_t^R & \text{if } E_{t-2}\Delta p_{t-1} = \Delta p_{t-1} \\ \Delta p_t^D & \text{otherwise} \end{cases} \qquad (2.72)$$

Hence if actual inflation in the previous period accords with expectations, wage setters expect the central bank to perform in line with its announced rule for period t. If the previous period's inflation does not accord with expectations, wage setters expect instead that the central bank will inflate at the higher discretionary rate Δp_t^D. If the central bank follows its rule every period then it also validates expectations each period. Thus the central bank maintains its *reputation* or *credibility* in each period. However, if the central bank cheats during period t, then the second part of equation (2.72) says that next period's expectations are $E_t\Delta p_{t+1} = \Delta p^D_{t+1}$. Then, if in period t+1 the central bank chooses Δp^D_{t+1} (which is optimal given expectations at time t), actual and expected inflation rates coincide, although at the discretionary levels.

Accordingly, the first part of equation (2.72) says that at time t+1 wage setters anticipate the rules outcome for period t+2, $E_{t+1}\Delta p_{t+2} = {}_{t+1}\Delta p_{t+2}$.

In other words the punishment from violating the rule during period t is that the discretionary solution obtains during period t+1. But, credibility is restored as of period t+2 as though no previous violation has occured. Hence Barro and Gordon's trigger strategy mechanism, in which wage setters use their inflationary expectations as a device to deter the central bank from producing the discretionary rate of inflation, specifies only one period's worth of 'punishment' for each 'crime'.[38]

The central bank minimizes (2.70) subject to wage setters' behaviour. In considering whether to cheat today, it compares the difference between the *temptation* to do so, with the discounted value of the loss in next period's welfare because of increased inflationary expectations (the enforcement not to cheat).

Suppose that the central bank has credibility in period t. If the central bank cheats then its best choice of inflation is

$$\Delta p_t^{CH} = \frac{\varepsilon}{1-\beta} \tag{2.61}$$

Following the same procedure as in Section VII.2 the central bank now gains the temptation

$$E_{t-1}L_t^R - L_t^{CH} = \frac{1}{2}\frac{\varepsilon}{1-\beta} - \Delta p^2 \tag{2.73}$$

The cost of this violation is that discretion, rather than the rule applies for period t+1. Hence, the central bank realizes next period the loss

$$L_{t+1}^D = \varepsilon\tilde{u} + \frac{\varepsilon}{2(1-\beta)^2} \tag{2.54}$$

rather than

$$L_{t+1}^{R} = \varepsilon\tilde{u} + \frac{1}{2}\,\Delta p^2 \tag{2.74}$$

The expected present value of the difference is

$$qE_{t-1}\,L_{t+1}{}^{D} - L_{t+1}{}^{R} = \frac{q}{2}\,\frac{\varepsilon^2}{(1-\beta)^2} - \Delta p^2 \tag{2.75}$$

Following Barro and Gordon (1983a, p. 109) we refer to the difference between these losses as the *enforcement* not to renege on the rule. The central bank abides by the rule during period t — that is, sets $\Delta p_t = {}_{t-1}\Delta p_t{}^R = \Delta p$ — if the enforcement is at least as great as the temptation.

Hence in equilibrium rules satisfy the enforceability restriction

$$E_{t-1}\,(L_t{}^R - L_t{}^{CH}) \leq qE_{t-1}\,(L_{t+1}{}^D - L_{t+1}{}^R) \tag{2.76}$$

The lowest credibly sustainable rate of inflation in found by substituting (2.73) and (2.75) in (2.76), equating the two sides and solving for Δp.[39] The solution is

$$\Delta p = \frac{1-q}{1+q}\,\frac{\varepsilon}{1-\beta} \tag{2.77}$$

This rate is higher than the first-best zero inflation rate but *lower* than the discretionary rate that would occur in the absence of deterrence.

$$0 < \frac{1-q}{1+q}\,\frac{\varepsilon}{1-\beta} < \frac{\varepsilon}{1-\beta} \qquad \text{for} \quad 0 < q \leq 1 \tag{2.78}$$

Note that the higher the discount factor q, the lower Δp. The reason is that a relatively high value of q (a low rate of discount of future costs) strengthens the enforcement. Therefore even in the absence of commitments a second-best lower rate of inflation can be credibly sustained by an appropriate deterrence mechanism. This completes the Section on repeated games.

VIII AMBIGUITY, CREDIBILITY AND PRIVATE INFORMATION ABOUT THE RELATIVE CONCERN FOR PRICE STABILITY

VIII.1 The Backus and Driffill Analysis

In the Barro and Gordon (1983a) framework wage setters and the central bank are assumed to have the same information. Backus and Driffil (1985) however, extended a finitely repeated version of the Barro and Gordon policy game to a situation in which wage setters are uncertain about the preferences of the central bank. Using the notation of this chapter, in particular wage setters are uncertain about the parameter ε, that is the weight of unemployment relative to inflation stabilization in the preferences of the central bank.

Hence, the critical element in the Backus and Driffill analysis is private information about the relative concern for price stability:[40] when the central bank announces its intention to fight inflation wage setters are uncertain whether this is in fact the case, or whether it is simply an attempt to manipulate their expectations. Backus and Driffill point out that a weakness of the Barro and Gordon analysis is that the punishment strategy utilized by wage setters (equation (2.61)) is essentially arbitrary.[41]

Consequently there is an infinite number of possible reputational equilibria with no mechanism for choosing among them. In order to avoid these problems Backus and Driffill apply the Kreps and Wilson (1982a, 1982b)[42] analysis of reputation to a finitely repeated version of the Barro and Gordon policy game. For ease of exposition we consider the two-period version of Backus and Driffill as presented in Persson and Tabellini (1990, pp. 56—66). Hence the following draws heavily on their work. The behaviour of wage setters is captured by the usual Phillips curve equation

$$u_t = \tilde{u} - \frac{1}{1-\beta}(\Delta p_t - E_{t-1}\Delta p_t) \qquad (2.21)$$

The central bank minimizes

$$\sum_{t=1}^{2} q^{t-1}[\frac{1}{2}(\Delta p_t)^2 + \varepsilon u_t] \qquad (2.79)$$

As stated before, a central assumption is that wage setters do not know the true value of the weight ε in the central bank's loss function (2.79).

The central bank is one of two types: 'wet' (W) with $\varepsilon > 0$, or 'hard-nosed' (HN) with $\varepsilon = 0$. In the latter case the central bank is irrevocably committed to pursuing a zero inflation policy.

At the start of the game in period 1, wage setters assign a prior probability x_1 to the event that the central bank is hard-nosed.

$$x_1 = \text{Prob}\,(\text{HN} \mid t{=}1) \tag{2.80}$$

and $(1 - x_1)$ to the complementary event that the central bank is wet. Since the central bank knows its own type the game is one of private information about the relative concern for price stability.

In the Backus and Driffill framework, monetary policy signals the central bank's preferences. By observing policy in period 1, wage setters learn something about the true value of ε. Wage setters' beliefs, x_1, are revised according to Bayes' rule.[43] Period 2 nominal wages are then set on the basis of the posterior beliefs, x_2.

Let $\tilde{\rho}_t = \text{Prob}(\Delta p_t = 0 \mid \varepsilon > 0)$ be the period t probability assigned by wage setters to the event that the wet type tries to masquerade as being hard-nosed by playing zero inflation. If wage setters observe the policy $\Delta p_1 = 0$ or $\Delta p_1 = \varepsilon/(1-\beta)$,[44] Bayes' rule suggests how to rationally update these prior beliefs.

$$x_2 = \text{Prob}(\text{HN} \mid \Delta p_1) = \frac{x_1 \text{Prob}(\Delta p_1 \mid \text{HN})}{\text{Prob}(\Delta p_1)} \tag{2.81}$$

Hence the posterior probability that the central bank is hard-nosed is given by the prior multiplied by the conditional probability to observe the policy Δp_1 given that the central bank is hard-nosed ($\varepsilon = 0$), divided by the unconditional probability to observe the policy Δp_1.

Clearly, if the 'discretionary' policy $\Delta p_1 = \varepsilon/(1-\beta)$ is observed, (2.81) gives

$$x_2 = \frac{x_1 \cdot 0}{(1 - x_1)(1 - \tilde{\rho}_1)} = 0 \tag{2.82}$$

since a hard-nosed policymaker (an 'inflation hawk') never inflates. However, if zero inflation ('the rule') is observed, (2.81) gives

$$x_2 = \frac{x_1 \cdot 1}{x_1 + \tilde{\rho}_1 (1 - x_1)} \tag{2.83}$$

Since the hard-nosed central banker chooses zero inflation with probability 1 and the wet type chooses it with probability $\tilde{\rho}_1$.

In equilibrium $\tilde{\rho}_1$ must be equal to the true probability chosen by a wet central bank in period 1.[45] Inserting this equilibrium requirement in (2.82) we have the following (rational) private learning process

$$x_2 = \begin{cases} \dfrac{x_1}{x_1 + \rho_1(1 - x_1)} & \text{if } \Delta p_1 = 0 \\ 0 & \text{otherwise} \end{cases} \tag{2.84}$$

Note that x_2 is a natural measure of central bank *reputation*. If a positive inflation rate is observed in period 1, then the reputation of being hard-nosed is destroyed and $x_2 = 0$. If, on the other hand, zero inflation is observed, then the central bank could really be hard-nosed; or it could simply pretend to do so — that is it could be masquerading — in order to maintain or enhance its reputation. Since only a non-masquerading wet central bank inflates, and if it does at the 'discretionary' one shot rate $\varepsilon/(1—\beta)$, expected inflation is

$$E_{t-1}\Delta p_t = (1 - \rho_t)(1 - x_t) \frac{\varepsilon}{1 - \beta} \tag{2.85}$$

From (2.85) it can be seen that the higher x_t the lower expected inflation. This is the source of the central bank's reputational incentives. As pointed out by Persson and Tabellini (1990, p. 61) in the last period (period 2), a wet central bank has no incentive to maintain its reputation. Hence it always sets

$$\Delta p_2^W = \frac{\varepsilon}{1 - \beta} \tag{2.86}$$

Thus, $\rho_2 = 0$ and

$$E_1 \Delta p^W{}_2 = (1—x_2)\ \varepsilon/(1—\beta) \tag{2.87}$$

Subtracting (2.87) from (2.86) unanticipated inflation is $x_2\varepsilon/(1-\beta)$. Hence unemployment in period 2 is

$$u_2^W = \tilde{u} - \frac{x_2\varepsilon}{(1-\beta)^2} \tag{2.88}$$

Substituting (2.86) and (2.88) in (2.49) the wet central bank's loss is

$$L_2^W = \varepsilon[\tilde{u} + \frac{(1-2x_2)\varepsilon}{2(1-\beta)^2}] \tag{2.89}$$

Taking the first derivative of (2.89) with respect to x_2, we find that it is given by

$$\frac{\partial L_2^W}{\partial x_2} = -\frac{\varepsilon^2}{(1-\beta)^2} < 0 \tag{2.90}$$

We can expand (2.90) as

$$\frac{\partial L_2^W}{\partial x_2} = \frac{\partial E_1 \Delta p_2^W}{\partial x_2} \cdot \frac{\partial u_2}{\partial E_1 \Delta p_2^W} \cdot \frac{\partial L_2^W}{\partial u_2} < 0 \tag{2.91}$$

From (2.91) it can be seen that an increase in the central bank's period 2 reputation reduces its loss in period 2 because a higher reputation decreases inflationary expectations which in turn decrease unemployment.[46]

Hence the Backus Driffill model features a trade-off between the short-run benefits of inflation and the long-run costs of losing its reputation. This trade-off can be expressed algebraicly using Barro and Gordon's (1983a) concepts of temptation and enforcement.

If the central bank inflates in period 1 the implied expected value of the loss function is

$$E_0 L_1^W = \varepsilon[\tilde{u} - \frac{\varepsilon}{2}(1-\beta)^2 + \frac{1}{1-\beta} E_0 \Delta p_1] \tag{2.92}$$

rather than

$$E_0L_1^{HN} = \varepsilon[\tilde{u} + \frac{1}{1-\beta}E_0\Delta p_1] \tag{2.93}$$

Following the set-up of Section VII.2 we refer to the difference between these losses as the *temptation.* In the present case we have

$$E_0[L_1^{HN} - L_1^{W}] = \frac{\varepsilon^2}{2(1-\beta)^2} \tag{2.94}$$

Note that this expression is exactly the same as the temptation in Section VII.2 (see equation (2.64)). The cost of inflating in period 1 rather than following a zero inflation policy is that the central bank's reputation in period 2, x_2, is zero rather than $x_1/(x_1 + \rho_1(1-x_1))$ (see the learning mechanism (2.84)).

Hence the central bank realizes in period 2 the loss

$$L_2^{W} = \varepsilon[\tilde{u} + \frac{\varepsilon}{2(1-\beta)^2}] \tag{2.95}$$

rather than

$$L_2^{HN} = \varepsilon[\tilde{u} + \frac{(1-2x_2)\varepsilon}{2(1-\beta)^2}] \tag{2.96}$$

The expected present value of the difference is

$$qE_0[L_2^{W} - L_2^{HN}] = \frac{qx_2\varepsilon^2}{(1-\beta)^2} \tag{2.97}$$

Following Barro and Gordon (1983a, p. 109) we refer to the difference between these losses as the *enforcement*.

Persson and Tabellini (1990, p. 62) point out that (2.97) plays the same role as the enforcement of the Barro Gordon model, be it that here it is due to a genuine change of beliefs rather than to an artificial 'punishment' by wage setters.

Whether the reputational incentives are strong enough depends on the enforceability restriction.

$$E_0[L_1^{HN} - L_1^{W}] \lesseqqgtr qE_0[L_2^{W} - L_2^{HN}] \tag{2.98}$$

They point out that depending on the value of q different equilibria may emerge.[47]

The general point however is that reputation can sustain low-inflation monetary policy, even in a finite-horizon set up. Hence Backus and Driffill (1985, p. 537) suggest that governments may try to appoint central bankers with reputations for fighting inflation, even if their own preferences place positive weight on unemployment. By doing so they minimize the costs associated with uncertainty about policy and with the credibility problem wet central banks have with noninflationary policies.

As pointed out by Cukierman (1986, p. 8) the Backus and Driffill analysis is restricted by the fact that the policy maker can be one of only two unchanging types. As a consequence, once a reputation is destroyed it cannot be rebuilt. Those features are inconsistent with the observed frequent reversals in the rate of monetary growth in the United States, England and other democracies. Therefore Cukierman and Meltzer (1986) extend the Backus and Driffill model in the sense that policy-maker's objectives are allowed to change continuously through time and to assume an infinite number of values. In addition, Cukierman and Meltzer analyse the effect of the precision of monetary control on the choice of policies. They conceive of credibility as the speed with which wage setters detect changes in the policy maker's objectives. Their analysis is the subject of the next subsection.

VIII.2 The Cukierman and Meltzer Analysis

Cukierman and Meltzer (1986) (CM) extend the Backus and Driffill model in the sense that policymaker's objectives are allowed to change continuously through time and to assume an infinite number of values. In this section we summarize their findings. A slightly different version of the CM model is presented in Cukierman (1992), chapter 9.[48] The behaviour of wage setters is captured by the Phillips curve

$$u_t = \tilde{u} - (\Delta m_t - E_{t-1}\Delta m_t) \tag{2.99}$$

Hence unemployment deviates from the natural rate to the extent that there are unanticipated boosts to monetary growth. For analytic convenience CM work with a slope coefficient normalized at unity.[49] Also they switch to an infinite horizon environment. Hence the central bank minimizes

$$E_0 \sum_{t=0}^{\infty} q^t[\tfrac{1}{2}(\Delta m_t)^2 + \varepsilon_t u_t] \qquad (2.100)$$

Note that equation (2.100) is a more general version of the analogous equation in the Backus and Driffill model. Apart from (2.100) being stated in terms of monetary growth rather than inflation, the major difference is that ε, the weight of unemployment stabilization relative to inflation stabilization, is time dependent. In the CM analysis ε rather than being restricted to either being wet ($\varepsilon > 0$) or hardnosed ($\varepsilon = 0$), can now take an infinite number of values.

Equations (2.101) and (2.101) specify the stochastic behaviour of the parameter ε and indicate that central bank objectives exhibit a certain degree of persistence

$$\varepsilon_t = \tilde{\varepsilon} + e_t \qquad (2.101)$$

$$e_t = \rho e_{t-1} + v_t^e \quad 0 < \rho < 1 \qquad v^e \sim N(0, \sigma_v^2) \qquad (2.102)$$

where $\tilde{\varepsilon}$ is a positive publicly known constant and e_t a first-order Markoff process whose realization is known only to the central bank. Thus, the central bank's aversion to unemployment is not constant over time, but varies in a serially correlated fashion.

Monetary growth immediately effects inflation. However, there is a stochastic error in monetary control, so that,

$$\Delta m_t = \Delta m_t^D + \psi_t \qquad \psi \sim N(0, \sigma_\psi^2) \qquad (2.103)$$

where Δm_t, Δm_t^D are actual and planned monetary growth.

The information structure is as follows. The coefficients q and ρ and the variances σ_v^2 and σ_ψ^2 are common knowledge. The central assumption in the CM framework is the following. The central bank knows exactly what it wants to achieve currently, that is, the value of ε_t and v_t, whereas wage setters do not observe ε_t directly but can draw inferences about the policymaker's objectives from observations of past monetary growth. Hence, like in the Backus and Driffill analysis the central bank has private information about its objectives.

The timing of events is as follows. Wage setters sign annual nominal contracts at the beginning of each year before monetary policy is chosen for that year. They take the information they have about the central bank's objectives and its behaviour into account in forming their expectations. In the second stage the central bank chooses Δm_t^D, taking the wage contracts and the associated expectations as given. In the third and final stage the control error for the period realizes and the rate of monetary growth is determined by equation (2.103).

The central bank picks that part of monetary growth that it controls so as to minimize (2.100). This gives rise to a discretionary decision rule in which the actual rate of monetary expansion depends on the current state of the central bank's objectives (ε_t) and on the current state of the control error (ψ_t).

Wage setters know the structure of the decision rule but do not know the current state e_t of the central bank's objectives. However they utilize information on all past rates of monetary growth to form a minimum variance estimate of the rate of monetary expansion for the period.[50] As pointed out by Cukierman (1992, p. 168) the central bank's decision rule depends on the process of expectations formation, whilst this process in turn depends on the central bank's decision rule. Cukierman and Meltzer (1986, p. 1105) show that the solution to the central bank's decision problem in equation (2.100) is[51]

$$\Delta m^D_t = c_0\tilde{\varepsilon} + c_1 e_t \qquad (2.104)$$

where c_0, c_1 are positive constants that depend on the parameters of the central bank's objective function and the precision of monetary control. When equation (2.104) is substituted in equation (2.103), actual monetary growth can be expressed as

$$\Delta m_t = c_0\tilde{\varepsilon} + c_1 e_t + \psi_t \qquad (2.105)$$

As stated before the CM model assumes that wage setters do not know the current state of the central bank's objectives. Wage setters however do know the central bank's decision rule in equation (2.105) and have observed Δm_t in each period up to and including the previous one. Since Δm_t has some degree of persistence, past values of monetary growth convey noisy but meaningful information about future monetary growth to wage setters. The noise is induced by the control error ψ_t.

CM show that the optimal predictor for future monetary growth adjusts slowly to actual changes in observed money growth; specifically

$$E_{t-1}\Delta m_t = \sum_{j=0}^{\infty} \lambda^j [(1-\rho)c_0\tilde{\varepsilon} + (\rho-\lambda)\Delta m_{t-1-j}] \quad 0<\lambda<1 \qquad (2.106)$$

Equation (2.106) specifies that expected monetary growth is a geometrically distributed lag, with decreasing weights, of weighted averages of the unconditional mean money growth $c_0\tilde{\varepsilon}$ and actually observed past rates of money growth Δm_{t-1-j}. The parameter λ is determined by the degree of persistence in the central bank's objectives (ρ), the precision of monetary control (σ_ψ^2) and the degree of instability in the central bank's objectives as measured by σ_v^2. The weight λ in equation (2.106) measures the degree of sluggishiness in expectations. Hence, the higher is λ the more attention wage setters pay to the distant past, and the slower the speed at which they recognize that a change in the central bank's objectives has actually occurred.

Since CM conceive of *credibility* as this speed of learning, the higher λ the lower credibility. In addition CM show that λ is a decreasing function of σ_v^2 and an increasing function of σ_ψ^2.[52] Hence, using this measure of credibility, the more precise monetary control is (the lower σ_ψ^2) the higher is credibility. Note that this characterization of credibility differs from the Backus and Driffill model of the previous section. In the latter model credibility or reputation is a *state variable*. It is the current subjective probability assigned by wage setters to the event that the policymaker is hard-nosed. Here credibility is a *parameter*.

At this point it is useful to compare CM with the Barro and Gordon (1983a) model as presented in Section VII.1. Equation (2.104) specializes to Barro and Gordon's discretionary solution (equation (2.51)) when asymmetric information is removed from the model.

Formally, asymmetric information is eliminated when for a given (non zero) σ_ψ^2 the variability of the central bank's objectives σ_v^2 is zero. In this case the weight of unemployment relative to inflation stabilization in the preferences of the central bank, ε_t, is common knowledge. The distributional assumptions on v imply that $\varepsilon_t \sim N(\tilde{\varepsilon}, \sigma_\varepsilon^2)$. The (asymptotic) variance of ε can be obtained from (2.101) and (2.102), it is given by[53]

$$\sigma_\varepsilon^2 = \frac{\sigma_v^2}{1-\rho^2} \qquad (2.107)$$

Hence, if $\sigma_v^2 = 0$, $\sigma_\varepsilon^2 = 0$ and $\varepsilon_t = \tilde{\varepsilon}$. Hence, in this case the solution of Cukierman and Meltzer (1986, p. 1107) specializes to

$$\Delta m_t^D = \tilde{\varepsilon} \qquad (2.108)$$

This equation can be obtained from the Barro and Gordon model by setting $\varepsilon = \tilde{\varepsilon}$, $\beta = 0$ and $\Delta m_t = \Delta p_t$ in equation (2.51).

To this point the level of noise in the control of money was considered to be a technologically given parameter. Suppose however, that technology only puts a lower bound $\underline{\sigma}_{\psi}^2$ on the variance of the control error. The central bank can choose any $\sigma_{\psi}^2 \geq \underline{\sigma}_{\psi}^2$. CM assume for simplicity $\underline{\sigma}_{\psi}^2 = 0$. The central bank sets the value of σ_{ψ}^2 once and for all so as to minimize the long-run expected value of its loss function (2.100). The choice of this variance determines *the politically optimal level of ambiguity* in the conduct of monetary policy, since a higher choice of σ_{ψ}^2, conveys more ambiguous signals to wage setters.

By manipulating the monetary control parameter, σ_{ψ}^2, the central bank affects the speed at which wage setters become aware of changes in central bank objectives and therefore the average value of benefits from monetary surprises.

In particular an increase in ambiguity increases the benefits from economic stimulation, that is the benefits from u being smaller than ũ, but it also increases the average inflation rate which is bad from the central bank's point of view. The level of ambiguity is chosen by weighting the effects of those two conflicting elements on the central bank's objectives. As stated by Goodhart (1994, p. 108), the higher σ_{ψ}^2 the more dust is thrown into the eyes of wage setters, and the central bank's current intentions can be forecast less well from past monetary growth; hence the is less value to the authorities to restrain inflation now to gain greater counter-inflation credibility in the future. According to Goodhart this gives the basic trade-off that emerges clearly from the CM analysis. The more dust, pervasive uncertainty, that the public encounters, the greater the power, and the leeway, that the central bank has to carry out surprise monetary actions with beneficial effects on unemployment, but the less their resulting credibility and the higher mean inflation. Hence, the CM analysis is one of the first papers that features the important trade-off between *credibility* and *flexibility*. By choosing more noisy monetary control procedures the central bank loses credibility but gains the flexibility to lower unemployment by surprise inflation.

This trade-off has also been investigated in the context of models with private information about the economy by Canzoneri (1985) and Rogoff (1985). Their models are the subject of the next section.

IX PRIVATE INFORMATION ABOUT THE ECONOMY: CREDIBILITY VERSUS FLEXIBILITY

IX.1 The Canzoneri Model

Now we move on to a setting in which the central bank has private information about the economy. This is neatly modelled by Canzoneri (1985). Suppose the central bank has forecasts of money demand that are private information. In this case the following scenario may apply. Monetary aggregates surge ahead of expected or targeted rates: the central bank claims that it is accommodating a perceived increase in money demand in order to stabilize the price level; wage setters counter that the central bank is running an inflationary policy to expand employment; a period of credibility building ensues, which may focus upon the personalities of policymakers, targeting produres, or even proposals for legislative reform. A key element in this scenario is that wage setters cannot verify the central bank's claim; the central bank's forecast of money demand is *private information*. Canzoneri models this scenario as a non-cooperative game which can be seen as an extension of the Barro and Gordon model outlined in Section VII.

The behaviour of wage setters is captured by the Phillips curve

$$u_t = \tilde{u} - (\Delta p_t - E_{t-1}\Delta p_t)^{54} \qquad (2.109)$$

The central bank minimizes

$$L_t = \tfrac{1}{2}(\Delta p_t)^2 + \frac{\varepsilon}{2}(u_t)^2 \qquad (2.110)$$

Equation (2.110) is the specification of the central bank's loss function employed throughout the remainder of this book. The central bank stabilizes inflation and unemployment around their target values (which here are normalized at zero).

Again the parameter ε measures the weight of unemployment relative to inflation stabilization in the preferences of the central bank. The model is closed with a simple quantity equation

$$m_t - p_t = \tilde{y} + v_t \qquad (2.111)$$

where m_t is the log of the money supply, $\tilde{y}$ is the equilibrium or natural rate of output and v_t is a stochastic disturbance to money demand.[55]

First differencing, (2.111) becomes

$$\Delta m_t - \Delta p_t = \Delta v_t \qquad (2.112)$$

If the disturbance to money demand follows a random walk,

$$v_t = v_{t-1} + \delta \qquad \delta \sim N(0, \sigma^2_\delta) \qquad (2.113)$$

Then (2.112) becomes

$$\Delta m_t - \Delta p_t = \delta_t \tag{2.114}$$

where δ_t is the white noise innovation.

Now we come to the information structure of the game. The central assumption in the Canzoneri model is that information is *asymmetric*. Wage setters do not see δ_t at the time they sign wage contracts but the central bank has forecasts of money demand that are private information. Hence the central bank has some forecast of δ_t. More specifically, let δ_t be decomposed into s_t and ψ_t,

$$\delta_t = s_t + \psi_t \tag{2.115}$$

where s_t is the central bank's forecast of δ_t, and ψ_t is its forecast error. The forecast s_t is private central bank's information and is not observed by wage setters. The timing of events is as follows. Wage setters form $E_{t-1}\Delta m_t$ on the basis of their knowledge of the central bank's loss function and their expectation that δ_t (and s_t and ψ_t) is zero. Next, the central bank sets Δm_t to minimize its loss function (2.110), knowing $E_{t-1}\Delta m_t$ and its own forecast of δ_t.

Ex post, wage setters can calculate δ_t from (2.112) for they will then observe both Δm_t and Δp_t. However, since information is asymmetric, they cannot decompose δ_t into the central bank's forecast, s_t, and the forecast error, ψ_t.

The equilibrium can now be found as follows. From the first order conditions for a minimum of L_t taking $E_{t-1}\Delta m_t$ as a fixed parameter we obtain the central bank's reaction function to wage setters' expectations

$$\Delta m_t = \frac{\varepsilon}{1+\varepsilon}[\tilde{u} + E_{t-1}\Delta m_t - E_{t-1}\Delta v_t] + \Delta v_t \tag{2.116}$$

Taking expectations conditional on information available to wage setters at t−1 of (2.116) gives

$$E_{t-1}\Delta m_t = \varepsilon\tilde{u} \tag{2.117}$$

Equation (2.117) is the reaction function of wage setters. Upon substituting (2.117) into (2.116), noting that wage setters cannot forecast shocks to velocity ($E_{t-1}\Delta v_t = 0$) and that the central bank uses s_t as a signal for Δv_t we obtain the discretionary rate of monetary expansion under private information

$$\Delta m_t^{DP} = \varepsilon\tilde{u} + s_t \tag{2.118}$$

where superscript DP denotes discretion under private information.

Substituting (2.113) and (2.118) into (2.112) we get the discretionary rate of inflation

$$\Delta p_t^{DP} = \varepsilon\tilde{u} - \psi_t \tag{2.119}$$

Hence unexpected inflation is

$$\Delta p_t^{DP} - E_{t-1}\Delta p_t^{DP} = -\psi_t \tag{2.120}$$

Finally, the level of unemployment can be found by substituting (2.120) into (2.109)

$$u_t^{DP} = \tilde{u} + \psi_t \tag{2.121}$$

Now the outcome will be compared with the benchmark case of *symmetric information*. In the latter case the central bank is as ignorant as the private sector about shocks to money demand. Setting $s_t = 0$ in equation (2.118) we obtain the discretionary rate of monetary expansion under symmetric information

$$\Delta m_t^{DS} = \varepsilon\tilde{u} \tag{2.122}$$

where superscript DS denotes discretion under symmetric information. Proceeding as before the DS-regime counterparts of equations (2.119) and (2.121) are

$$\Delta p_t^{DS} = \varepsilon\tilde{u} - \delta_t \tag{2.123}$$

$$u_t^{DS} = \tilde{u} + \delta_t \tag{2.124}$$

We are now prepared to evaluate both information structures from the perspective of society. Substituting the results relevant for the central bank ((2.119) and (2.121), (2.123) and (2.124)) into the central bank's loss function (2.110) and taking expectations we obtain

$$E_{t-1}L_t^{DP} = \frac{1+\varepsilon}{2}[\varepsilon\tilde{u}^2 + \sigma_\psi^2] \tag{2.125}$$

$$E_{t-1}L_t^{DS} + \frac{1+\varepsilon}{2}[\varepsilon\tilde{u}^2 + \sigma_\delta^2] \qquad (2.126)$$

Subtracting (2.125) from (2.126) the per-period difference in welfare losses between the symmetric information regime and the private information regime is given by

$$E_{t-1}[L_t^{DS} - L_t^{DP}] = \frac{1+\varepsilon}{2}[\sigma_\delta^2 - \sigma_\psi^2] \qquad (2.127)$$

Since $\sigma^2_\delta > \sigma_\psi{}^2$ welfare losses under symmetric information are higher than under private information.

The reason is that with private information the central bank is left with more *flexibility* to accommodate s_t, before it passes on to inflation and unemployment; this benefits society as a whole.

However, as stated at the beginning of this section under private information the central bank is faced with a credibility problem. Suppose the central bank sets a high Δm_t, claiming to be accommodating an unexpectedly high money demand; wage setters charge that it is instead running an inflationary policy to increase employment, and a credibility breakdown ensues. If the central bank's forecast of money demand is private information, the central bank's adherence to mere stabilization policy cannot be verified directly. Hence, then the problem becomes the trading off of the *flexibility* needed for stabilization with the *credibility* constraint required for eliminating the inflation bias; this problem is the main subject of the next subsection.

IX.2 Optimal Commitment in Monetary Policy: the Rogoff-Lohmann Analysis

Rogoff (1985) considers an alternative approach to the time consistency problem. He demonstrates that society can make itself better off by selecting an agent to head the central bank who is known to place a greater weight on inflation stabilization (relative to unemployment stabilization) than is embodied in the social loss function L.

Suppose that in period t-1 society (the principal[56]) selects an agent to head the central bank in period t. The reputation of this individual is such that if he is appointed to head the central bank, he will minimize the following loss function.

$$I_t = \frac{(1+d_2)}{2}(\Delta p_t)^2 + \frac{\varepsilon}{2}(u_t)^2 \qquad (2.128)$$

When d_2 is strictly greater than zero, then this agent places a greater relative weight on inflation stabilization than society does. Note that if $d_2 = 0$ equation (2.128) reduces to the social loss function (2.110).

The central bank minimizes (2.128) subject to the Phillips curve

$$u_t = \tilde{u} - (\Delta p_t - E_{t-1}\,\Delta p_t + \mu_t)^{57} \tag{2.129}$$

where

$$\mu_t = v^{\mu}_t \qquad v^{\mu}_t \sim N\,(0, \sigma^2_{\mu}) \tag{2.130}$$

As in the Canzoneri (1985) analysis the central bank here has *private information* about the economy. This fact is reflected in the timing of the game.

First nominal wage contracts are signed. In the present set-up nominal wage contracts are reflected in expected inflation. Next, the productivity shock (v^{μ}_t) realizes. This shock is unknown to wage setters at the time contracts are signed but is observed by the central bank. After observing the shock the central bank sets monetary policy (the inflation rate). Finally unemployment is determined.

The algorithm for deriving the time-consistent equilibrium is as follows. Substituting the Phillips curve (2.129) in the loss function (2.128), from the first order conditions for a minimum of (2.128), i.e. $\partial I_t/\partial \Delta p_t = 0$, we obtain the central bank's reaction function to wage-setter's expectations

$$\Delta p_t^I = \frac{\varepsilon}{(1+d_2)+\varepsilon}\tilde{u} + \frac{\varepsilon}{(1+d_2)+\varepsilon}E_{t-1}\Delta p_t^I - \frac{\varepsilon}{(1+d_2)+\varepsilon}v_t^{\mu} \tag{2.131}$$

where superscript I denotes the independent central bank regime. Taking expectations conditional on information at t-1 of (2.131) gives

$$E_{t-1}\Delta p_t^I = \frac{\varepsilon}{(1+d_2)}\tilde{u} \tag{2.132}$$

Equation (2.132) is the reaction function of wage-setters. Upon substituting (2.132) in (2.131) we get the solution for the inflation rate

$$\Delta p_t^I = \frac{\varepsilon}{(1+d_2)}\tilde{u} - \frac{\varepsilon}{(1+d_2)+\varepsilon}v_t^{\mu} \tag{2.133}$$

A comparison of inflation under discretion ($d_2 = 0$) and (2.132) shows that average inflation (the inflationary bias) will be lower under an independent central bank. This result confirms the intuition that credibly increasing the central banker's commitment to inflation stabilization reduces the discretionary rate of inflation.

Subtracting (2.132) from (2.133) we obtain the following expression for unanticipated inflation.

$$\Delta p_t^I - E_{t-1}\Delta p_t^I = \frac{-\varepsilon}{(1+d_2)+\varepsilon} v_t^v \tag{2.134}$$

Substituting (2.134) in (2.129) we get the solution for unemployment

$$u_t^I = \tilde{u} - \frac{(1+d_2)}{[(1+d_2)+\varepsilon]} v_t^{\mu} \tag{2.135}$$

Now we evaluate central bank independence as an institutional device to overcome the time-inconsistency problem. We show that for society the optimal central banking institution depends on the balance between *credibility* and *flexibility*.

As in the Canzoneri model the problem is the trading off of the flexibility needed for stabilization with the credibility constraint required for eliminating the inflation bias. To see this following Rogoff (1985, pp. 1175-1176), we whall first develop a notation for evaluating the expected value of society's loss function under the independent central bank regime 'I', $E_{t-1}L_t^I$.[58]

$$E_{t-1}L_t^I = \tfrac{1}{2}(\varepsilon\tilde{u}^2) + \Pi^I + \Gamma^I \tag{2.136}$$

where $\Pi^I \equiv \tfrac{1}{2}(\Delta\tilde{p}_t^I)^2$ and $\Delta\tilde{p}_t^I$ is the mean inflation rate as determined by equation (2.132).

$$\Gamma^I = \tfrac{1}{2}E_{t-1}\,\{\varepsilon[v_t^{\mu} + \Delta p_t^I - E_{t-1}\Delta p_t^I)]^2 + (\Delta p_t^I - E_{t-1}\Delta p_t^I)^2\}$$

The first component of $E_{t-1}L_t^I$, $\tfrac{1}{2}\varepsilon\tilde{u}^2$ is nonstochastic and invariant across monetary regimes. If represents the deadweight loss due to the labour market distortion ($\tilde{u} > 0$).[59] This loss cannot be reduced through-monetary policy in a time-consistent rational expectations equilibrium.

The second term depends on the mean inflation rate. This term is also nonstochastic but does depend on the choice of monetary policy regime.

The final term, Γ^I, represents the 'stabilization' component of the loss function. It measures how succesfully the central bank offsets disturbances to stabilize unemployment and inflation around their mean values. By subsituting the relevant results ((2.133) and (2.135)) into (2.136) and abstracting from the (regime invariant) deadweight loss, one gets

$$\Pi^I + \Gamma^I = \frac{\varepsilon^2}{2(1+d_2)^2}\tilde{u}^2 + \frac{\varepsilon[\varepsilon+(1+d_2)^2]}{2[(1+d_2)+\varepsilon]^2}\sigma_\mu^2 \tag{2.137}$$

To solve for the value of d_2 that minimizes $E_{t-1}L_t^I$, differentiate (2.137) with respect to d_2

$$\frac{\partial E_{t-1}L_t^I}{\partial d_2} = \frac{\partial \Pi^I}{\partial d_2} + \frac{\partial \Gamma^I}{\partial d_2} \tag{2.138}$$

$$\frac{\partial \Gamma^I}{\partial d_2} = \frac{\varepsilon^2 d_2}{[(1+d_2)+\varepsilon]^3} \tag{2.139}$$

$$\frac{\partial \Pi^I}{\partial d_2} = \frac{-\varepsilon^2\tilde{u}^2}{(1+d_2)^3} \tag{2.140}$$

From (2.140) it can be seen that increasing the central bank's commitment to inflation stabilization decreases the credibility component of the social loss function. On the other hand, from (2.139) it follows that having a more independent central bank increases the stabilization component of the loss function. Hence, optimal commitment in monetary policy involves trading off the credibility gains associated with lower average inflation versus loss of flexibility due to a distorted response to output shocks.

Rogoff (1985, p. 1178) using an envelope theorem shows that the ideal agent, that is the central banker that maximizes social welfare, places a large but finite weight on inflation stabilization.[60] Hence, the optimal central banking institution is characterized by $0 < d_2^* < \infty$.

Following the Rogoff paper, in an interesting contribution Flood and Isard (1989) propose that the central bank be motivated to follow a simple zero-inflation rule in 'normal' times and to deviate from the rule when large output shocks are realized. Hence they propose a mixed strategy that combines a simple verifiable rule with discretion. The proposed arrangement mitigates the loss of *flexibility* arising from the lack of response to output shocks, at the cost of lower *credibility* arising from reintroducing an inflationary bias into monetary policy.

Flood and Isard's proposal is implemented if the central bank commits to the simple rule $\Delta p_t = 0$[61] and incurs a strictly positive but finite cost if she reneges on the rule. Using the notation of this book their framework may be summarized as follows. The political principal sets the cost d_5 in the central bank's loss function

$$L_t^{CB} = \tfrac{1}{2}(\Delta p_t)^2 + \frac{\varepsilon}{2}(u_t)^2 + d_5 \, DUM \tag{2.141}$$

where superscript CB denotes central bank.

This loss function is identical to the social loss function (2.110) except for the additive cost term. This cost is incurred by the central bank if it deviates from the simple zero inflation rule; DUM is a dummy variable, which takes on the value of unity if the central bank deviates from the rule, and zero otherwise.

The time sequence in the Flood and Isard model is as follows. After the central bank's political principal has set d_5 wage setters form inflationary expectations $E_{t-1}\Delta p_t$. Then the shock v_t^{μ} is realised. Finally, the central bank sets the inflation rate Δp_t. The central bank either follows the simple zero inflation rule or deviates from it (at cost d_5) to set the inflation rate at its discretion.

In a comment on Flood and Isard's paper Lohmann (1990) shows that the optimal degree of commitment to the simple rule d_5^* will depend crucially on the probability distribution of the shock v_t^{μ}. Since we assumed a normal distribution, in the context of this Chapter the optimal degree of commitment depends on the variance of the shock σ_{μ}^2. The reason for this is that the higher the variance of productivity shocks, the greater the need for a flexible response to output shocks.[62]

Note that in the Lohmann (1992) version of the Flood and Isard (1989) proposal considered here in normal times the central bank is motivated to follow a *zero* inflation rule. Using the formal apparatus of the Rogoff (1985) model Flood and Isard propose that the central bank be motivated to be *fully independent* ($d_2 = \infty$ in equation (2.131)) in 'normal' times and to behave in a purely discretionary manner ($d_2 = 0$ in equation (2.131)) when large output shocks are realized. The problem for the central bank's political principal is then to set d_5 in such a manner that the expected value of the social loss function is minimized.

Hence the proposed institutional arrangement can be parametrized as a fully independent central bank supplemented by an escape clause[63] ($d_2 = \infty$ and $0 < d_5 < \infty$).

In a recent paper Lohmann (1992) sheds some new light on the trade off between credibility and flexibility. Her paper can be seen as a mix of the Rogoff (1985) model and the Flood and Isard (1989) proposal. She examines the optimal design of a central banking institution that lends credibility to a low-inflation monetary policy while allowing for a flexible policy response to unforeseen contingencies.

The policymaker grants partial independence to a conservative central banker, who places a higher weight on inflation stabilization than the policymaker. If the policymaker retains the option to override the central banker's decisions at some strictly positive but finite cost, she induces the central bank to implement a nonlinear policy rule.[64]

In normal times, the central bank sets the inflation rate independently at his discretion. In extreme situations, he implements a flexible escape clause: the larger the output shock, the more the central banker accommodates the policymaker's ex post demands in order to avoid being overridden. Using the notation of this book the Lohmann framework may be summarized as follows.

The policymaker sets the parameter d_2 in the central banker's loss function (2.128). In addition, the policymaker's commitment to the central banker is explicitly formalized by the introduction of the additive cost term into the policymaker's loss function (2.141). Hence, in the Lohmann model the cost d_5 is incurred by the *policymaker* and not by the *central bank*. She assumes that the policymaker can choose a cost d_5, which she incurs when she *ex post* overrides the central banker's monetary policy decisions. The set of central banking institutions is then characterized by two variables: the central banker's additional weight d_2 on inflation stabilization, $d_2 \in \mathrm{IR}$, and the cost d_5 incurred by the policymaker when overriding the central banker, $d_5 \in [0, \infty\rangle$. The model of delegation consists of three stages:

Stage 1. The policymaker chooses the central banker's additional weight d_2 on the inflation goal and sets the cost d_5 of overriding the central banker.

Stage 2. Wage setters form inflationary expectations $E_{t-1}\Delta p_t$.

Stage 3. (i) The output shock v_t^{μ} is realized. (ii) The central banker sets the inflation rate. (iii) Either the policymaker accepts the inflation rate set by the central banker; or she pays the cost d_5 of overriding the central banker and resets the inflation rate. (iv) Inflation Δp_t and unemployment u_t are realized.

In the institutional design stage the policymaker[65] commits to a central banking institution (d_2, d_5). The wage setters, the policymaker, and the central banker play a noncooperative game in the second and third stages. The players' equilibrium strategies are a function of the institutional parameters d_5 and d_2. Under the optimal insititutional arrangement, the noncooperative game played is that in which the equilibrium outcome minimizes the policymaker's expected loss, evaluated at the institutional design stage. The model is solved by backwards induction.

Lohmann shows that the optimal central banking institution (d_2^*, d_5^*) which minimizes the policymaker's expected loss at the institutional design stage is characterized by $0 < d_2^* < \infty$, $0 < d_5^* < \infty$. Hence the policymaker appoints a central banker who places a higher but finite weight on inflation stabilization, and she retains the option to override the central banker's decisions at some strictly positive but finite cost.

This arrangement minimizes the credibility loss[66] induced by the inflationary bias and the distortionary response to the output shock. Lohmann's result on optimal commitment in monetary policy implies that the institution of a partially independent conservative central banker dominates a number of other arrangements which are contained in the set of feasible central banking institutions: discretion ($d_2 = 0$ or $d_5 = 0$), full commitment to the simple zero-inflation rule ($d_2 = \infty$ and $d_5 = \infty$), and the Rogoff (1985) model ($0 < d_2 < \infty$ and $d_5 = \infty$). Hence Rogoff's model corresponds to the case where the policymaker faces an infinite cost of overriding a political appointee.

The conclusion of the Lohmann model is that by extending the Rogoff model with an escape clause the policymaker obtains lower losses because of an improved balance between credibility and flexibility. By now, the most recent developments in the so-called optimal contract literature (Persson and Tabellini (1993), and Walsh (1993)) claim that optimal contracts between governments and central bankers may eliminate the trade-off between credibility and flexibility altogether; zero average inflation and an optimal response to supply shocks can be achieved simultaneously. This literature is the subject of the next section.

X OPTIMAL CONTRACTS FOR CENTRAL BANKERS

As pointed out by Persson and Tabellini (1993) and Walsh (1993) the issue of central bank design can also be seen as one that involves structuring a *contract* between the central bank and the government. They show that a contract between the government and the central banker in which the central banker's remuneration - the central bank's transfer - declines in proportion to inflation can attain the first best equilibrium.[67] Not only does this contract remove the inflationary bias of monetary policy, but the central bank's countercyclical policy is optimally active.

Hence, the trade-off between credibility and flexibility as emphasized by Rogoff and others is eliminated. The intuition behind this result is straightforward. In the standard Barro-Gordon model,[68] the inflationary bias is constant across states of nature, a contract therefore only needs to raise the marginal cost of inflation to the central banker by a constant amount, leaving the central banker free to respond with discretion to economic disturbances. The contract can be interpreted as an inflation targeting rule even though such rules are normally thought to be suboptimal in the presence of supply shocks.[69]

Persson and Tabellini (1993) owe a great deal of inspiration to Walsh and they consider some of the same issues. However, their framework - while more general than the standard Barro-Gordon model employed by Walsh - makes it more difficult to relate their results to the existing literature. Therefore, in reviewing the contract literature we restrict attention to Walsh (1993).[70]

Using the notation of this book his framework may be summarized as follows. The behaviour of wage-setters is captured by the Phillips curve

$$u_t = \tilde{u} - (\Delta p_t - E_{t-1}\Delta p_t + \mu_t) \tag{2.129}$$

where

$$\mu_t = v_t^{\mu} \qquad\qquad v_t^{\mu} \sim N(0, \sigma^2_{\mu}) \tag{2.130}$$

The central bank minimizes the social loss function

$$L_t = \tfrac{1}{2}(\Delta p_t)^2 + \frac{\varepsilon}{2}(u_t)^2 \tag{2.110}$$

Using (2.110), (2.129), (2.130) the reaction function of the central bank under discretion is given by

$$\Delta p_t^D = \varepsilon\tilde{u} - \frac{\varepsilon}{1+\varepsilon} v_t^{\mu} \tag{2.142}$$

where superscript D denotes discretion and equation (2.142) is obtained by setting $d_2 = 0$ in equation (2.133). Following Lohmann (1992, p. 275) figure 2.1 graphs the inflation rate set under discretion and under the regime of full commitment to the simple zero inflation rule (R). Figure 2.1 clearly illustrates the conventional trade-off between rules and discretion.

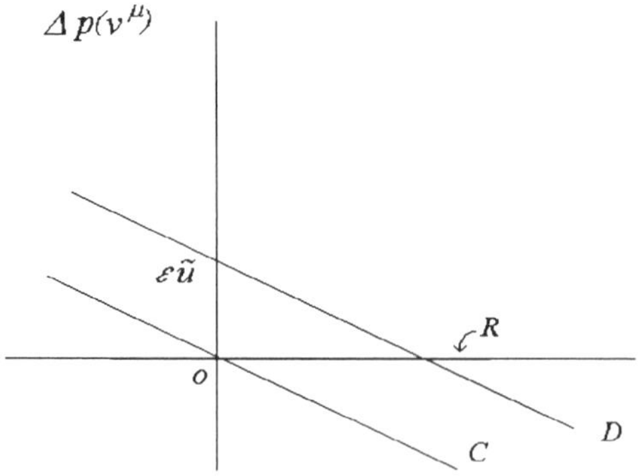

Figure 2.1 *Reaction functions under various monetary regimes*

Under the discretionary regime the central bank reacts optimally to the supply shock (the slope of the reaction function = $-\varepsilon/(1+\varepsilon)$); that is it has full *flexibility*, but this is at the expense of the *credibility* loss associated with an inflationary bias (the intercept term $\varepsilon\tilde{u}$).

On the other hand under full commitment to a zero inflation rule (ε = 0 or $d_2 = \infty$) the central bank solves its credibility problem (the intercept term is zero), but loses flexibility (the slope term is also zero).

As stated earlier an appropriately drawn up contract between the government and the central bank may serve to obtain a first best equilibrium, a rules-cum-discretion solution[71] that combines zero inflation (a zero intercept term) with an optimal countercyclical policy (the slope term should be $-\varepsilon/(1+\varepsilon)$).

In Figure 2.1 the first best state-contingent policy rule with commitments is denoted by C, where the superscript C stands for commitment.

Accordingly, the first-best state-contingent rule is given by

$$\Delta p_t^C = -\frac{\varepsilon}{1+\varepsilon} v_t^{\mu} \tag{2.143}$$

As is well known, the policy rule given by equation (2.143) is time inconsistent and therefore not credible (Persson and Tabellini (1990, p. 21), Lohmann (1992, p. 275)) if implemented by a central bank whose objective funtion is given by equation (2.110). However, now we will consider a contract that changes the central bank's incentive structure such that (2.143) emerges as its optimal strategy.

Suppose that at the institutional design stage t = t - 1 the government (the political principal) establishes a contract with the central bank under which the central bank is rewarded or penalized on the basis of observable macroeconomic outcomes. Suppose the central bank's transfer, T_t, depends on the actual inflation rate.[72]

The objective of the central bank then becomes one of choosing Δp_t to maximize

$$-L^{CB}_t = T_t - L_t \tag{2.144}$$

where L is the social loss function (2.110). The first order condition for the central bank can be solved to show that

$$\Delta p_t^D = \frac{\varepsilon}{1+\varepsilon}\tilde{u} + \frac{\varepsilon}{1+\varepsilon} E_{t-1}\Delta p_t^D - \frac{\varepsilon}{1+\varepsilon} v_t^{\mu} + \frac{1}{1+\varepsilon}\frac{\partial T_t}{\partial \Delta p_t^D} \tag{2.145}$$

Taking expectations conditional on information at t-1 of (2.145) yields

$$E_{t-1}\Delta p_t^D = \varepsilon\tilde{u} + \frac{\partial T_t}{\partial \Delta p_t^D} \tag{2.146}$$

Substituting (2.146) in (2.145) we get the solution for the time-consistent inflation rate

$$\Delta p_t^D = \varepsilon\tilde{u} - \frac{\varepsilon}{1+\varepsilon} v_t^{\mu} + \frac{\partial T_t}{\partial \Delta p_t^D} \tag{2.147}$$

Thus, the central bank can be induced to implement the optimal commitment policy (2.143) under discretion if

$$\Delta p_t^D = \Delta p_t^C \tag{2.148}$$

Substituting (2.146) and (2.145) into (2.148) gives

$$\frac{\partial T_t}{\partial \Delta p_t^D} = -\varepsilon\tilde{u} \tag{2.149}$$

This suggests the optimal transfer function will take the form

$$T_t(\Delta p_t) = c_0 - \varepsilon\tilde{u}\Delta p_t \tag{2.150}$$

Equation (2.150) is like a targeting rule in which the central bank is penalized based on the observed rate of inflation. The target rate of inflation is equal to zero.[73]

Since the transfer is linear in inflation, it has the effect of raising the marginal cost of inflation to the central bank by a constant amount. Since wage-setters expect the central bank to set Δp_t to equate the marginal benefit and marginal cost of inflation, the contract serves to reduce the rate of inflation.

As pointed out by Walsh (1993, p. 13) in the standard analysis of monetary policy, the inflationary bias arises because the central bank fails to account for the effect of its systematic behaviour on wage setters' expectations. This externality is overcome by making the transfer decline with the realized rate of inflation. By raising the marginal cost of inflation to the central bank, the contract causes the central bank to *internalize* this externality. Because the inflationary bias is independent of v_t^{μ}, the contract is not contingent on v_t^{μ}.

Thus, it is not necessary for the government to verify the central bank's observations of v_t^{μ}. Under the contract given by equation (2.150) there is no trade-off between lowering average inflation and inducing an optimal stabilization response to shocks. Thus, the trade-off between *credibility* and *flexibility* emphasized by Rogoff (1985), Lohmann (1992) and others disappears. This completes the section on the contracting approach to central bank design. We now move on to the summary and the conclusions of this survey.

XI SUMMARY AND CONCLUSIONS

In this section we will summarize the rules versus discretion debate and try to make an assessment.

During the early debate the gold standard prevailed. Therefore in this period the debate was most often about how this simple rule for monetary policy could reduce the variability of activity and prices. However, as was pointed out in Section II the actual functioning of the gold standard involved the monetary authorities in a high degree of discretion.

After World War II the Keynesian Revolution shifted emphasis for concern for the stability imposed by insitutions to the idea that central banks should act to offset specific events. The choice between monetary and fiscal policies depended on the structural coefficients of the deterministic Keynesian system viz the slopes of the IS- and LM curves. Keynesians shifted the focus from institutional design to the problem of how to achieve full employment by appropriately timed and quantified government action.

We showed in Section IV how Friedman attacked the Keynesian framework. Because of incomplete or incorrect information and various lags, policymakers not bound by a constant money growth rule would be tempted into *excess activism*, destabilizing rather than stabilizing the economy.

Was the literature in the 1950s dominated by Friedman's contentions, the 1960s saw the (expectations augmented) Phillips curve and the associated debate. A typical model used at that day for the analysis of various policy rules was presented in Section V.2. There it was shown that an integral (feedback) policy rule outperforms a constant money growth rate rule by removing rather than introducing oscillations from the adjustment path. Hence, as concerns activist policy in the context of an expectations augmented Phillips curve, the principal conclusion is that some activist policy can potentially improve on the performance of a constant money growth rate rule.

The analysis of Sections IV-VI seem to justify one major conclusion: the pre-1977 literature proved indecisive. Using the first class of arguments, that is excess activism, it was not proved that rules were better than discretion. This point has also been stressed by Argy (1988, p. 155): 'Much of the theoretical analysis in the end proved inconclusive. Everything depended on how dynamics were represented and how policy reacted.' Argy's view is shared by Fischer. According to Fischer (1990, p. 1169) the pre-1977 arguments of principle for rules lacked any convincing demonstration that rules might be systematically better than discretion.

However, the notion of *dynamic inconsistency* importantly changed the debate. This is because in the post 1977 debate a rule represents a means of overcoming the time-inconsistency problem.

In Section VII it was shown that in the Barro and Gordon (1983a) model time consistent monetary policy has an inflationary bias: it results in an excessive level of inflation with no gains in the form of systematic lower unemployment. Therefore the central bank would clearly like to find ways to credibly commit to lower inflation (possibly a constant money growth rule), as this could reduce her welfare losses. The trouble with the latter policy is that it is time inconsistent. This is the dilemma described by Kydland and Prescott. The socially optimal monetary policy strategy (zero inflation) is time inconsistent, while the time consistent policy is socially sub-optimal.

Much of the succeeding literature has dealt with the development of credible commitment technologies. Barro and Gordon (1983a) and Backus and Driffill (1985) showed that repeated interaction between wage setters and the central bank can give rise to reputational forces that may substitute for formal rules.

However, in the Barro and Gordon model of Section VII the expectation formation strategy of wage setters to deter the central bank from producing the discretionary rate of inflation is essentially arbitrary. This limitation is overcome in the Backus and Driffil (1985) and Cukierman-Meltzer (1986) models of Section VIII.

In the Backus and Driffill model expectations play the same role, however there they are due to genuine changes of beliefs (Bayesian learning) rather than to an artificial punishment strategy.

Cukierman and Meltzer extend the Backus and Driffill model in the sense that the central bank's objectives are allowed to change continuously through time and to assume an infinite number of values. In addition they analyse the effect of the precision of monetary control on the choice of policies.

They conceive of credibility as the speed at which wage setters learn about changes in the central bank's objectives. The latter speed depends on the precision of monetary control. Viewing the variance of the control error as a choice parameter, we get the basic trade-off that emerges from the Cukierman and Meltzer analysis. The higher the level of ambiguity (the variance of the control error), the more uncertainty that wage setters encounter and the greater the power and the leeway that the central bank has to carry out surprise monetary actions with beneficial effects on unemployment, but the less their resulting credibility and the higher mean inflation.

Hence, the Cukierman Meltzer analysis is one of the first papers that features the important trade-off between *credibility* and *flexibility*. By choosing more noisy monetary control procedures the central bank loses credibility but gains the flexibility to stimulate employment by surprise inflation.

In Section IX this trade-off has been investigated in the context of models with private information about the economy.

The Rogoff (1985) model is a fine example of a model in which - dynamic inconsistency issues notwithstanding - there is an important role for activist stabilization policy. Rogoff demonstrates that society can make itself better off by selecting an agent to head the central bank who is known to place a greater weight on inflation stabilization (relative to unemployment stabilization) than is embodied in the social loss function.

However, because the central bank has private information about productivity shocks it also pays for society to have the central bank partly accommodate these shocks before they pass on to inflation and unemployment. As in the Canzoneri (1985) model, the problem is the trading off of the flexibility needed for stabilization with the credibility constraint required for eliminating the inflation bias.

Also in Section IX we discussed the contribution of Lohmann (1992) who shows that the appointment of a conservative central banker (as in the Rogoff model) supplemented with the option to override the central banker (an escape clause) in case of large output shocks, dominates a number of other institutional arrangements proposed to balance credibility and flexibility.

Finally, in Section X we discussed the recent developments in the so-called optimal contract literature. Persson and Tabellini (1993) and Walsh (1993) claim that optimal contracts between governments and central bankers may eliminate the trade-off between credibility and flexibility altogether; zero average inflation and an optimal response to supply shocks can be achieved simultaneously.

The contract may serve to obtain a first best equilibrium, a rules *cum* discretion solution, that combines the benefits of rules (solution of the credibility problem) with those of discretion (optimally active stabilization policy). Attractive as this result may seem, we do not expect it to settle the rules versus discretion debate. Rather, paraphrasing Capie, Goodhart and Schnadt (1994, p. 112) we expect this debate to continue to echo, through the history of central banking.[74]

APPENDIX A2:STABILISATION POLICY UNDER OVERLAPPING WAGE CONTRACTS

Following the work of Sargent and Wallace a lot of research has been devoted to the robustness of the policy invariance result. Following Fischer (1977b) we will show that the rational expectations hypothesis is a necessary but not a sufficient condition for the policy invariance result to hold. Fischer examines the consequences of introducing multiperiod wage contracts, where nominal wages cannot be renegotiated every period, but are valid over two time periods. The model we employ to analyse the policy non-neutrality in the presence of rational expectations is identical to the one in Section VI except for the wage-setting relation. Hence we have

$$y_t = \beta l_t + \mu \qquad \mu \sim N(0, \sigma_\mu^2) \tag{2.33}$$

$$l_t = \frac{-1}{1-\beta}(w_t - p_t - \mu_t) \tag{2.34}$$

$$y_t = m_t - p_t \tag{2.12}$$

Wage—setting no longer follows the pattern described in (2.18), but instead

$$w^1_t = E_{t-1}\, p_t - (1-\beta)\, l^*$$

and

$$w^2_t = E_{t-2}\, p_t - (1-\beta)\, l^*$$

where w^1 represents wage contracts negotiated at time $t - 1$ based upon the minimization of $E_{t-1}\,(l_t - l^*)^2$ subject to (2.34) and w^2 represents wage contracts negotiated at time $t - 2$ based upon the minimization of $E_{t-2}\,(l_t - l^*)^2$.

Fischer assumes that half of all wage contracts in the economy are negotiated in alternate years. Therefore at time t the average nominal wage is given by

$$w_t = \tfrac{1}{2}E_{t-2}\, p_t + \tfrac{1}{2}E_{t-1}\, p_t - (1-\beta)\, l^* \tag{A2.1}$$

We obtain the aggregate supply function by substitution of (A2.1) in (2.34) and the resulting equation in (2.33)

$$y_t = \frac{\beta}{1-\beta}(p_t - 1/2(E_{t-2}\, p_t + E_{t-1} p_t)) + \tilde{y} + \frac{1}{1-\beta}\mu_t \tag{A2.2}$$

Equilibrium in the goods market prevails when (A2.2) is equal to (2.12) implying that the price level is being governed by the following expectational equation

$$p_t = \frac{\beta}{2}E_{t-2}\, p_t + \frac{\beta}{2}E_{t-1}\, p_t + (1-\beta)(m_t - \tilde{y}) - \mu_t \tag{A2.3}$$

Taking expectations of both sides of (A2.3) conditional on information at time $t - 2$ we get

$$E_{t-2}\, p_t = E_{t-2}\, m_t - \tilde{y} \tag{A2.4}$$

whilst at time $t - 1$ we get

$$E_{t-1} p_t = E_{t-1} m_t - \tilde{y} \tag{A2.5}$$

Hence the average expected price level for period t is

$$1/2(E_{t-2} p_t + E_{t-1} p_t) = 1/2(E_{t-2} m_t + E_{t-1} m_t) - \tilde{y} \tag{A2.6}$$

Subtracting (A2.6) from (A2.3) we get the following relation between the average forecast error and unanticipated shocks

$$p_t - 1/2(E_{t-2} p_t + E_{t-1} p_t)$$

$$= (1 - \beta)(m_t - 1/2(E_{t-1} m_t + E_{t-2} m_t)) - \mu_t \tag{A2.7}$$

As in Section VI we assume that the central bank wishes to stabilize unemployment around the natural rate of unemployment by adopting

$$m_t = d_1 \mu_{t-1} + \omega_t \qquad \omega_t \sim N(0, \sigma_\omega^2) \tag{2.41}$$

Taking expectations of both sides of (2.41) conditional on information at time t — 2 we get

$$E_{t-2} m_t = 0 \tag{A2.8}$$

Whilst at time t — 1 we get

$$E_{t-1} m_t = d_1 \mu_{t-1} \tag{A2.9}$$

Subtracting $1/2E_{t-1} m_t$ from (2.41) we get the following expression for unforeseeable monetary policy

$$m_t - ½(E_{t-1} m_t + E_{t-2} m_t) = \frac{d_1}{2} \mu_{t-1} + \omega_t \tag{A2.10}$$

Substituting (A2.10) in the expression for the average forecast error (A2.7) and the resulting equation in (A2.2) yields

$$y_t - \tilde{y} = \beta \omega_t + \mu_t + \frac{\beta d_1}{2} \mu_{t-1} \tag{A2.11}$$

Contrast (A2.11) with (2.44), its equivalent in the New-Classical model. The difference between these equations is the term $(\beta d_1/2)\mu_{t-1}$ at the extreme right-hand side of (A2.11). With staggered contracts monetary policy can affect real output due to the presence of d_1 in (A2.11).

The policy invariance result disappears because at the beginning of period t half of the wage constracts in the economy cannot be reopened. They have been entered into at the end of period t — 2 and have one more year to run. In the last year of operation of that contract, the monetary authorities react to the disturbance μ_{t-1}. It is precisely this reaction which could not have been anticipated at time t — 2 since $E_{t-2} m_t = 0$. Hence given the predetermined second-period nominal wage, the value of d_1 will affect the real wage for the second period of the contract and thus output.

Now we link the Fischer analysis to the Phillips curve debate. Substituting the nominal wage (A2.1) in the labour demand function (2.34) we get the following expression for employment

$$l_t = \frac{1}{1-\beta}(p_t - \tfrac{1}{2}(E_{t-2}\, p_t + E_{t-1}\, p_t) + \mu_t) + l^* \qquad \text{(A2.12)}$$

Subtracting (A2.12) from the labour force l^s, using that $u \equiv l^s - l$, yields the expectations augmented Phillips curve

$$u = \tilde{u} - \frac{1}{1-\beta}(p_t - \tfrac{1}{2}(E_{t-2}\, p_t + E_{t-1}\, p_t) + \mu_t) \qquad \text{(A2.13)}$$

Substituting (A2.10) in (A2.7) and the resulting equation in (A2.13) we get the following relation for unemployment

$$u - \tilde{u} = \omega_t + \frac{d_1}{2}\mu_{t-1} \qquad \text{(A2.14)}$$

From (A2.14) it can be seen that in the presence of overlapping wage contracts the short-run Phillips curve trade-off between inflation and unemployment is reestablished. For the deviation of unemployment from its natural rate now also depends on the degree of discretion d_1.

If the monetary authorities wish to minimize the variance of unemployment around its natural rate they have to find that value of d_1 in (2.41) that minimizes

$$\text{Var}\,(u_t - \tilde{u}) = \sigma_\omega^2 + \tfrac{1}{4}\, d_1^2 \sigma_\mu^2 \qquad \text{(A2.15)}$$

It can be easily seen that the optimal policy in this instance is to set $d_1 = 0$, which in terms of equation (2.41) implies the adoption of a fixed money supply rule. This result derives from the assumption that all disturbances hitting the economy are purely random. Since such disturbances cannot be offset by counter-cyclical policy, setting $d_1 > 0$ makes matters worse by making activity more volatile around its steady state. However, following Fischer it can be shown that if there are lag patterns in the productivity disturbance a feedback rule again dominates a fixed rule. For suppose that productivity follows a simple random walk

$$\mu_t = \mu_{t-1} + v_t^{\mu} \qquad v_t^{\mu} \sim N(0, \sigma_v^2) \tag{A2.16}$$

and the objective of the authorities is to stabilize activity (y) around its natural rate. Substituting (A2.16) in (A2.11) we get[75]

$$y_t - \tilde{y} = \beta\omega_t + (1 + \frac{\beta d_1}{2})\mu_{t-1} + v_t^u \tag{A2.17}$$

Taking variances yields

$$Var(y - \tilde{y}) = \beta^2\sigma_\omega^2 + \sigma_v^2 + (\frac{2 + \beta d_1}{2})^2\sigma_\mu^2 \tag{A2.18}$$

If the authorities wish to minimize (A2.18) a fixed money supply rule is now suboptimal. The optimal value of d_1 is obtained from the first-order condition for a minimum of

$$\tfrac{1}{4}\beta^2 d_1^2 + \beta d_1 + 1 \tag{A2.19}$$

Hence the optimal state contingent rule is now one which sets $d_1 = \frac{-2}{\beta}$. Thus, the optimal policy rule becomes

$$m_t = \frac{-2}{\beta}\mu_{t-1} + \omega_t \tag{A2.20}$$

Hence in order to stabilize output around its natural rate the central bank offsets persistent shocks to productivity by manipulating the money supply.

NOTES

1. This characterization of the distinction between rules and discretion is based on McCallum (1987, p. 10).
2. It needs to be emphasized that the issue of rules vs discretion is not the same as the issue of activist vs nonactivist policy. This is important because leading undergraduate textbooks e.g. Mishkin (1992, p. 682) continue to muddle together the two distinct issues.
3. Prime Minister Peel was of the Currency School persuasion.
4. This goes back to the analysis of Hume (1875).
5. On the actual operation of the gold standard see Bordo and Schwartz (1984) and M. June Flanders (1990).
6. See Sijben (1990).
7. Carlson (1988, p. 3).
8. For an in-depth discussion of Fed policy in the *Great Depression* see Wheelock (1992).
9. In this paper we do not address the instrument problem. See Poole (1970).
10. Simons (1948, pp. 160-162), the original appeared in Simons (1936).
11. See for example Lerner (1944).
12. Tobin (1990, p. 2) points out that before the *Tinbergen framework* was properly understood the idea was to throw everything available at the problem of the moment, depression, unemployment or war-generated inflation. Against unemployment, for example, spend more on public works, cut taxes, print more money, and lower interest rates - all.
13. This assumption is relaxed in Section VI.
14. Of course monetary and fiscal policy are not always independent instruments. If printing money is the only way to finance government deficits, then there is no monetary policy independent of fiscal policy. For an analysis along these lines see Chapter 5.
15. The variance of a linear function of two stochastic variables is obtained from $\mathrm{Var}(\alpha x + \beta y) = \alpha^2 \mathrm{Var}(x) + \beta^2 \mathrm{Var}(y) + 2\alpha\beta \mathrm{Cov}(x, y)$, see for instance Cuddy (1974, p. 15).
16. The value of β is taken from Alogoskoufis (1994, p. 211).
17. Moreover, Blanchard and Fischer (1989, p. 582) point out that if the coefficients in (2.1) - (2.6) are stochastic - i.e. when there is multiplier-uncertainty [Brainard (1967)] - the optimal policy-rule will be less activist.
18. According to Humphrey (1985) Phillips was far from the first to postulate an inflation-unemployment trade-off or to draw the curve bearing his name. Humphrey states that at least ten precursors are neglected. Humphrey associates the folowing authors with the pre-history of the Phillips Curve: Hume (1752b), Thornton (1802), Fisher (1926), Tinbergen (1936, 1951), Klein and Golberger (1955), Brown (1955) and Sultan (1957).
19. As pointed out by Smyth (1994d, p. 6), in their paper Samuelson and Solow used the expression 'Phillips curve'. This may have been the first use of the term.
20. Holmes and Smyth (1970) show that there is no justification to assume it possible to draw a line linking excess demand for labour and the unemployment rate.
21. Following Argy (1988, p. 148) we label this case 'simplistic Monetarism'.
22. A necessary and sufficient condition for global stability is $\beta < 1$.
23. In setting up the expectations augmented Phillips curve framework, I borrowed fairly heavily from the recent survey of Alogoskoufis (1994).

24. Again the model is stable since ex hypothesi $\beta < 1$.
25. A recent (New-Keynesian) interpretation views the NAIRU as the rate of unemployment at which the claims of workers to real wages and firms to real profits are recoonciled and inflation is constant. See Carlin and Soskice (1990, p. 136).
26. Typical papers are Ferguson and Gupta (1981) and Keller and Review (1981).
27. The expectations augmented Phillips Curve model consist of equations (2.1) (2.2) (2.12) (2.20) and (2.23).
28. However, Keuzenkamp (1991) notes that thirty years earlier a model with explicitly rational expectations was published by Tinbergen (1932). Hence, Tinbergen being the founding father of activist macroeconomic policy also anticipated the stick by which this research programme was hit most severely much later.
29. In the presence of overlapping wage contracts as analysed by Fischer (1977b) the short-run trade-off is reestablished. For an analysis along these lines see the appendix to this chapter.
30. Accordingly the central bank cares about the (conditional) variance of inflation and the *level* of unemployment. This specification follows Barro and Gordon (1983a, p. 104), in Chapter 4 we switch to the more complicated form in which both arguments are quadratic.
31. With the more complicated form of the loss function used in Chapter 4, Δp_t would depend also on $E_{t-1}\Delta p_t$ and $\tilde{u}$.
32. Depending on operating procedures the policymakers set the money stock or the interest rate. However, it is simpler to think of the central bank to choose inflation directly. For a lucid exposition of monetary policy games with the money stock as a policy instrument see Canzoneri and Henderson (1991).
33. Monetary policy cannot reduce unemployment below its natural rate.
34. With a more complicated form of the loss function, the result for Δp_t^{CH} generally differs from that under discretion Δp_t^D.
35. Barro and Gordon (1983a) do not analyse this regime.
36. With a loss function in which both arguments are quadratic in general the ranking of regimes will depend on ε.
37. This table is based on a similar one in Sijben (1992).
38. For a critical look at deterrence via trigger strategies see Cukierman (1992, pp. 209-210).
39. Since this is a quadratic equation there are two roots, the smallest of which corresponds to the minimum credibly sustainable inflation. See Barro and Gordon (1983, p. 112).
40. This terminology follows Cukierman (1992, pp. 323-325).
41. To say this in more technical terms using the Folk theorem of supergames any rate of inflation below $\varepsilon/(1-\beta)$ can be sustained by an appropriately chosen triger strategy. See Cukierman (1992, p. 209).
42. The Kreps and Wilson (1982b) analysis of reputation is in the field of industrial organization and deals with the question about whether or not entry occurs in a monopolistic market.
43. Bayes' rule is $\text{Prob}(A \mid B) = \left(\text{Prob}(B \mid A) \cdot P(A)\right)/\text{Prob}(B)$ see for instance Berck and Sydsaeter (1991, p. 149).
44. Recall that $\varepsilon/(1-\beta)$is the one-shot optimum policy. See equation (2.51).
45. For more details see Persson and Tabellini (1990, p. 64) especially their footnote 52.
46. Note that with the more complicated loss function used in Chapter 4, in which both arguments are quadratic, Δp_2^W would depend also on $E_1\ \Delta p_2^W$ and hence on x_2.
47. The equilibrium may be separating ($q < ½$), pooling ($q > ½x_1$) or semi-separating ($½ \le q \le ½x_1$). See Persson and Tabellini (1990, pp. 63-64).
48. According to Goodhart's (1994) review of *Central Bank Strategy, Credibility and Independence: Theory and Evidence*, Chapter 9 is the most important central chapter

of the book.

49. Equation (2.99) is obtained by setting $\Delta p_t = \Delta m_t$ and $\beta = 0$ in equation (2.21).
50. The signal extraction exercise is dependent on the relative variances of e, the stochastic process influencing the central bank's preferences, and ψ, the stochastic error in the money control process.
51. The following draws heavily on Cukierman (1986).
52. $\lambda \equiv b/2 - \sqrt{1/4b^2 - 1}$ where $b \equiv \rho + (1+r)/\rho$ and 52. $r \equiv c_1^2\, \sigma_v^2/\sigma_\psi^2$.
53. See Bartlett (1962, p. 145) and appendix A to Schaling and Smyth (1994).
54. Equation (2.109) is obtained by setting $\beta = 0$ in equation (2.21).
55. With β being set equal to zero (see the previous note) full consistency with section 6 (especially equation (2.36)) implies that $\tilde{y} = 0$. The latter implication does not influence further results in this section.
56. The political principal is the set of politicians who have the power to bring about changes in the institutional arrangements underlying the making of monetary policy.
57. Equation (2.129) is obtained by setting $\beta = 0$ in equation (2.45) and adding and subtracting p_{t-1}.
58. The derivation of this expression can be found in appendix C of Chapter 7. By setting $\beta = 0$ and A = I in this derivation one obtains equation (2.136).
59. In the context of the model of Section V.2 a positive natural rate of unemployment follows from the assumption that ℓ^*, the target employment level of wage-setters is smaller than the effective labour force ℓ^s. Hence the natural rate of unemployment is inefficiently high. See also Section III.2 of Chapter 4.
60. Using the notation of this book the proof of the Rogoff theorem can be found in Section V1.1 of Chapter 7 for the (more general) case that $\beta > 0$.
61. Strictly speaking Flood and Isard consider rules of the form $\Delta p_t^R(\Delta p) = \Delta p$. Here, following Lohmann (1992) we focus on a simple zero inflation rule.
62. By similar reasoning d_5^* will also depend on ε and $\tilde{u}$. For instance, a higher natural rate of unemployment implies a higher time consistent rate of inflation and consequently a higher credibility problem for society. We leave a formal proof for further research.
63. The use of terminology here is somewhat different than in Lohmann (1992). Using the notation of this book Lohmann views the parameter d_2 as the degree of 'conservativeness' and the parameter d_5 as the degree of central bank independence. Neumann (1991) gives a detailed account of the various meanings of central bank independence.
64. For an interesting variant of the Lohmann model, based on the revenue motive for monetary expansion, see Lippi and Swank (1994).
65. This is different from the Rogoff model where in the insitutional design stage *society* appoints a central banker that is 'too conservative'.
66. Lohmann speaks here of a deadweight loss induced by the inflationary bias. We reserve the term deadweight loss for the component of the expected loss that is invariant across monetary regimes. This component is associated with the labour market distortion.
67. Fischer (1994, p. 39) points out that one example of such a contract occurs when the salary of the governor is fixed in nominal terms during his or her term of office, as for the Bank of England and the Reserve Bank of New Zealand.
68. This is the Rogoff model of the previous section for the case that $d_2 = 0$.
69. In Chapter 7 inflation targeting is parametrized as full commitment to a zero inflation rule.
70. In fact we focus on a 'bare bones' version of Walsh (1993). In particular we do not consider such issues as the role of the central bank's announcements of its private information or reappointment. Also, we treat the inflation rate as a directly controllable policy instrument.
71. This terminology follows Minford (1993).

72. In Walsh (1993) the transfer also depends on a publicly observed noisy signal on the supply shock. Using the notation of this book we have $s_t = v_t^{\mu} + \psi_t$ where s and ψ are the signal and the normally distributed measurement error. Hence, the expected value of v^{μ} conditional on s will equal $\sigma^2_{\mu} s/(\sigma^2_{\mu} + \sigma^2_{\psi})$. In this section we assume $\sigma_{\psi}^2 \rightarrow \infty$, hence $E_{t-1}\, v_t^{\mu} = 0$.
73. In Walsh (1993, p. 12) the target rate of money growth depends on the central bank's forecast of the supply shock. Since we assumed this forecast to be zero (see the previous footnote), the target rate of inflation is zero.
74. For a survey of recent developments in the context of financial stability see Sijben (1994).
75. A better avenue would be to reconsider the optimization procedure used to derive (A2.1). However for convenience we take a short cut and simply plug in the new disturbances in the surprise-supply function.

3. Central Bank Independence in Twelve Industrial Countries

I INTRODUCTION

As stated in Chapter 2 the theoretical rationale for central bank independence finds its origin in the ongoing 'rules versus discretion' debate. Governments and central banks may be tempted to impart an inflationary bias to the economy thereby sacrificing long-term welfare to short-run political gains. The associated time-consistency problem can be overcome by legislative rules and by setting up politically independent central banks. Hence one would expect central bank independence to be an important determinant of policy choices and, through them, of economic performance.

In order to test this hypothesis one needs quantitative measures of central bank independence. The first attempt to quantify central bank independence is Bade and Parkin (1988) who used a number of legal attributes from central bank laws to create measures of political and financial independence for twelve countries during the floating exchange rate years 1972 to 1986. Alesina (1988, 1989) extended their sample of industrial countries by using institutional information provided by Fair (1980) and Masciandaro and Tabellini (1988). A subsequent attempt to quantify central bank independence was made by Grilli, Masciandaro and Tabellini (1991) who compared the monetary regimes of eighteen industrial countries by focusing on political and economic independence. Recently, broadly based measures of legal independence for over sixty countries (including LDCs) have been developed in Cukierman (1992) and Cukierman, Webb and Neyapti (1992).[1]

By confronting the legal measures (indices) with macroeconomic data these studies try to verify whether and to what extent central bank independence matters for economic performance. Typically, the results of this literature are stated in terms of correlations between indices on the one hand, and inflation, output growth and interest rates on the other hand.[2] We survey the empirical evidence on central bank independence in Chapter 4.

For now, it needs to be emphasized that empirical results are particularly sensitive to the numerical values of indices. (Swinburne and

Castello-Branco (1991)).

These values are dependent on; (i) criteria used in the examination of central bank laws (statutes); (ii) the interpretation of the relevant statute as to whether a central bank meets this criterion, i.e. possesses a certain attribute; and (iii) the way these attributes are aggregated to a composite index of central bank independence.

Of course there is no non-arbitrary way of choosing criteria. Also the interpretation of the relevant statute is a delicate matter because one has to make a distinction between purely formal or legal issues, and more substantive issues regarding the conduct of monetary policy. Again in making this distinction there is an unavoidable arbitrariness. For each economist when building an index of this kind is somewhat biased in favour of his/her own country, because the greater acquaintance with the case brings recognition of the greater freedom of behaviour acquired in current practice by the national central bank compared to the formal rule. Finally as pointed out by Grilli, Masciandaro and Tabellini (1991, p. 367) there is no non-arbitrary way of aggregating these criteria or attributes to a composite index. Hence, there are unavoidable subjective elements in the construction of indices of central bank independence.

In order to view these elements in a broader perspective this Chapter compares the indices of central bank independence as presented in Bade and Parkin (1988), Alesina (1988, 1989) and Grilli, Masciandaro and Tabellini (1991).[3] Such a comparison does not yet exist in the literature. We focus on three aspects: (a) is the index based on the best possible interpretation of the central bank law within the context of monetary policy making;[4] (b) is the index consistent in using all relevant criteria in determining the independence of each central bank; (c) are the indices of the various authors different or not?

In order to answer the questions mentioned above, the Chapter is organized as follows. We analyse the competence of central banks on the base of central bank laws within the context of monetary policy making. Twelve industrial countries are examined: Australia, Belgium, Canada, France, Germany, Italy, Japan, the Netherlands, the United Kingdom, the United States, Sweden and Switzerland.[5] We describe the central bank laws of these countries focusing on three areas: (i) relationships between central banks and government in the formulation of monetary policy; (ii) procedures for appointing the board of the central bank, and; (iii) formal responsibilities (objectives) of the central bank with respect to monetary policy. This description can be found in the appendix. After a critical examination of the existing indices in Section II, in Section III we construct a new index of central bank independence. This index is used to reach a critical perspective of other indices.[6] For instance, according to this index we qualify the Bank of Japan as less independent than Alesina (1988, 1989), while for the Nederlandsche Bank the reverse applies. Finally, our conclusions can be found in Section IV.

II INDICES OF CENTRAL BANK INDEPENDENCE

II.1 Bade and Parkin's Courageous Attempt

A seminal paper concerning indices of central bank independence is Bade and Parkin (1988) (BP). The paper investigates the cross-country relationship between monetary policies and the laws which establish and delimit the powers of central banks. The study is empirical and deals with the experience of twelve industrial countries (Australia, Belgium, Canada, France, Germany, Italy, Japan, the Netherlands the United Kingdom and the United States, Sweden and Switzerland) during the floating exchange rate years 1972 to 1986.[7]

They describe the central bank laws of the twelve countries focusing on three features: (i) the relationship between central banks and government in the formulation of monetary policy; (ii) the procedures for appointing the board of the central bank, and; (iii) the financial and budgetary relations between the central bank and the government.

On the basis of features (i) and (ii) BP classify the twelve central banks according to their degrees of policy independence. On the basis of feature (iii) they identify the degree of financial independence from government. In this paper we focus on features (i) and (ii). BP's description of financial and budgetary relations is discussed in Eijffinger and Schaling (1992). BP conclude that central banks which are independent both in policy making and in the appointment of directors deliver a lower rate of inflation than other central bank types.

On the basis of feature (i) the relationship between central banks and government in the formulation of monetary policy[8] and feature (ii) the procedures for appointing and removing central bank directors, BP construct their index of policy independence. The degree of policy independence is determined using three criteria:

1. Is the bank the final policy authority?
2. Is there no government official (with or without voting power) on the bank board?
3. Are more than half of the board appointments made independent of the government?

Since each criterion can be met or not, 2^3 potential policy types can be distinguished. This is summarized in Table 3.1.

Table 3.1 Central bank laws: policy types

Bank is final policy authority *1*	No government official on bank board *2*	Some board appointments independent of government [1] *3*	Potential central bank type[2]	Central bank type does exist	Policy type
—	—	*	(a)	no	—
—	*	*	(b)	no	—
*	—	*	(c)	no	—
*	—	—	(d)	no	—
—	—	—	(e)	yes	1
—	*	—	(f)	yes	2
*	*	—	(g)	yes	3
*	*	*	(h)	yes	4

1) Operationalized as proportion of members *not* appointed directly or indirectly by the government. ≥ 11/21.

2) It should be noted that the letters have nothing to do with similar symbols used in other tables.

However, BP find that in all cases were the government is responsible for the formulation of monetary policy, it also appoints over 12/14 of the policy board. That is, there is no central bank which makes some board appointments independent of the government, although it is not in charge of monetary policy. Therefore, types (a) and (b) do not exist. Moreover, a central bank being itself in charge of monetary policy and also having a government official on its board (types (c) and (d)), does not exist.[9] Therefore, the potential policy types (a)-(d) do not occur in reality. This means that no actual central bank corresponds to the first four configurations of institutional features.

So, only the bottom half of Table 3.1 is relevant for the construction of the BP index of policy independence. The overall degree of policy independence is determined by a combination of attributes 1. - 3. It should be noticed that there is no non-arbitrary way of aggregating them. However, from Table 3.1 it can be easily seen that BP choose the simplest one: they simply summed the attributes possessed by the central bank, meaning that each attribute is weighted equally. Thus, the four remaining (existing) central bank types are ranked from 1 (least independent) to 4 (most independent) depending on the number of asterisks. For instance, the least independent central bank (zero asterisks) is not in charge of monetary policy, has a government official on the board, and does not make any board appointments independent of government.

BP's ranking of the twelve central banks can be found in the first column of Table 3.2.

BP now turn to an investigation of the relationship between central bank types and monetary policy. In their analysis of monetary policy they focus on two aspects; its inflationary stance (level) and the variability (variance) of inflation. The inflationary stance is measured by the average rate of change of consumer prices (CPI).

Concerning policy variability, what is of interest is the variability of inflation as well as output and employment. However, BP point out that if they were to measure variability of policy by examining both nominal and real variability, inevitably conflicting rankings would result from cross-country differences in slopes of short-run trade-offs between output and inflation.[10] Regarding these trade-offs well outside the scope of their study, they examine only the variability of inflation.[11]

Furthermore, consider Table 3.2 which permits a direct examination of the relationship between policy independence and monetary policy. From Table 3.2 it appears that there is no association between any of the policy types and the measure of variability of policy presented.

Moreover, consider the association between categories of central bank independence and the inflation performance. From Table 3.1 it is clear that the first category (policy type 1) differs from the second only in the presence of a governnment official on the bank board. According to BP it is immediately apparent that there are no discernible differences in inflation rates between the first two groups. The third and fourth groups (Japan, United States, Germany and Switzerland) are the independent central banks.

Table 3.2 Average inflation and its variability grouped according to central bank policy type: flexible exchange rate period 1972-1986

		Inflation rate		Policy variability	
Country	Type	Percent	Rank	Standard deviation	Rank
Australia	1	9.9	(10)	3.2	(7)
Belgium	2	7.1	(6)	3.0	(5)
Canada		7.9	(7)	2.8	(3)
France		9.5	(9)	3.2	(7)
Italy		14.0	(12)	4.6	(10)
Netherlands		5.8	(3)	3.0	(5)
Sweden		8.9	(8)	2.5	(2)
United Kingdom		11.2	(11)	6.0	(11)
Japan	3	6.6	(4)	6.1	(12)
United States		6.9	(5)	3.5	(9)
Germany	4	4.3	(1)	2.0	(1)
Switzerland		4.4	(2)	2.8	(3)

BP think it striking that the two most independent central banks, those of Germany and Switzerland, have delivered a lower inflation rate than the intermediate central banks of Japan and the United States. Also, BP point out that the mean inflation rate of the eight government dominated central banks (policy types 1 and 2) is in excess of ten percent; thus although the U.S. and Japanese inflation rates are well within two standard deviations of that mean, those of Switzerland and Germany are signficantly below the mean.

On the basis of these facts BP conclude that there is an association between the degree of central bank policy independence and the average rate of inflation. By and large, the more independent the central bank, the lower the inflation rate.[12]

II.2 Alesina's Extension

Bade and Parking's work has been integrated in the positive theory of economic policy[13] by Alesina (1988, 1989). Alesina uses the BP index of policy independence to illustrate the relationship between the degree of politico-instititutional stability and economic performance. Alesina extends BP's sample of industrial countries to include New Zealand, Spain, Denmark, Norway and Finland, by using institutional information provided by Masciandaro and Tabellini (1988) and Fair (1980), respectively. Alesina likewise concludes that there is an inverse relationship between the degree of independence of central banks and the average inflation rate (Alesina (1988, p. 41)).[14] Alesina's results can be summarized in Table 3.3.[15]

Table 3.3 Inflation and central bank independence (1973-1986)

	Average inflation	Alesina index of central bank independence	Bade Parkin index of central bank independence
Italy	13.7	1.5	2
UK	10.7	2	2
Australia	9.7	1	1
France	9.2	2	2
Sweden	8.7	2	2
Canada	7.8	2	2
Belgium	6.9	2	2
US	6.9	3	3
Japan	6.4	3	3
Netherlands	5.5	2	2
Switzerland	4.1	4	4
Germany	4.1	4	4

As can be easily seen from this Table, the numerical values of the 'Alesina index of central bank independence' are identical to those of the BP index of policy independence, except for the case of Italy. Alesina has the following argument for classifying Italy as 1.5 rather than 2, as in BP:

> 'Bade and Parkin's classifications disregard institutional changes in the period considered. The Italian Central Bank obtained more economic independence in 1982. Given this change we classified Italy as 1.5 rather than 2, as in Bade-Parkin.'[16]

Therefore, Alesina's argument contains two major elements:

1. Criticism of BP for their disregard of institutional changes
2. The identification of institutional changes with changes in economic independence.

The first element of Alesina's criticism has implications for the way of aggregating the attributes which make up his index. We will return to this issue later. The second element is based on Tabellini's (1988) account of the divorce ('divorzio') between the Treasury and the Italian Central Bank in 1981. After divorce the CICR[17] no longer obliged the Banca d'Italia to absorb all excess supply of short-term Treasury bills. This step decreased the scope for accommodating monetary policy by monetary financing of government deficits and increased the independence of Banca d'Italia.

In the preceding sub-section we saw that the BP index of policy independence is determined by the total number of statutory attributes ('asterisks') concerning policy making and the appointment of directors (BP (1. - 3.)). If the Alesina index is an extension of the BP policy index, in the sense that it is 'richer' and more informative, it must follow that:

1. Alesina implicitly uses a fourth criterium say A4: Is the central bank not required to absorb excess supply of short-term Treasury bills?
2. The Alesina indicator of central bank independence is determined by a combination of attributes (1. — 3.) and A4.

Having four BP policy types combined with criterion A4 yields 4 × 2 = 8 potential policy-economic types.

From this Table it can be seen that, according to Alesina, only five central bank types can be discerned among the twelve industrial countries. These existing central bank types can be found in the bottom half of Table 3.4.

Again, there is no non-arbitrary way to aggregate attributes BP 1. - 3. and A4, i.e. to rank these types from least independent to most independent. However, from Table 3.4 it can be easily seen that Alesina did not follow BP in summing the attributes possessed by the central bank. For if he had, Banca d'Italia would have been qualified as type 3 (upgrade) rather than type 1.5 (downgrade).[18]

Table 3.4 Alesina types and central bank laws

(See note below)

BP policy type	Criterion A4 met?	Potential central bank type	Central bank type does exist? (a)	Alesina type (a)
1	*	(a)	no	—
3	*	(b)	no	—
4	*	(c)	no	—
1	—	(d)	yes	1
2	*	(e)	yes	1.5
2	—	(f)	yes	2
3	—	(g)	yes	3
4	—	(h)	yes	4

(a) See Table 3.3

Therefore, if the Alesina index is internally consistent, it can be considered asymmetrical in the sense that attributes are not weighted equally.

From Table 3.4, reflecting our assumption that criterion A4 was applied to all the twelve industrial countries, it follows that:

1. All central banks, except Banca d'Italia, are forced to accommodate fiscal policy with monetary policy.[19]
2. Notwithstanding the former Banca d'Italia, being Alesina type 1.5, is less independent than the central banks of France, Sweden, Belgium, Canada, the Netherlands and the United Kingdom. All of them are of the type 2 category.

Since 1 is obviously counterfactual it follows that the Alesina (1988, 1989) synthetic indicator of central bank independence is internally inconsistent (Reductio ad absurdum). However, if the Alesina index is internally inconsistent, i.e. it is not the case that in determining the independence of each central bank all relevant criteria are used, the numerical values in table 3.4 cannot be compared and therefore do not qualify as 'indices' of central bank independence.

II.3 The Broad Index of Grilli, Masciandaro and Tabellini

A recent index of central bank independence is that of Grilli, Masciandaro and Tabellini (1991) (GMT). They compare the monetary regimes of eighteen industrial countries (Australia, Austria, Belgium, Canada, Denmark, France, Germany, Greece, Ireland, Italy, Japan, the Netherlands, New Zealand, Portugal, Spain, Switzerland, the United Kingdom and the United States) during the post-war period (1950-1989) by focusing on political and economic independence of the central bank.[20]

Like BP and Alesina, they find that in countries with more politically independent central banks inflation is on average lower and less variable. On the other hand, GMT find no indication that the monetary regime matters for real economic performance.

According to GMT, political independence is the capacity to choose the final goal of monetary policy, such as inflation or the level of economic activity. The latter capacity is primarily determined by the following features:

1. Relationships between central banks and government in the formulation of monetary policy
2. Procedures for appointing the board of the central bank
3. Formal responsibilities (policy goals) of the central bank with respect to monetary policy.

On the basis of features 1. - 3. GMT construct their index of policy independence. The degree of policy independence is determined using eight criteria:[21]

1. Is the governor not appointed by the government?
2. Is the governor appointed for more than five years?
3. Are all board members not appointed by the government? (Compare with BP 3: are some board appointments made independent of the government?)
4. Is the board appointed for more than five years?
5. Is there no mandatory participation of a government representative in the board? (Compare with BP 2: is there no government official on the bank board?)
6. Is there no government approval of monetary policy required? (Compare with BP 1: is the bank the final policy authority?)
7. Are there statutory requirements that the bank pursues monetary stability among its goals?
8. Are there legal provisions that strengthen the bank's position in case of conflicts with the government?

The overall index of policy independence is determined by a combination of the attributes 1. - 8. Again, there is no non-arbitrary way of aggregating them. Like Bade and Parkin, GMT choose the simplest one: they simply summed the attributes possessed by the central bank. Thus, each attribute is weighted equally. The eighteen central banks are ranked from 1 (least independent) to 6 (most independent). GMT's results can be summarized in Table 3.5.[22]

Table 3.5 Political independence of central banks

Countries		Appointments			Relationship with government		Constitution		Index of political independence
	1	*2*	*3*	*4*	*5*	*6*	*7*	*8*	*9*
Australia		*					*	*	3
Belgium				*					1
Canada	*	*					*	*	4
France		*		*					2
Germany		*		*	*	*	*	*	6
Italy	*	*	*		*				4
Japan							*		1
Netherlands		*		*	*	*	*	*	6
Switzerland		*			*	*	*	*	5
U.K.					*				1
U.S.				*	*	*	*	*	5
Sweden	—	—	—	—	—	—		—	—

Notes:

1 = Governor *not* appointed by government

2 = Governor appointed for > 5 years

3 = *All* the Board *not* appointed by government

4 = Board appointed for > 5 years

5 = No mandatory participation of government representative in the Board

6 = No government approval of monetary policy formulation is required

7 = Statutory requirements that central bank pursues monetary stability among its goals

8 = Legal provisions that strengthened the central bank position in conflicts with the government are present

9 = Overall index of political independence, constructed as the sum of the asterisks in each row

From this Table it can be seen that the GMT policy index is richer, i.e. more informative, than the BP index of political independence. The GMT is more informative because more criteria are taken into account. BP use only three criteria, whilst GMT consider eight attributes. It can be easily seen that GMT criteria 5 and 6 are identical to BP criteria 2 and 1. One is tempted to make a similar inference concerning GMT criterion 3. However, concerning the appointment of directors GMT require all board members not to be appointed by the government, whilst BP require only ≥ 11/21[23] of board members not to be appointed by the government. Therefore, GMT's criterion 3 is more strict than BP's criterion 3.

II.4 Grilli, Masciandaro and Tabellini versus Bade and Parkin

In order to compare GMT's findings with these of BP, we restrict attention to attributes 3, 5 and 6 of GMT. Since aggregation procedures are identical, differences in numerical values of the BP and GMT indices are dependent on:

(a) differerences in the interpretation of the central bank laws with respect to GMT attributes 5 and 6 (or BP attributes 1 and 2);
(b) the difference between GMT attribute 3 and BP attribbute 3.

We label differences (a) and (b) respectively as interpretation effect and criterion effect. Thus numerical differences depend on both these effects. The total effect is decomposed in Table 3.6.

With respect to the interpretation effect, from Table 3.6 it can be seen that GMT and BP differ in their interpretations of the central bank laws of Canada, France, Belgium, Japan, and the Netherlands. Canada, France, and Belgium are downgraded (—1), because contrary to BP GMT believe a government representative to be present on the central bank boards. The Nederlandsche Bank is upgraded (+1), because unlike BP, GMT consider the central bank to be the final authority in policy making. The differences are most striking in the case of Japan. The Bank of Japan is severely downgraded (—2), because GMT believe that the government has an official on the bank board, while according to BP there is no official. GMT are also of the opinion that the government is the final authority in policy making, contradicting BP.
We will return to these differences in Section IV.

With respect to the criterion effect, by using a stricter version of BP 3, GMT change the ranking of the Bundesbank, Banca d'Italia and the Swiss National Bank vis à vis BP. Both the Bundesbank and the Swiss National Bank are downgraded (-1), whilst Banca d'Italia is upgraded (-1)

Table 3.6 Grilli, Masciandaro and Tabellini vs Bade-Parkin

Country	GMT Policy type	BP Policy type	Interpretation effect	Criterion effect	Difference
(See note below)	(a)	(b)	(c)	(d)	(e)
Australia	1	1			
Belgium	1	2	-1		-1
Canada	1	2	-1		-1
France	1	2	-1		-1
Germany	3	4		-1	-1
Italy	3	2		+1	+1
Japan	1	3	-2		-2
Netherlands	3	2	+1		+1
Switzerland	3	4		-1	-1
UK	2	2			
US	3	3			
Sweden	-	2			

(a) (Number of asterisks in columns 3, 5 and 6 of Table 3.5) + 1.
(b) See Table 3.2
(c) (Number of asterisks in columns 5 and 6 of Table 3.5 + number of asterisks in column 3 of Table 3.1) + 1 — BP Policy Type.
(d) (Number of asterisks in columns 1 and 2 of Table 3.1 + number of asterisks in column 3 of Table 3.5) + 1 — BP Policy Type.
(e) (c) + (d) = total difference between GMT and BP.

(+1). It should be noticed that because the BP type 4 banks (Germany and Switzerland) do not meet GMT criterion 3, they become intermediate banks. That is, in terms of political independence, they get the same status as the Federal Reserve (BP type 3). This is intuitively not very appealing. Neither is the fact that Banca d'Italia is the only central bank that meets GMT criterion 3. Therefore, we conclude that by introducing a very strict criterion concerning the appointment of directors, GMT severely bias the ranking of the central banks of Germany, Switzerland and Italy.

III TOWARDS A NEW INDEX OF POLICY INDEPENDENCE

III.1 A New Index of Policy Independence

Following GMT, we identify policy independence with the capacity of the central banks to choose the final goals of monetary policy. This capacity is primarily determined by the following features:

1. The procedures for appointing the board of the central bank.
2. The relationship between central banks and government in the formulation of monetary policy.
3. Formal responsibilities (policy goals) of the central bank with respect to monetary policy.

On the basis of features 1. - 3. we construct a new index, which is called the Eijffinger-Schaling (ES) index of policy independence. The degree of policy independence is determined using three criteria:

1. Is the bank the sole final policy authority (b), is this authority not entrusted to the central bank alone (b/g), or is it entrusted completely to the government (g)?
2. Is there no government official (with or without voting power) on the bank board?
3. Are more than half of the board appointments made independent of the government?[24]

Now we can distinguish 3 × 2 × 2 = 12 potential policy types. This is summarized in Table 3.7.

The first four types are the BP potential types (a)-(d). In Section III it was shown that these types do not exist. For the sake of convenience we repeat the argument. A central bank being itself in charge of monetary policy and also having a government official on its board (types (c) and (d)) does not occur in reality. Besides, there is no central bank that in spite of its not being in charge of monetary policy, makes some board appointments independent of the government. Therefore, types (a) and (b) do not exist.

From our examination of central bank laws in the Appendix, it follows that this argument includes the 'twin-authority' central banks, i.e. the central banks which have some but incomplete policy authority (b/g). That is, a 'twin-authority' central bank that has a government official on its board (type e) does not exist. Finally, there is no twin-authority bank that makes some board appointments independent of the government.

Table 3.7 Eijffinger — Schaling Policy Types

Bank is final policy authority *1*	No government official on bank board 2	Some board appointments independent of government *3*	Potential central bank type	Central bank type does exist	Policy type
— (g)	—	*	(a)	no	—
— (g)	*	*	(b)	no	—
** (b)	—	*	(c)	no	—
** (b)	—	—	(d)	no	—
* (b/g)	—	—	(e)	no	—
* (b/g)	*	*	(f)	no	—
* (b/g)	—	*	(g)	no	—
— (g)	—	—	(h)	yes	1
— (g)	*	—	(i)	yes	2
* (b/g)	*	—	(j)	yes	3
** (b)	*	—	(k)	yes	4
** (b)	*	*	(l)	yes	5

Consequently potential types (f) and (g) do not exist either. So, only the bottom part of Table 3.7 is relevant for the ES index of policy independence. The overall degree of policy independence is determined by a combination of attributes ES 1 - 3. Contrary to BP and GMT, we do not weigh each attribute equally. This becomes clear if we take a look at ES 1. If policy making is exclusively entrusted to the central bank a country gets two asterisks. If it is not exclusively entrusted to the central it gets one asterisk. Finally, if the government is the sole authority in policy making it gets zero asterisks. Therefore, regarding our first criterion the maximum amount of asterisks is higher (two) than that with respect to criteria ES 2 and 3 (one). This means that criterion 1 has a weight of 2/4, two times the weight of the other criteria (1/4). Hence, our index is asymmetrical in the sense that attributes are not weighted equally.

We have the following argument in favour of asymmetrical weighting. Like GMT, the ES index of policy independence is based on:

1. The relationship between central banks and government in the formulation of monetary policy.
2. The procedures for appointing the board of the central bank.
3. Formal responsibilities (policy goals) of the central bank with respect to monetary policy.

However, GMT separately assess features 1 and 3. For example, the following conclusions can be drawn considering the Reserve Bank of Australia. From Table 3.5 it follows that according to GMT the Reserve Bank Act of 1959 contains provisions that the central bank pursues monetary stability (GMT 7) among its goals. On the other hand, according to Table 3.5, the government is the final policy authority (GMT 3). Therefore, GMT assess the contents of the final goals of monetary policy (GMT 7) irrespective of the capacity to choose these goals (GMT 6). By their separate assessment GMT allow for a one for one trade-off between the capacity to pursue a monetary policy goal and the contents of such a goal. That is, restricting attention to GMT 6 and 7, a subservient central bank with provisions for monetary stability is as independent as an autonomous central bank without these provisions. Of course, this trade-off is a natural consequence of symmetrical weighting.

Like GMT, the ES index of policy independence is based on features 1. - 3. However, we want to avoid the mentioned trade-off phenomenon. Therefore, feature 1, the final authority in policy making, is assessed in conjunction with feature 3, the policy goals of monetary policy. That is, the extent to which a central bank is regarded to be the sole policy authority (ES 1), also depends on the presence of statutory requirements concerning monetary stability. Hence, we think a double weight (2/4 vs 1/4) with respect to ES 1 can be justified.

III.2 Comparison with the Literature

The five remaining (existing) central bank types are ranked from 1 (least independent) to 5 (most independent) according to the number of asterisks. Our findings are summarized in Table 3.8. In order to facilitate comparison with the literature we include BP's results.

Table 3.8 Eijffinger - Schaling vs Bade—Parkin

Country	ES policy type	BP policy type	BP A. policy type	Interpretation effect	Criterion effect	Difference ES-BP
(See note below)	(a)	(b)	(c)	(d)	(e)	(f)
Australia	1	1	1	0	0	0
Belgium	3	2	2	+1	0	+1
Canada	1	2	2	—1	0	—1
France	2	2	2	0	0	0
Germany	5	4	5	0	+1	+1
Italy	2	2	2	0	0	0
Japan	3	3	4	—1	+1	0
Netherlands	4	2	2	+2	0	+2
Switzerland	5	4	5	0	+1	+1
VK	2	2	2	0	0	0
US	3	3	4	—1	+1	0
Sweden	2	2	2	0	0	0

(a) (Number of asterisks in columns 1, 2 and 3 of Table 3.7) + 1.

(b) See Table 3.2

(c) BP Asymmetrical Policy Types; BP types if BP 1 has two times the weight of BP 2 and 3. (b = **).

(d) ES —/— BPA.

(e) BPA —/— BP.

(f) (d) + (e)

Again, differences in numerical values are dependent on both interpretation and criterion effects. In order to isolate the criterion effect we construct 'BP Asymmetrical Policy Types' (BPA). The latter types result when BP outcomes are entered into our (asymmetrical) aggregation procedure. For instance, consider Japan. According to BP the bank is the final policy authority. In terms of our aggregation procedure this means two asterisks, rather than one. Therefore as a consequence of the higher relative weight attached to this criterion the Bank of Japan becomes BP (asymmetrical) type 4. Now the total difference between ES and BP can be decomposed according to the following formula:

$$ES - BP = (ES - BPA) + (BPA - BP) \tag{3.1}$$

where the first term on the right hand side is the interpretation effect and the second term is the criterion effect. From Table 3.8 it follows that the interpretation effects (see column (d)) concern Belgium, Canada, Japan, The Netherlands and the United States.

The National Bank of Belgium is upgraded (+1), because we regard it a twin-authority (b/g) rather than a government dominated institution (g). This is because the bank gained more independence by the reform of the money market and monetary instruments in January 1991 (see Section I).

Table 3.9 Eijffinger — Schaling vs Grilli—Masciandaro—Tabellini

Country	ES Policy type	GMT Policy type	ES—BP	BP-GMT	Difference ES-GMT
(See note below)		(a)	(b)	(c)	(d)
Australia	1	1	0	0	0
Belgium	3	1	+1	+1	+2
Canada	1	1	—1	+1	0
France	2	1	0	+1	+1
Germany	5	3	+1	+1	+2
Italy	2	3	0	—1	—1
Japan	3	1	0	+2	+2
Netherlands	4	3	+2	—1	+1
Switzerland	5	3	+1	+1	+2
VK	2	2	0	0	0
US	3	3	0	0	0
Sweden	2	—	0	—	—

(a) See Table 3.6.

(b) See column (f) Table 3.8.

(c) See column (e) Table 3.6 (signs must be reversed).

(d) (b) + (c).

The Bank of Canada is downgraded (—1) because, contrary to BP, we find a government official on the board, namely the Deputy Minister of

Finance (without voting power). The Bank of Japan is downgraded (-1) because unlike BP we consider it to be a twin-authority (b/g) rather than a bank dominated (b) institution. The Nederlandsche Bank is upgraded (+2), because we consider it independent in policy making (b) rather than dependent (g) as a consequence of the only formal right of the Minister of Finance to give directions to the Bank. Finally, the Federal Reserve System is downgraded because unlike BP (b), we consider it a twin-authority institution (b/g).

In Table 3.9 our findings are confronted with GMT's. Also, the total difference between ES and GMT may be decomposed, taking the following formula:

$$ES - GMT = (ES - BP) + (BP - GMT) \qquad (3.2)$$

where the first term on the right hand side is decomposed in Table 3.9 and the second term is decomposed in Table 3.6.

IV CONCLUSIONS

The theoretical rationale for central bank independence finds it origin in the ongoing 'rules versus discretion debate'. A recent kind of analysis employed in this longstanding debate is to assess central bank independence by means of the tools of quantitative indices. Numerical values of these indices are dependent on (i) criteria used in the examination of central bank laws (statutes), (ii) the interpretation of the relevant statute as to whether a central bank meets this criterion, i.e. possesses a certain attribute, and (iii) the way these attributes are aggregated to a composite index of central bank independence. Since in principle features (i) - (iii) are arbitrary there are unavoidable subjective elements in the construction of indices of this kind.

In order to view these elements in a broader perspective we compare the major indices of central bank independence as presented in Bade and Parkin (1988) (BP), Alesina (1988, 1989) and Grilli, Masciandaro and Tabellini (1991) (GMT). Also we construct a new index of central bank independence. This index is then used to reach a critical perspective of the mentioned indices and to re-assess central bank independence in twelve industrial countries.

Our findings regarding the existing indices can be summarized as follows. Alesina (1988, 1989) made some serious mistakes in updating Bade and Parkin (1988). Hence, the Alesina revision of the position of the Banca d'Italia implies counterfactual statements concerning e.g monetary accommodation of government deficits. Therefore, the Alesina revision is ad hoc and his index inconsistent. Furthermore, GMT and BP differ in their interpretations of the central bank laws of Canada, France, Belgium, Japan, and the Netherlands. These differences refer to both the presence of government officials on the bank board, and the final authority in policy making. Also, by using a very strict criterion with respect to the appointment of directors GMT change the ranking of the Bundesbank, Banca d'Italia and the Swiss National Bank vis à vis that by BP.

Finally, in re-assessing central bank independence in twelve industrial countries we qualify Banca d'Italia as less independent than GMT, while for the Nationale Bank van België, the Banque de France, the Bundesbank, Bank of Japan, the Nederlandsche Bank and the Schweizerische Nationalbank the reverse applies.

APPENDIX A3: CENTRAL BANK LAWS IN TWELVE INDUSTRIAL COUNTRIES

This appendix contains the source material behind Section III.1 (including Tables 3.7 and 3.8). It provides information on the final authority in monetary policy making, on the presence of government officials on the bank board, on the number of board members not appointed by the government, and on the presence of statutory requirements concerning monetary stability.

A3.1 Sweden

Established in 1668, the Sveriges Riksbank is the oldest central bank in the world. Although this central bank is legally independent of the government, it is not in practice. The legal base for the policy making by the Riksbank is the Sveriges Riksbank Act ('Lag för Sveriges Riksbank') of 1934.[25] The Act provides no specific objectives for the central bank, like in other countries.

In practice, monetary policy is a part of the economic policy by the government and fits into this 'to quite the same degree as where this obligation has been given a legal basis'.[26]

According to Article 1 of the Act, the Riksbank is directly subordinated to the Riksdag (parliament) and formally independent. Furthermore, Article 32 states the following: 'The Directors may not receive instructions with regard to the administration of the Riksbank from anyone except the Riksdag and its Banking Committee in cases in which that Committee is competent to give instructions on behalf of the

Riksdag'.[27]

In addition to this Act, the Riksdag approved special regulations, such as the Credit Policy Instruments Act of 1974, in which 'a government authorization is required before the Riksbank may exercise its powers'.[28] Thus, the policy making by the Riksbank is influenced considerably by the government through these special regulations, in particular by the Ministry of Finance and Economics.[29]

The Board of Directors ('Bankofullmäktige') of the Riksbank has eight members, of which seven are appointed by the Riksdag for a period of three years.[30] These Directors appoint a Governor, who plays only a representative role, for a period of five years and elect among themselves a Chairman on recommendation of the government. The Board takes decisions by a majority with a decisive vote of the Chairman. However, until 1976 and in 1982 Social-Democratic governments used to appoint the Chairman, mostly a former (Deputy) Minister of Finance or Economics.

A3.2 United Kingdom

The Bank of England, established in 1694, was nationalized by the Bank of England Act of 1946.[31] This Act provides only information on the appointment of the Court of Directors and the right to give instructions to the Bank of England.

According to Article 4 (1): 'The Treasury may from time to time give such directions to the Bank as, after consultation with the Governor of the Bank, they think necessary in the public interest'. At the introduction of the Act it was stressed that this right to give directions was not meant to lead to 'any day-to-day interference by the Government or the Treasury with the ordinary work of the Bank'.[32] The right was to be used merely in 'exceptional and unusual cases', which has never occured until now.

It was the Banking Act of 1979 (revised in 1987) that formulated the responsibilities of the central bank. The first task of the Bank of England is the (prudential) supervision of the banking system. 'Other activities of the Bank governed by statute include its note-issuing powers, its management of the Exchange Equalisation Account on behalf of the Treasury, and its duties as banker to the Government and as Government's agent in managing the National Debt'.[33] Nevertheless, monetary policy is regarded as a component of economic policy and therefore conducted by the government with the central bank as its major adviser. As stated in a memorandum by the Bank: 'Economic policy is the responsibility of the Government and is determined by Ministers. Policy decisions are, however, the end product of the assimilation and discussion of studies, forecasts, advice and proposals available to Ministers from a wide range of sources, in which processes the Bank of England has a role to play which can be distinguished from that of Government departments'.[34]

The Bank of England is managed by the Court of Directors, which is made up of the Governor, the Deputy Governor and sixteen Directors.[35] All members are appointed by the Crown on the recommendation of the Prime Minister. The term of office for the Governor and the Deputy Governor is fixed at five years and for the Directors at four years. Four of these Directors are full-time Executive Directors, the other twelve being part-time External Directors who represent various sectors of society: the business sector, the banking system, the insurance industry and the trade unions. The last may be asked to make recommendations. The Governor is chairman of the Court of Directors, heads the day-to-day operations by the Bank and plays the most important role in formulating advice or proposals to the government.[36]

A3.3 France

Established in 1803, the Banque de France was nationalized under the Law of December 2, 1945, which 'had been decided and passed in the perspective of a greater subordination of the Banque de France to the State'.[37] After discussions between its Governor and the Minister of Finance regarding central bank independence,[38] as a compromise the Statutes of the Banque de France ('Les Statuts de la Banque de France') of January 3, 1973 were introduced. These Statutes define in rather general terms the policy goals of the central bank and its relationship with the government.[39] According to Article 1 of the Statutes: 'The Banque de France is the institution which, in the framework of the economic and financial policy of the nation, receives from the State the general mission of watching over the currency and credit'. Thus, the government determines the economic and financial policy to which the monetary policy has been subordinated. Further, Article 4 states: that 'It contributes to the preparation and participates in the implementation of the monetary policy that has been decided by the Government and with the assistance, within the framework of its competence, of the Conseil National du Crédit'. Although the central bank is legally always subject to directions from the government, its Governor implements in consultation with the Minister of Finance the monetary policy in practice.[40] Founded in 1945 as an institution to broaden the political and social base for monetary policy, the Conseil National du Crédit with its 51 members, chaired by the Minister of Finance, advises the Governor (who is his vice-chairman), but is not directly involved in the monetary policy making.

The Banque de France is headed by the Governor, who is supported by two Deputy Governors. Both the Governor and the Deputy Governors are appointed by the President of the Republic after consultation with the Cabinet for an indefinite period, which makes their position rather vulnerable. In practice, the term of office is limited to 5-7 years.[41] In France the Governor has a strong personal responsibility in conducting the management, which may be viewed as a factor that increases his flexibility in negotiations.[42] The Governor is also chairman of the Conseil Général consisting of twelve other members, among them the Deputy Governors. One member is elected by the staff of the Banque and the remaining nine are appointed by the Cabinet on the nomination of the Minister of Finance, representing the economic and financial sectors of society. The Minister also appoints two government auditors with the power to object to decisions by the Conseil Général.[43] The Conseil Général supervises all activities of the Banque and must approve afterwards its administration, and agreements and treaties with other authorities.

A3.4 The Netherlands

The Nederlandsche Bank was established in 1814 and only nationalized in 1948. The statutory task of the Dutch central bank regarding monetary policy is embedded in the Bank Act ('Bankwet') of 1948.[44] Article 9 (1) of this Act states that 'The Bank shall have as its duty to regulate the value of the Dutch currency in such a way as will be most conducive to the nation's prosperity and welfare, and in doing so seek to keep the value as stable as possible'. Further, Article 9 (3) of the Act reads: 'It shall supervise the credit system in pursuance of the Act on the Supervision of the Credit System'. The latter Act gives the Bank the power to implement rules to be followed by credit institutions in their lending. Thereby, the policy goal of the Nederlandsche Bank is to stabilize the internal and external value of the currency, i.e. price level and exchange rate, but not as a sole and independent objective.[45]

The Bank Act also provides for a procedure, if a conflict should arise between the government and the Bank with respect to monetary policy. According to Article 26 (1) of this Act: 'In cases, that our Minister (of Finance) may consider it necessary for the purpose of coordinating monetary and financial policy of the Government and the policy of the Bank, he may give, after consultation with the Bank Council, the necessary directions to the Governing Board to attain those objectives'. Although the Minister of Finance legally has the right to give directions to the central bank, the application of this right is always considered by both authorities as an ultimate remedy ('ultimum remedium') because of the very complicated procedure to solve the conflict.[46] Article 26 reflects the democratic principle that the Minister of Finance is responsible for central bank policy to the parliament. Ultimately, it is to the parliament to assess whether the policy pursued by the Bank must be deemed 'conducive to the nation's prosperity and welfare'. The Minister of Finance has never exercised the right to give directions until now. He and the Governing Board of the Bank are compelled to reach agreement with each other and, thus, the independence of the Bank is sufficiently guaranteed by Article 26.[47]

The Nederlandsche Bank is managed by the Governing Board ('Directie') being composed of the President, the Secretary and presently three Executive Directors.[48] They are nominated by a joint meeting of the Governing Board and Supervisory Board ('Raad van Commissarissen') and appointed by the Crown on the proposal of the Cabinet for a fixed period of seven years. In practice, these nominations were always accepted by the Crown.[49] The Supervisory Board consisting of twelve members, appointed by the Minister of Finance, supervises the Governing Board. Finally, the Bank Council ('Bankraad') of seventeen members is chaired by the Royal Commissioner ('Koninklijk Commissaris') and may seek information from the Bank and offer independent advice to the Minister of Finance.

A3.5 Belgium

Established in 1850, the National Bank of Belgium ('Nationale Bank van België') is owned half by the state and half by the public.[50] The legal base for the functioning of the Belgian central bank are the Organic Law ('Organieke Wet') and the Statutes of 1939, which provide no specific objectives for the Bank.[51] Article 29 of the Organic Law states the following: 'The Minister of Finance shall have the right to supervise all the operations of the Bank. He may object to the execution of any measure which would be contrary to the Law, the Statutes or the interests of the State. This supervision shall be entrusted to a Government Commissioner'. According to Article 30 of this Law: 'The Government Commissioner is appointed by the Crown. He shall supervise all the operations of the Bank. He may suspend and report to the Minister of Finance, every decision that would be contrary to the Laws, the Statutes or the interests of the State'.[52] Therefore, the National Bank of Belgium can not be considered as formally independent of the government. The Bank is forbidden to pursue targets conflicting with the general objectives of the government.[53] Nevertheless, the relationship between the central bank and government has changed, in favour of more independence, by the reform of the money market and monetary policy instruments which started on January 29, 1991. The reform was intended to improve the access to the market for Treasury bills, to introduce a regime of primary dealers and to innovate and extend the monetary policy instruments. As a consequence of this reform, the responsibility of the central bank for monetary policy was more clearly defined and its touch with financial markets on behalf of policy making improved.[54]

The Board of Directors ('Bestuurscomité') of the National Bank of Belgium is made up of the Governor and three to six Directors of which one acts as Deputy Governor. The Governor and Directors are appointed by the Crown for a fixed period of five and six years respectively. The Board of Directors is chaired by the Governor and collectively responsible for the management of the Bank and the formulation of monetary policy. It may change the discount rate and the rate for advances in a case of emergency, but must report to the Council of Regency ('Regentenraad'). The Council of Regency determines, however, the policy goals of the Bank and deals with general questions concerning the Bank, the currency, credits and the economic development.[55] The Council of Regency consists of the Board of Directors and ten Regents elected by the General Meeting of Shareholders for a period of three years, representing the Minister of Finance (3), financial institutions (2), trade unions (2) and organisations of industry, commerce and agriculture (3). The Governor is chairman and has a decisive vote.

A3.6 Germany

The legal predecessors of the Deutsche Bundesbank were the Reichsbank, established in 1876, and the Bank Deutscher Länder, founded together with the introduction of the Deutsche Mark by the currency reform of 1948. The Deutsche Bundesbank was established by the Deutsche Bundesbank Act ('Gesetz über die Deutsche Bundesbank') of 1957.[56] Its main policy goals are provided for in Article 3 of this Act: 'The Deutsche Bundesbank shall regulate the amount of money in circulation and of credit supplied to the economy, using the monetary powers conferred on it by this Act, with the aim of safeguarding the currency, and shall arrange for the handling by banks of domestic and external payments'. Article 3 clearly reflects the special responsibility of the central bank for maintaining the internal and external value of the currency, i.e. price level and exchange rate.[57]

The relationship between the Bundesbank and the federal government is embedded in Article 12 of the Act reading: 'Without prejudice to the performance of its functions, the Deutsche Bundesbank shall be required to support the general economic policy of the Federal Government. In exercising the powers conferred on it by this Act it shall be independent of instructions from the Federal Government'. Thus, Article 12 guarantees the independence of the central bank regarding monetary policy making. It should be noticed that the Act does not cover any procedures in case of a major conflict between the Bundesbank and the federal government. Nevertheless, Article 13 of the Act provides for certain procedures for the coordination of monetary and economic policy and for consultation between central bank and government as independent bodies. According to Article 13 (2,3) members of government may attend meetings of the Central Bank Council, without voting right, and the President of the Bank those of the government on invitation.[58]

The Central Bank Council ('Zentralbankrat') of the Deutsche Bundesbank is made up of the Directorate ('Direktorium') and the Presidents of the Landeszentralbanken (main offices). The Council determines monetary policy under chairmanship of the President or Deputy President of the Bundesbank and meets every two weeks.[59] The Directorate, consisting of the President, Deputy President and at the maximum eight (now four) other members, implements the decisions taken by the Central Bank Council. The at most ten members of the Directorate are appointed by the President of the Federal Republic on the nomination of the Federal Government, while the eleven Presidents of the Landeszentralbanken are appointed by him on the nomination of the Bundesrat based on a proposal by the Government of the Land concerned, all after consultation of the Central Bank Council. Both the members of the Directorate and the Presidents of the Landeszentralbanken have a maximum term of office of eight years which is usually realized.[60] During this term they can not be removed from office on political grounds. The appointment of the members of the Central Bank Council reflects also a large degree of independence of the Bundesbank.

A3.7 Japan

Established in 1882, the Bank of Japan was reorganized by the Bank of Japan Law of 1942.[61] According to Article 1 of this Law: 'The Bank of Japan has for its object the regulation of the currency, the control and facilitation of credit and finance, and the maintenance and fostering of the credit system, pursuant to the national policy, in order that the general economic activities of the nation might adequately be enhanced'. The latter part of Article 1 may be taken to mean 'to foster the stable development of the Japanese economy'.[62] Thus, the main objectives of the Bank are to stabilize the value of the currency and to maintain orderly credit conditions. Regarding the relationship between the central bank and government, Article 43 states that: 'The competent Minister (of Finance) may, if deemed particularly necessary for the attainment of the object of the Bank of Japan, order the Bank to undertake any necessary business, or order alterations in the By-Laws as well as other necessary actions'. Although the Minister, formally, has the right to give instructions, in practice this right has never been used as a result of the regular, informal contacts between Bank management and government.[63] With respect to its main goal, price stability, the actual influence of the Bank is much greater than what is legally defined. For example, the Bank of Japan has been fairly succesful in advocating the liberalization of Japanese financial markets and in arguing for a more market-oriented implementation of monetary policy, which the Ministry of Finance has resisted for a long time.[64] The influence of the Ministry is, above all, based on financial regulation (regulatory leverage) and decreases gradually by financial liberalization. However, the Bank of Japan derives its influence mainly from guiding the financial markets (market leverage), which increases by the strengthening of market forces. Thereby, the independence of the central bank has continued to grow.[65]

The highest policy-making body of the Bank of Japan is the Policy Board, consisting of the Governor, two representatives from the Ministry of Finance and Economic Planning Agency (without voting right) and four other members, representing banking (2), commerce and industry (1), and agriculture (1). The Governor and the other members of the Policy Board are appointed by the Cabinet for a period of five and four years respectively. Since 1969, the Governor has been chosen alternately from Bank officials and former Ministry of Finance officials.[66] The Governor conducts the operations of the Bank according to the directions of the Policy Board and heads the Executive Board, which further includes two Deputy Governors (formerly one), at least three Executive Directors and two Executive Auditors (now six and four respectively), and a number of Counsellors.[67] The Deputy Governors are appointed by the Cabinet for five years, while the other members of the Executive Board by the Minister of Finance on recommendation of the Governor for two to four years. Despite the fact that the Policy Board is, from a legal point of view, the most important policy making body, the major responsibility for formulating monetary policy resides with the Executive Board.[68]

A3.8 Italy

The Banca d'Italia, established in 1893, is owned partially, through public financial institutions, by the State.[69] The legal base for its functioning are the Statutes ('Statuto della Banca d'Italia') of 1936, which provide no specific objectives for the central bank.[70] The relationship between the Banca d'Italia and the government is embedded in Article 20 of the Statutes stating that the Board of Directors ('Comitato') is just responsible for the general management of the central bank and not for monetary policy making. Furthermore, Article 25 reads: 'He (the Governor) shall make proposals to the Minister of the Treasury concerning change in the discount rates and in the interest rate on advances'. Obviously, the Governor prepares monetary policy and the Minister of the Treasury has to approve it formally.[71]

The Statutes of 1936 were amended in 1947 by providing the Banca d'Italia with supervision on the financial system and by the foundation of the Interministerial Committee for Credit and Savings ('Comitato Interministeriale per il Credito e il Risparmio' or CIRC).[72] According to Article 1 of the Decree of 1947, the CICR, 'whose duty it shall be to supervise, at the highest level, the safeguarding of savings, the carrying on of credit activities, and exchange matters', will give directives to the central bank for its operations. The CIRC is made up of the most important ministers and the Governor, and chaired by the Minister of the Treasury. In general, this committee determines the goals of monetary policy with the Banca d'Italia in an advisory role. The central bank has always been integrated with economic policy making, which explains why it scarcely had any conflict with the Treasury. Until the mid-seventies the central bank was, clearly, subordinated to the government. However, from 1975 on the Banca d'Italia paid more attention to gaining independence with respect to monetary policy.[73]

The Governor, having a personal responsibility for the implementation of monetary policy, is appointed by the Board of Directors of the Banca d'Italia, for an indefinite term of office. The Board of Directors consists of thirteen Directors, elected by the General Meeting of Shareholders at the thirteen regional offices of the central bank for a fixed period of three years, the Governor with a casting vote and a representative of the Ministry of the Treasury as an observer without voting right. Although the appointment of Governor and Directors seems to be independent of the government, Article 19 of the Statutes of 1936 states that: 'Appointments and dismissals must be approved by decree of the President of the Republic on the proposal of the President of the Council of Ministers in agreement with the Minister of the Treasury, the Council of Ministers having been heard'.

A3.9 Switzerland

Established in 1905, the Swiss National Bank ('Schweizerische Nationalbank') has enjoyed a high degree of independence from the government, reflecting the deep-rooted distrust of the Swiss public in centralized approaches to policy making.[74]

The main policy goals of the Swiss central bank are provided for in Article 2 (1) of the Federal Law on the Swiss National Bank ('Bundesgesetz über die Schweizerische Nationalbank') of 1953: 'The principal task of the National Bank shall be to regulate the country's monetary circulation, facilitate payments transactions, and implement a credit and monetary policy serving the general interests of the country. It shall advise the Federal authorities in monetary matters.'[75] The central bank interprets this Article as a mandate to achieve and to maintain a stable price level, which view is shared by the federal government and largely accepted by the public.[76] The relationship between the Swiss National Bank and the federal government ('Bundesrat') is one of legal and administrative separation. The National Bank Law does not contain any provision giving the government influence on monetary policy making. In case of important policy decisions, both authorities should consult each other, but mutual consent is not required.[77] The independence of the central bank is also guaranteed by Article 63, limiting the competence of the federal parliament to approving an increase in the Bank's basic capital and that of the federal government to appointing representatives to the Bank Council, the members of the Directorate, their deputies and the managers of the branch offices, and to other formal approvals.

The Bank Committee ('Bankausschuss') is the principal policy making body of the Swiss National Bank and has the right to participate in the setting of the Bank's official lending rates.[78] Representing the various parts (cantons) of the country, this Bank Committee is made up of the Chairman and the Deputy Chairman of the Bank Council ('Bankrat') and eight other members, which are appointed by the Bank Council for a fixed period of four years. The Bank Council, consisting of forty members, is responsible for the supervision and control of the Bank's management, but plays a limited role with respect to monetary policy. Its Chairman, Deputy Chairman and twenty-three other members are appointed by the federal government and the remaining fifteen members are elected by the General Meeting of Shareholders also for a period of four years.[79] Thus, only one-fifth of the Bank Committee and five-eighths of the Bank Council are directly appointed by the federal government. Finally, the highest managing and executive authority is the Directorate ('Direktorium') of the Bank, which is composed of three members elected by the federal government, on recommendation of the Bank Council, for a fixed term of six years.[80] The government also appoints among these three members a President and a Vice-President, although there is a collective responsibility.

A3.10 Australia

The Commonwealth Bank of Australia was established in 1911, initially as a trading bank. Steps toward the acquisition of central banking powers were taken in the 1920s, especially in 1924. Again, during the Great Depression of the 1930s, it began to acquire further central banking responsibilities (e.g. for the exchange rate) and, under emergency powers in World War II, established *inter alia* exchange control and a wide range of credit controls. These were continued under the Banking Act 1945.[81] Then in 1959, central banking functions were separated from trading bank operations and a new Reserve Bank of Australia was established.

The functions of its Board are set out in Article 10 (2) of the Reserve Bank Act of 1959[82]

> 'It is the duty of the Board, within the limits of its powers, to ensure that the monetary and banking policy of the Bank is directed to the greatest advantage of the people of Australia and that the powers of the Bank under this Act, the Banking Act 1959 and the regulations under that Act are exercised in such a manner as, in the opinion of the Board, will best contribute to: the stability of the currency of Australia, the maintenance of full employment in Australia and the economic prosperity and welfare of the people in Australia'.

Thus, the threefold policy goal of the Reserve Bank also includes the fostering of economic activity and employment. Regarding monetary policy making the central bank is bound to inform the federal government on a regular base: 'The Governor and the Secretary to the Department of the Treasury shall establish a close liaison with each other and shall keep each other fully informed on all matters which jointly concern the Bank and the Department of the Treasury' (Article 13). In practice, the relationship between the Reserve Bank and the federal government is characterized by both formal and informal contacts. Nevertheless, the Bank is completely subordinated to the Secretary of the Treasury, being the final competent authority with respect to monetary policy. In case of differences of opinion between the central bank and the Treasury, Article 11 (2) states that 'the Treasurer and the Board shall endeavour to reach agreement'.[83]

Furthermore, according to Article 50 (1) of the Banking Act of 1959 the Reserve Bank's setting of rates on discounts and advances needs to be approved by the Treasury.[84] So, the central bank is more or less an agent of the government.

The Reserve Bank Board, responsible for implementing monetary policy, consists of the Governor, the Deputy Governor, the Secretary to the Treasury as an ex officio member and seven other members. The government official on the Board has a voting right. The Governor and Deputy Governor are appointed by the Governor-General (the executive branch of the federal government) for a term of office, not exceeding seven years. The seven other members comprise at most two members who are officers of the Bank or Public Service, holding office 'during the pleasure of the Governor-General',[85] and at least five members selected from the academic, agricultural and general business sector by the Governor-General for a fixed period of five years. The Governor is chairman of the Board and has a casting vote.

A3.11 United States

Established in 1913, the Federal Reserve System is a federal government authority comprising the twelve Federal Reserve Banks, whose shares are owned by commercial banks being its members, and formerly (until 1935) the Federal Reserve Board as its main policy making body. The legal base for its functioning was embedded in the Federal Reserve Act of 1913.[86] The Preamble of this Act constituted the powers of the Federal Reserve System: 'To provide for the establishment of Federal Reserve Banks, to furnish an elastic currency, to afford means of rediscounting commercial paper, to establish a more effective supervision of banking in the United States, and for other purposes'. By the Banking Act of 1933 the Federal Reserve Board was granted more autonomy vis-à-vis the Federal Reserve Banks and the Federal Open Market Committee (FOMC) was created to make policy recommendation to the Board for conducting open market operations.[87] Further, the Banking Act of 1935 replaced the Federal Reserve Board by the Board of Governors and strengthened its position by removing the Secretary of the Treasury and the Treasurer from the Board. Through the 'Accord' of 1951 the Federal Reserve gained more autonomy as a consequence of its agreement with the Treasury that its open market policy should no longer support the market for government debt.[88] The goals of the central bank regarding monetary policy were clearly formulated in Section IIA of the 1977 amendment to the Act by stating that: 'The Board of Governors of the Federal Reserve System and the Federal Open Market Committee shall maintain long run growth of the monetary and credit aggregates commensurate with the economy's long run potential to increase production, so as to promote the goals of maximum employment, stable prices, and moderate long-term interest rates'. So, the Federal Reserve should aim both at price stability and at economic activity and employment.[89] Furthermore, the Humphrey-Hawkins Act of 1978 was meant to improve the coordination of economic and monetary policy between the federal government, Congress (parliament) and Federal Reserve by reporting requirements for the central bank to Senate and House of Representatives at semi-annual hearings on the Board's and FOMC's objectives and plans with respect to the growth of monetary and credit aggregates.[90] In practice, both the Federal Reserve and the government have a shared responsibility for monetary policy making. Although the central bank maintained the same degree of formal autonomy, it lost some of its independence after the mid-1960's.[91]

The Board of Governors of the Federal Reserve System, acting as its highest policy making body, is composed of seven members which are selected in order to maintain a geographical balance and a balance between bankers and non-bankers. These seven Governors are appointed by the President of the United States for a fixed period of fourteen years, with approval by the Senate. After a full term of office the Governors may not be reappointed. The President appoints two members of the Board of Governors as Chairman and Vice-Chairman for a fixed period of four years.[92] Political influence on the appointment of the Board is minimalized by the long term of office, exceeding more than three administrations, and the impossibility of dismissal on political grounds. Furthermore, the formulation of global monetary targets its carried out by the FOMC.[93] The FOMC is made up of the Board of Governors and five of the twelve Presidents of the Federal Reserve Banks. The President of the Federal Reserve Bank of New York, conducting open market operations and exchange market interventions on behalf of the System, is an ex officio member of the FOMC. The other four members are elected for a period of one year on a rotating basis. The Presidents of the twelve Federal Reserve Banks are appointed by the Board of Directors of each Bank, with consent of the Board of Governors.[94]

A3.12 Canada

The Bank of Canada, only established in 1935, had its functioning originally based on the Bank of Canada Act of 1934.[95] The policy goals of the Canadian central bank were given in the Preamble of this Act, reading: 'Whereas it is desirable to establish a central bank in Canada to regulate credit and currency in the best interests of the economic life of the nation, to control and protect the external value of the national monetary unit and to mitigate by its influence fluctuations in the general level of production, trade, prices and employment, so far as may be possible within the scope of monetary action, and generally to promote the economic and financial welfare of the Dominion'. Until 1967, this Act did not confine the threefold task of the central bank regarding monetary policy making.[96] However, in 1967 the relationship between the Bank of Canada and the federal government was changed by the introduction of the Bank of Canada Act of 1967.[97] This was caused by a major conflict of the Governor with the Minister of Finance on the implementation of monetary policy. The Governor, wanting to conduct a restrictive policy, was forced to resign. The Act of 1967 gave the Minister of Finance the right to promulgate instructions to the Bank and, therefore, the ultimate authority for monetary policy. Article 14 (1) of the revised Act states that: 'The Minister and the Governor shall consult regularly on monetary policy and on its relation to general economic policy'. Furthermore, Article 14 (2) continues: 'If, notwithstanding the consultations provided for in Subsection (1) there should emerge a difference of opinion between the Minister and the Bank concerning the monetary policy to be followed, the Minister may, after consultation with the Governor in Council (executive branch of government), give to the Governor a written direction concerning monetary policy, in specified terms, and the Bank shall comply with such directive'. Although the Minister of Finance has, up to now, never used his right to give instructions, this possibility has severely affected the independence of the central bank after 1967.

The highest policy making body of the Bank of Canada is its Board of Directors, consisting of the Governor, Deputy Governor, twelve Directors and the Deputy Minister of Finance as an ex officio member without voting power.[98] Both the Governor and the Deputy Governor are appointed by the Directors, with the approval of the Governor in Council, for a fixed period of seven years. The Minister of Finance appoints the twelve Directors,[99] with the consent of the Governor in Council, for a period of three years. The (Deputy) Governor and Directors may be reappointed. The Governor is the chief executive officer and supervises the Bank. Moreover, the Bank has an Executive Committee, which is competent to deal with any matter within the competence of the Board. The Executive Committee is composed of the Governor, Deputy Governor, two Directors and the Deputy Minister of Finance and mainly responsible for the implementation of monetary policy.

NOTES

1. As pointed out by Cukierman (1993, p. 272) there are often serious gaps, particularly in LDCs, between the letter of the law and its application. Indices that reflect some of these gaps are the actual (as opposed to the legal) term of office of the CB governor and the responses of experts on monetary institutions to a questionnaire on central bank independence.
2. Exceptions are Bade and Parkin (1988, pp. 21-23), and Schaling (1993).
3. A meaningful comparison of the indices of Cukierman (1992) (LVAU), and Cukierman, Webb and Neyapti (1992) (LVAW) with the other indices (BP, AL, GMT and ES) is practically impossible. The reason is that the LVAU and LVAW indices focus on different legal attributes from central bank laws than those included in the other indices. This point is also illustrated by Eijffinger and de Haan (1994, p. 34).
4. We focus on internal monetary policy, i.e. we take no account of the relations of governments and central banks in the conduct of exchange rate policy. We leave this for further research.
5. Eijffinger and van Keulen (1994) extend this sample to include Austria, Denmark, Finland, Hungary, Luxembourg, New Zealand, Norway, Poland, Portugal, Spain and the Czech republic.
6. In Eijffinger and Schaling (1993c) we restrict attention to this new index.
7. Bade and Parkin (1988, p. 18) point out that a commitment to a fixed exchange rate leaves monetary policy with the task of determining the stock of foreign reserves. Therefore, they think it pointless to look to the effects of central bank laws on monetary policy in a fixed exchange rate era. Empirical support for this view can be found in de Haan and Sturm (1992).
8. BP's results concerning both the relationship between the central bank and the government in monetary policy making and the procedures for appointing and removing central bank directors are extensively discussed in Eijffinger and Schaling (1992a, pp. 18-20).
9. Of course, in this case the presence of a government official without voting power on the policy board would not make much sense.
10. For an examination of aggregate demand policy and exchange rate policy rules in a multi-country Phillips-curve framework see Taylor (1982).
11. Even though interest rates are the proximate instruments of monetary policy, according to Bade and Parkin (1988, p. 19) there is no inherent inconsistency in using the variability of inflation as the appropriate measure of the variability of policy. Short-term interest rates are typically manipulated with a view to achieving a particular behaviour for the growth rate of various monetary aggregates, and these aggregates are further regarded as appropriate intermediate targets in achieving predictable and less variable inflation. A diagrammatic presentation of this line of reasoning is given in Eijffinger and Gerards (1990, p. 13).
12. This tentative conclusion is given formal content by estimating first order autoregres-

sions for inflation (where all the coefficients on lagged inflation were restricted to be equal) with inclusion of a dummy variable for the German and Swiss central bank type, see Bade and Parkin (1988, p. 21-23).

13. Alesina supports the rational partisan theory, a theory that combines Hibbs' (1977) partisan theory with rational expectations macroeconomic theory.
14. This research was also published in the Report by the European Commission '*One market, one money*'. See Commission of the European Communities (1990, pp. 97-98).
15. For ease of comparison we focus on the BP sample, skipping New Zealand, Spain, Denmark, Norway and Finland.
16. See: Alesina (1988, p. 42). However, Tabellini (1988a, p. 96) states this change to have taken place in the summer of 1981.
17. See Section II.
18. Correspondence with Alesina did not clarify the weighting procedure of Alesina (1988, 1989).
19. Note that this assertion follows from our (counterfactual) hypothesis that the Alesina index is internally consistent.
20. According to Grilli, Masciandaro and Tabellini, economic independence is the capacity to choose the instruments of monetary policy. Their treatment of economic independence is extensively discussed in Eijffinger and Schaling (1992a).
21. To facilitate comparison corresponding BP criteria are given in italics.
22. Again, for ease of comparison we focus on the BP sample, skipping Austria, Denmark, Greece, Ireland, New Zealand, Portugal and Spain.
23. The threshold for meeting BP's criterion 3 is the composition of the Central Bank Council of the Bundesbank.
24. Following BP this criterion is operationalized as: proportion of members not appointed directly or indirectly by the government $\geq 11/21$.
25. See Aufricht (1967, pp. 663-671). The last revision of this Act was made in 1988.
26. From Skanland (1984, p. 16).
27. Aufricht (1967, pp. 668-669).
28. In Sveriges Riksbank, Credit and Foreign Exchange, 1990.
29. See Fair (1979, p. 40).
30. See Sveriges Riksbank, Annual Report 1990, p. 5.
31. See Aufricht (1967, pp. 185-192).
32. From Eizenga (1991, p. 4). Eizenga (1991) distinguishes three differences between the right to give instructions in the United Kingdom and that prevailing in the Netherlands.
33. See Cairncross (1988, p. 68).
34. Memorandum by the Bank of England, 'The relationship between the Bank of England and the Treasury', G.B. House of Commons, Treasury and Civil Services Committee, Session 1979-1980, Memorandum on monetary policy, 1980, pp. 177-180 (in particular paragraph 14).
35. According to Article 2 (1) of the Bank of England Act of 1946.
36. See Fair (1979, p. 41) and Eizenga (1991, pp. 6-7).
37. Translated from: Koch (1983, p. 371). The Law of December 2, 1945 is given by: Aufricht (1967, pp. 199-210).
38. See Bouvier (1988, pp. 96-97).
39. In Banque de France, *La Banque de France et la Monnaie*, Paris, 1986, pp. 149-157.
40. See Eizenga (1990, pp. 2,12); Eijffinger (1991, pp. 3-4).
41. From Skanland (1984, p. 13).
42. From Skanland (1984, p. 13).
43. See Fair (1979, p. 39) and Eizenga (1990, pp. 4-5).
44. This Act is given in Wetten Binnenlands Geldwezen, Zwolle, 1979, pp. 5-27. See

also Eizenga (1983, p. 10).

45. See Eijffinger (1986, pp. 8-9) and Eizenga (1987, p. 12).
46. This procedure is extensively discussed by: A.M. de Jong, *De Wetgeving nopens De Nederlandsche Bank*, 1814-1958, een historische studie, The Hague, 1960.
47. From Eizenga (1987, pp. 13-14).
48. Article 22 of the Bank Act provides the possibility to appoint at most five Executive Directors. The Governing Board has a collective responsibility for the Bank's management.
49. See also Eizenga (1987, p. 14).
50. The latter half is held by various authorities and, thus, under indirect control of the government.
51. The Organic Law and Statutes are revised on January 2 and 23, 1991. See *Belgisch Staatsblad*, January, 25 and 29, 1991.
52. This Commissioner is mostly the highest Ministry of Finance official.
53. However, Fair (1979, p. 37) is of the opinion that 'in practice the National Bank is largely independent'.
54. See Hervorming van het monetair beleidsinstrumentarium, aspecten en documenten, Belgische Vereniging van Banken, No. 114, January 1991, p.25.
55. According to Articles 63 and 64 of the Statutes of 1939.
56. See The Deutsche Bundesbank - Its monetary policy instruments and functions, *Deutsche Bundesbank Special Series*, No. 7, 2nd edition, Frankfurt-am-Main, October 1987, pp. 105-130.
57. For an interpretation Eizenga (1987, pp. 2-12) and Eijffinger (1991, pp. 3-5).
58. In practice, these members only attend Central Bank Council meetings with important issues. See Skanland (1984, p. 18).
59. The Central Bank Council has a collective responsibility.
60. The minimum term of office is two years. See Eizenga (1987, p. 4).
61. This Law was amended in 1949 to found the Policy Board, the highest policy making body of the Bank. See Aufricht (1961, pp. 423-448).
62. An interpretation is given by Suzuki (1987, pp. 305-312).
63. Suzuki (1987, p. 314) means 'In reality, the management of monetary policy is carried out under the responsibility of the Bank of Japan from an independent point of view'.
64. See Cargill (1989, p. 38).
65. For an analysis of this process Eijffinger & van Rixtel (1992, p. 24).
66. See also *The Economist*, Central Banks: America v. Japan - The rewards of independence, January, 25, 1992, p. 22.
67. From The Bank of Japan, *Annual Review 1991*, Tokyo, 1991, pp. 35-36.
68. The Policy Board formally adopts the decisions of the Executive Board. See: Cargill (1989, pp. 27-28).
69. From Fair (1979, p. 39).
70. See Aufricht (1967, pp. 421-440).
71. Recently, the Italian parliament approved a bill to give the central bank full authority regarding discount policy.
72. The Decree on the Interministerial Committee for Credit and Savings of 1947, in Aufricht (1967, pp. 453-455).
73. See Nardozzi (1988, p. 179).
74. From Rich (1989, p. 1).
75. This Law should be read in conjunction with Article 39 of the Federal Constitution amended in 1951. See Aufricht (1967, pp. 705-724).
76. For an interpretation Skanland (1984, p. 7) and Rich (1989, p. 7).
77. See also Skanland (1984, p. 22).
78. According to Rich (1989, p. 6), however, this right 'is not a significant as it may

seem at first sight because these rates no longer constitute important policy instruments in Switzerland'.

79. The federal government holds no shares. See Fair (1979, p. 41).
80. To the Directorate may be added deputies and department managers.
81. See Wilson (1952, pp. 33-99).
82. The Reserve Bank Act of 1959 is given by Aufricht (1961, pp. 53-71).
83. For the procedure to settle such conflicts: Article 11 (2) - 11 (7) of the Reserve Bank Act of 1959.
84. However, Masciandaro and Tabellini (1988, p. 149) mean that recently: 'the central bank has not formally promulgated regulations, but has informed the banks of its goals concerning the rates of interest, following discussions'.
85. According to Article 14 (3) of the Reserve Bank Act of 1959.
86. See also Board of Governors, The Federal Reserve System; Purposes and Functions, Washington, D.C., 1984. An interpretation can be found in *Cargill* (1989, pp. 21-32).
87. For the creation of the FOMC: Akhtar and Howe (1991, p. 364).
88. During the Second World War the stabilization of this market had become the principal function of the System. See Eizenga (1983, p. 4).
89. For a recent evaluation of the 'twin objectives' *The Economist*, Central Banks: America v. Japan - The rewards of independence, January, 25, 1992, pp. 22-23.
90. According to Eizenga (1983) 'this Act does not derogate from the independence of the FED with regard to its policies' (p. 6). He calls it 'independent within the government' (pp. 7-9).
91. See also Hetzel (1990, p. 170).
92. From Krooss and Samuelson (1969, pp. 2913-2914).
93. See Eizenga (1983, p. 2).
94. For legislative proposals to restructure it: Akhtar and Howe (1991, p. 358).
95. See Aufricht (1961, pp. 89-105).
96. According to Article 14 (1) of the Act of 1934, the Governor had power to veto any action or decision of the Board of Directors or Executive Committee, which could be overruled by the federal government.
97. In *The Revised Statutes of Canada*, 1970, Vol. 1, Ottawa, 1970.
98. Notice that the government official in the Board of Governors of the Reserve Bank of Australia, on the contrary, has voting power.
99. They will be selected from 'diversified occupations' and in practice, from different regions of Canada. See Fair (1979, p. 37).

4. Central Bank Independence: Theory and Evidence

I INTRODUCTION

The theoretical rationale for central bank independence finds its origin in the ongoing 'rules versus discretion' debate. Authors like Barro and Gordon (1983a) and Rogoff (1985) argue that governments and central banks are tempted to impart an inflationary bias to the economy, thereby sacrificing long-term welfare to short-run political gains. The associated time-consistency problem can be overcome by legislative rules and by setting up politically independent central banks. Hence, one would expect countries with independent central banks to have a lower sustainable rate of inflation.

In addition to the well-developed theoretical literature,[1] there are also some studies that compare actual monetary regimes between a large number of countries. The most comprehensive studies are Bade and Parkin (1988), Alesina (1988, 1989), Grilli, Masciandaro and Tabellini (1991), Cukierman (1992), Cukierman, Webb and Neyapti (1992), Eijffinger and Schaling (1992b, 1993a, 1994), Alesina and Summers (1993) and Eijffinger, Van Rooij, and Schaling (1994). It is striking that the conclusions of the latter are less clear-cut than the theoretical literature. For instance, contrary to Alesina and Summers, Bade and Parkin find no correlation between central bank independence and the variability of inflation. Next, unlike the prediction of the Rogoff (1985) model,[2] both Alesina and Summers and Grilli, Masciandaro and Tabellini find no association between central bank independence and (the variability of) real output growth.

In this Chapter on the basis of a single-stage Phillips-curve monetary policy game with private information about the economy[3] - i.e. supply shocks - we derive several propositions concerning the relationship between central bank independence and (the variance of) inflation and output growth. These propositions are tested for twelve industrial countries (Australia, Belgium, Canada, France, Germany, Italy, Japan, the Netherlands, Sweden, Switzerland, the U.K. and the U.S.) for the post-Bretton-Woods period (1972-1991). In testing the game-theoretic model we use the indices of central bank independence introduced in Chapter 3.

The main conclusions of this Chapter can be summarized as follows. First of all, both our model and estimation results give further support to the well-known inverse relationship between the degree of central bank independence and the level of inflation found by e.g. Alesina (1988, 1989) and Cukierman, Webb and Neyapti (1992). Secondly, contrary to Grilli, Masciandaro and Tabellini (1991) and Alesina and Summers (1993), we find little empirical evidence that the more independent the central bank is, the lower the variability of inflation. Thirdly, our estimation results reject clearly the proposition - implied by the Rogoff (1985) model - of a positive relation between independence and the variability of real output growth. In other words, inflation-averse central banks do not bear the costs of triggering recessions nor do politically sensitive central banks reap the benefits of avoiding recessions. Finally, no empirical relationship can be found between central bank independence and the level of real output growth in the long run. Hence, our empirical results support the proposition of Grilli, Masciandaro and Tabellini (1991) that having an independent central bank is like having a free lunch. There are benefits (lower inflation) but no apparent costs in terms of real output growth.

The plan of this chapter is as follows. In Section II we combine the Rogoff (1985) Phillips-curve monetary policy game with the Alogoskoufis (1994) model of wage and employment determination, to allow for persistence in the natural rate of output. In Section III we use this model to analyse the theoretical relationships of central bank independence with the means and variances of inflation and real output growth. Finally, in Section IV we confront the propositions from the game-theoretic model with empirical evidence using various indices of central bank independence.

II A SIMPLE CLOSED ECONOMY MACROMODEL

II.1 The Model

The main purpose of Sections II and III is to combine the Rogoff (1985) Phillips curve monetary policy game with the Alogoskoufis (1994) model of wage and employment determination, to allow for persistence in the natural rate of output. Next, following Cukierman (1992, pp. 415-431) we use this model to analyse the effects of central bank independence on the mean and variance of inflation and real output growth.

We assume that there are two types of agents, wage-setters and the central bank. Wage-setters unilaterally choose the nominal wage every time period, and the central bank controls monetary policy to determine the inflation rate.

The timing of events is as follows. Wage-setters sign annual nominal contracts (Gray (1976), Fischer, (1977a)) at the beginning of each year, before monetary policy is chosen for that year.

Wage-setters know the domestic monetary regime, i.e. they know the weight of inflation stabilization relative to employment stabilization in the preferences of the central bank. They take this information into account in forming their expectations. Finally, employment is determined by competitive firms. We now move on to the supply side of the model.

II.2 Wage and Employment Determination

Consider the following supply block which is a closed-economy version of Alogoskoufis (1994). Capital will be assumed fixed, and output is given by a short-run production function of the following type

$$y_t = \beta \ell_t + \mu_t \qquad 0 < \beta < 1 \tag{4.1}$$

where lower-case letters refer to logarithmic deviations from steady state values.[4] Thus, y is the log of output, ℓ the log of employment, and μ a measure of productivity. β is the exponent of labour and is less than unity.

Having described the level of output, it remains to specify how productivity evolves over time. We use a stochastic trend specification discussed in Stock and Watson (1988). This specification says that over the long run productivity will grow at some average rate, labelled g. However, shocks to productivity, ν_t^μ, can cause productivity growth to deviate from its mean. Moreover, these shocks are persistent with respect to the level of productivity: once perturbed by an ν_t^μ shock, μ_t will show no tendency to return to its trendline. Hence, the supply shocks are assumed to have permanent effects on the economy's productive capacity.[5] The mathematical expression for the stochastic trend specification is a random walk with drift

$$\mu_t = g + \mu_{t-1} + \nu_t^\mu \tag{4.2}$$

where g is the average (or expected) rate of growth of productivity (the drift of the μ-process), and ν^μ is a normally distributed productivity shock with zero mean and variance σ_μ^2. Without loss of generality we normalize σ_μ^2 at 1.

Firms determine employment by equalizing the marginal product of labour to the real wage $w_t - p_t$. This yields the following employment function

$$\ell_t = \frac{-1}{1 - \beta}(w_t - p_t - \mu_t) \tag{4.3}$$

where w is the log of the nominal wage and p the log of the price level.

The nominal wage is set at the beginning of each period and remains fixed for one period. The objective of wage setters is to stabilize employment around a target employment level $l_i^s \equiv \tilde{\ell}$. Denoting the log of the labour force by l^s, we assume $l_i^s < l^s$ Thus we employ the insider-outsider approach to the labour market (Blanchard and Summers (1986), Lindbeck and Snower (1986)).[6] Thus, wages in each period are set to minimize

$$E_{t-1} (\ell_t - \tilde{\ell})^2 \tag{4.4}$$

where E_{t-1} is the operator of rational expectations, conditional on information available at the end of period t − 1. The minimization of (4.4) is subject to the labour demand function (4.3).[7]

From the first-order conditions for a minimum of (4.4) subject to (4.3) the nominal wage is given by

$$w = E_{t-1}\, p_t + E_{t-1}\, \mu_t - (1 - \beta)\tilde{\ell} \tag{4.5}$$

Substituting (4.5) in the labour demand function (4.3), and the resulting equation in the production function, we get the following relation between employment, output and unanticipated shocks

$$\ell_t = \tilde{\ell} + \frac{1}{1 - \beta} (p_t - E_{t-1}\, p_t + \nu_t^{\mu}) \tag{4.6}$$

$$y_t = \beta\tilde{\ell} + \mu_t + \frac{\beta}{1 - \beta} (p_t - E_{t-1}\, p_t + \nu_t^{\mu}) \tag{4.7}$$

An unanticipated rise in prices $p_t - E_{t-1}\, p_t$ reduces the real wage, and causes firms to employ more labour. Thus, both aggregate employment and output exhibit a transitory deviation from their respective equilibrium or 'natural' rates $\tilde{\ell}$ and $\beta\tilde{\ell} + \mu_t$.[8]

On the other hand, an unanticipated shock to productivity increases the marginal product of labour, and given the real wage causes firms to employ more labour. Thus employment rises above $\tilde{\ell}$, and output rises on account of both the higher employment (transitory effect) and the higher productivity (permanent effect).

Subtracting (4.6) from the labour force ℓ^s, using the approximation that the rate of unemployment $u \approx \ell^s - \ell$, and adding and subtracting $p_{t-1}/(1 - \beta)$, we get the following expression for the short-run determination of unemployment.

$$u_t = \tilde{u} - \frac{1}{1 - \beta} (\Delta p_t - E_{t-1}\Delta p_t + \nu_t^{\mu}) \tag{4.8}$$

where $\tilde{u} = \ell^s - \tilde{\ell}$ and Δ is the first difference operator. $\tilde{u}$ can be thought of as the equilibrium of 'natural' rate of unemployment in this model. Thus, (4.8) is the well known expectations augmented 'Phillips curve'. Unemployment deviates from its equilibrium rate only to the extent that there are unanticipated shocks to inflation or productivity. Anticipated shocks to inflation and productivity are reflected in wages (equation (4.5)) and do not affect unemployment. We can now incorporate the Phillips curve in a monetary policy game. This is the subject of the next section.

III A STATIC GAME BETWEEN WAGE-SETTERS AND THE CENTRAL BANK

III.1 The Social Welfare versus the Political Approach to Central Bank Behaviour

In order to investigate optimal monetary policy - in which the inflation rate is treated as a directly controllable policy instrument[9] - consider a central bank that is concerned with both price stability and low unemployment. We assume a quadratic loss function, that penalizes both inflation and unemployment. More specifically we use

$$L_t = \frac{1}{2}(\Delta p_t - \Delta p^*)^2 + \frac{\varepsilon}{2}(u_t - u^*)^2 \tag{4.9}$$

where Δp^* and u^* are the inflation and unemployment targets of the central bank. The parameter ε measures the weight of unemployment stabilization relative to inflation stabilization in the preferences of the central bank. The central bank chooses Δp and wage-setters 'choose' $E_{t-1}\Delta p_t$.

As pointed out by Cukierman (1992, p. 27-28) the recent literature on monetary policy games has given two competing interpretations to the loss function of the monetary policymaker in equation (4.9). One part of the literature (Havrilesky (1987) and Mayer (1990)) views the central bank as a mediator between different interest groups that try to push monetary policy in various directions. On this view, the loss function (4.9) reflects a distributionally motivated political compromise mediated through the central bank between the advocates of employment stimulation and the advocates of price stability. The coefficient ε then measures the relative political clout of the two groups. The other part regards equation (4.9) as a social welfare function and the central bank as a benevolent social planner (Kydland and Prescott (1977), Barro and Gordon (1983a, 1983b), Rogoff (1985) and Canzoneri (1985)).

Since one of the main purposes of this Chapter is to combine the Rogoff (1985) model with union behaviour along the lines of Alogoskoufis (1994), we follow Rogoff's analysis and choose the social welfare approach to central bank behaviour.

As stated in Chapter 1 there is a world-wide tendency to establish more independent central banks. Therefore now, following Rogoff (1985, pp. 1177-1180), we consider central bank independence as an institutional response to the time-consistency problem. Rogoff demonstrates that society can make itself better off by selecting an agent to head the central bank who is known to place a greater weight on inflation stabilization (relative to unemployment stabilization) than is embodied in the social loss function L_t. He demonstrates that, in choosing among potential candidates, it is never optimal to choose an individual who is known to care 'too little' about unemployment.

Suppose, for example that in period t-1 society selects an agent to head the central bank in period t. The reputation of this individual is such that it is known that if he is appointed to head the central bank, he will minimize the following loss function

$$I_t = \frac{(1+d_2)}{2}(\Delta p_t)^2 + \frac{\varepsilon}{2} u_t^2 \quad 0 < d_2 < \infty \tag{4.10}$$

When d_2 is strictly greater than zero, then this agent places a greater relative weight on inflation stabilization then society does. Hence we view the coefficient d_2 as a measure of the political independence of the central bank. The higher d_2 the more independent the central bank.[10] An alternative approach is explicit modelling of the interaction of separate monetary and fiscal authorities. See e.g. Alesina and Tabellini (1987), Cukierman (1992, pp. 351-355) and Debelle and Fischer (1994). Cukierman identifies the degree of central bank independence with the central bank's impact on the discount rate (q)[11] of the policy maker. The higher the central bank independence, the larger will be the impact of the central bank's lower degree of time preference in actual policy.

Having a one shot game following Rogoff (1985) we define central bank independence as the additional weight placed on inflation stabilization. Note that if $d_2 = 0$ equation (4.10) reduces to the social loss function (4.9) and we obtain the results under the fully discretionary regime.

III.2 Time Consistent Inflation Policy

Following Alogoskoufis (1994, p. 204) we start with a cooperative game, i.e. we assume that the natural rate of unemployment is efficient. In the context of the model of Section II.1, this can be represented by the assumption that $\tilde{l}$, the target employment level of wage-setters is equal to l^s, the effective labour force. In the latter case the central bank has no incentive to try and reduce unemployment below its equilibrium rate. As there is no conflict between the unemployment targets of wage setters and the central bank, the policy game can be seen as a cooperative one.[12] This state of affairs is summarized in the first column of Table 4.1.

Table 4.1 Policy games and unemployment targets

Central bank	Wage-setters	
	$\tilde{l} = l^s$ $\tilde{u} = 0$	$\tilde{l} < l^s$ $\tilde{u} > 0$
$u^* = 0$	$u^* = \tilde{u}$	$u^* < \tilde{u}$
Natural rate	Efficient	Inefficient
Policy game	Cooperative	Non-cooperative

We now turn to the second column of Table 4.1, i.e. the situation where the equilibrium unemployment rate is inefficiently high. In what follows we show that then the equilibrium inflation rate becomes proportional to the natural rate of unemployment. In this case discretionary monetary policy is no longer a Pareto-equilibrium, due to the time-inconsistency of optimal monetary policy. Assuming that $\tilde{l} < l^s$, i.e. that $\tilde{u} > 0$ the central bank has incentives to systematically create inflation in order to reduce unemployment below its natural rate.

Substituting the Phillips curve (4.8) in the loss function (4.10) yields

$$l_t = (1+d_2)/2(\Delta p_t)^2 + \frac{\varepsilon}{2}\left[\tilde{u} - \frac{1}{1-\beta}\Delta p_t + \frac{1}{1-\beta}E_{t-1}\Delta p_t - \frac{1}{1-\beta}\nu_t^{\mu}\right]^2 \quad (4.11)$$

From the first order conditions for a minimum of (4.11), i.e. $\partial l_t / \partial \Delta p_t = 0$, we obtain the central bank's reaction function to wage-setter's expectations

$$\Delta p_t = \frac{\varepsilon(1-\beta)}{(1+d_2)(1-\beta)^2+\varepsilon}\tilde{u} + \frac{\varepsilon}{(1+d_2)(1-\beta)^2+\varepsilon}$$

$$E_{t-1}\Delta p_t - \frac{\varepsilon}{(1+d_2)(1-\beta)^2+\varepsilon}\nu_t^{\mu} \quad (4.12)$$

[13]

Taking expectations conditional on information at t − 1 of (4.12) gives

$$E_{t-1}\Delta p_t = \frac{\varepsilon}{(1+d_2)(1-\beta)}\tilde{u} \quad (4.13)$$

Equation (4.13) is the reaction function of wage-setters. Upon substituting (4.13) in (4.12) we get

$$\Delta p_t = \frac{\varepsilon}{(1+d_2)(1-\beta)}\tilde{u} - \frac{\varepsilon}{(1+d_2)(1-\beta)^2+\varepsilon}\nu_t^{\mu} \qquad (4.14)$$

Figure 4.1 shows the central bank's reaction function if $v_t^{\mu} = 0$, i.e. the average inflation rate as a function of the expected inflation rate.[14]

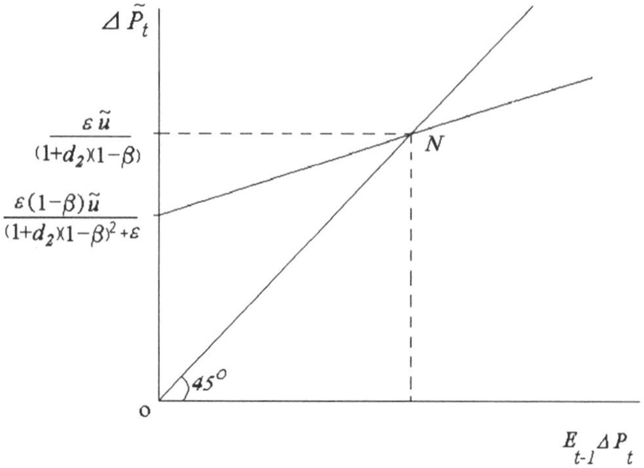

Figure 4.1 Actual and expected inflation with an inefficient natural rate

The only point at which expectations are rational is at point N, which represents the non-cooperative Nash equilibrium.

Denoting the average inflation rate by $\Delta\tilde{p}_t$, from (4.14) it follows that

$$\Delta\tilde{p}_t = \frac{\varepsilon}{(1+d_2)(1-\beta)}\tilde{u} \qquad (4.15)$$

Hence, at point N the inflation rate is above zero (the outcome in the cooperative case).

Subtracting (4.13) from (4.14) we obtain the following expression for unanticipated inflation

$$\Delta p_t - E_{t-1}\Delta p_t = \frac{-\varepsilon}{(1+d_2)(1-\beta)^2+\varepsilon}\nu_t^{\mu} \qquad (4.16)$$

Upon substituting (4.16) in (4.8) we get

$$u_t = \tilde{u} - \frac{(1+d_2)(1-\beta)}{(1+d_2)(1-\beta)^2 + \varepsilon}\nu_t^{\mu} \tag{4.17}$$

Equations (4.15) and (4.17) highlight the time inconsistency of optimal monetary policy. The monetary policy strategy of the central bank, i.e. equation (4.12) is time-consistent in the sense that at each point in time the inflation rate selected is best, given the current situation. However, as can be seen from equations (4.15) and (4.17), the resulting policy is socially sub-optimal. It is sub-optimal since it results in an excessive level of inflation, i.e. it produces an inflationary bias with no gains in the form of systematic lower unemployment. This completes the description of the non-cooperative Nash equilibrium.

III.3 Results for Inflation and its Variance

Following Cukierman (1992, pp. 351-355) in this section we investigate the effects of central bank independence on the mean and variance of inflation. Taking the first derivative of (4.15) with respect to d_2, we get

$$\frac{\partial \Delta \tilde{p}_t}{\partial d_2} = \frac{-\varepsilon \tilde{u}}{(1+d_2)^2(1-\beta)} < 0 \tag{4.18}$$

From (4.18) we derive Proposition (4.1).

Proposition 4.1: The more independent the central bank (the higher d_2) the lower the average inflation rate.

Proposition 4.1 is analogous to Cukierman's (1992, p. 354) proposition 18.1.

Note that the greater $1/(1-\beta)$ (that is, the greater the reduction in unemployment from unanticipated inflation in the expectations augmented Phillips curve (4.8)), the larger the natural rate of unemployment and the higher society's preferences for unemployment stabilization relative to inflation stabilization, the greater the inflation benefits of appointing independent central bankers.

We now consider inflation variability. Taking variances of (4.14), noting that $\sigma_{\mu}^2 = 1$, we get

$$\text{Var } \Delta p_t = \frac{\varepsilon^2}{[(1+d_2)(1-\beta)^2+\varepsilon]^2} \tag{4.19}$$

Taking the first derivative of (4.19) with respect to d_2, we get

$$\frac{\partial(\text{Var } \Delta p_t)}{\partial d_2} = \frac{-2(1-\beta)^2\varepsilon^2}{[(1+d_2)(1-\beta)^2+\varepsilon]^3} < 0 \tag{4.20}$$

From (4.20) we derive Proposition 4.2:

Proposition 4.2: The more independent the central bank (the higher d_2) the lower the variance of the inflation rate.

Proposition 4.2 is analogous to Cukierman's (1992, p. 354) proposition 18.2.

It is well known that inflation and its variance display a strong cross sectional positive relationship. This model proposes a causal theory in which those two variables are linked because of their common link to central bank independence.[15]

To give a numerical example, with β being about 0.7,[16] ε is 1 and d_2 equal to 4 we get Var Δp_t = 0.48. If the central bank is completely dependent (d_2 = 0), then Var Δp_t = 0.84. Thus the ratio of the variance of inflation with an independent central bank to the ratio without an independent central bank is 0.57. This example suggests that central bank independence may be a significant factor in explaining cross country differences in inflation variability.

By again differentiating (4.20) with respect to d_2, we find that

$$\frac{\partial^2(\text{Var}\Delta p_t)}{\partial d_2^2} = \frac{6(1-\beta)^4\varepsilon^2}{[(1+d_2)(1-\beta)^2+\varepsilon]^4} > 0 \tag{4.21}$$

Using (4.20) and (4.21) we obtain Figure 4.2.

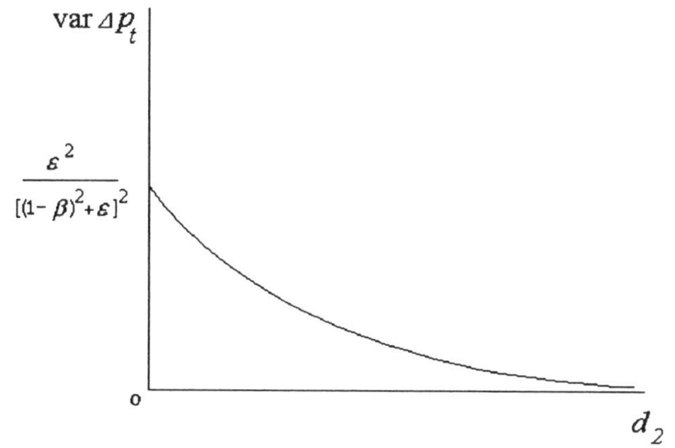

Figure 4.2 Central bank independence and the variance of inflation

This completes the description of the results on the mean and variance of inflation.

III.4 Results for Growth and its Variance

Cukierman's (1992, pp. 349-359) analysis does not contain any propositions about the relationship between central bank independence and (the variability of) output growth. This is not so in the present paper.

Adding and subtracting $\beta/(1-\beta)p_{t-1}$ from (4.7) yields

$$y_t = \beta\,\bar{l} + \mu_t + \frac{\beta}{1-\beta}\,(\Delta p_t - E_{t-1}\,\Delta p_t + \nu^{\mu}_{t}) \qquad (4.22)$$

If we employ $\tilde{y}_t$ as shorthand for $\beta\tilde{\ell} + \mu_t$ we get

$$y_t - \tilde{y}_t = \frac{\beta}{1-\beta}\,(\Delta p_t - E_{t-1}\Delta p_t + \nu^{\mu}_{t}) \qquad (4.23)$$

Equation (4.23) is the famous Lucas surprise supply function which says that unanticipated inflation and/or productivity shocks cause transitory deviations of output from its equilibrium (mean) level $\tilde{y}$.

Upon substituting (4.16) in (4.23) we get

$$y_t - \tilde{y}_t = \frac{(1+d_2)\beta(1-\beta)}{(1+d_2)(1-\beta)^2 + \varepsilon} v_t^{\mu} \tag{4.24}$$

Now we move from levels to growth rates, that is we now examine the effects of central bank independence on the growth rate of output and its variance.

Taking first differences of (4.24) we get

$$\Delta y_t - \Delta\tilde{y}_t = \frac{(1+d_2)\beta(1-\beta)}{(1+d_2)(1-\beta)^2 + \varepsilon} \Delta v_t^{\mu} \tag{4.25}$$

From (4.25) we derive proposition 4.3.

Proposition 4.3: The mean or average rate of growth of output is independent from the prevailing monetary regime (d_2).

Of course, this result is just a corollary of the natural rate property of the Alogoskoufis (1994) supply block.[17]

Taking variances of (4.25) we get[18]

$$\mathrm{Var}(\Delta y_t - \Delta\tilde{y}_t) = \frac{2(1+d_2)^2\beta^2(1-\beta)^2}{[(1+d_2)(1-\beta)^2 + \varepsilon]^2} \tag{4.26}$$

Taking the first derivative of (4.26) with respect to d_2 we get

$$\frac{\partial \mathrm{Var}(\Delta y_t - \Delta\tilde{y}_t)}{\partial d_2} = \frac{4\beta^2(1-\beta)^2(1+d_2)\varepsilon}{[(1+d_2)(1-\beta)^2 + \varepsilon]^3} > 0 \tag{4.27}$$

Again differentiating (4.27) with respect to d_2 we find that

$$\frac{\partial^2 \mathrm{Var}(\Delta y_t - \Delta\tilde{y}_t)}{\partial d_2^2} = \frac{4\beta^2(1-\beta)^2\varepsilon[\varepsilon - 2(1-\beta)^2(1+d_2)]}{[(1+d_2)(1-\beta)^2 + \varepsilon]^4} \tag{4.28}$$

By setting $(\varepsilon - 2(1-\beta)^2(1+d_2))$ equal to zero we find a point of inflection at

$d_2 = ((\varepsilon - 2(1-\beta)^2)/2(1-\beta)^2$. Using (4.27) and (4.28) we obtain Figure 4.3.

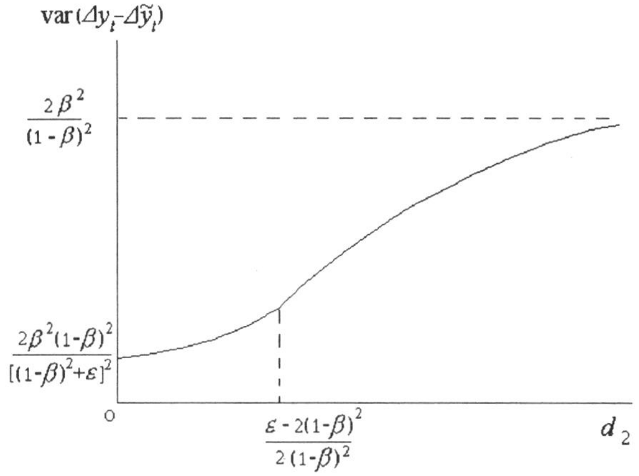

Figure 4.3 Central bank independence and the variance of output growth

From Figure 4.3 we derive proposition 4.4.

Proposition 4.4: The more independent the central bank (the higher d_2) the higher the variance of output growth around the natural rate of growth.

To give a numerical example with the same parameter values as before we get $Var(\Delta y_t - \Delta \tilde{y}_t) = 1.05$. If the central bank is completely dependent ($d_2 = 0$), then $Var(\Delta y_t - \Delta \tilde{y}_t) = 0.07$. Thus the ratio of the variance of output growth with an independent central bank to the ratio without an independent central bank is 15. This example suggests that central bank independence may be a significant factor in explaining cross country differences in the variability of real output growth.

Finally, we summarize the main propositions from this section in Table 4.2.

In order to confront these propositions with some cross-country evidence we can now move on to empirical testing. This is the subject of the next section.

Table 4.2 Central bank independence, growth and inflation

Inflation		Growth	
Mean	Variance	Mean	Variance
$\frac{\partial \Delta \tilde{p}_t}{\partial d_2} < 0$	$\frac{\partial \mathrm{Var}\, \Delta p_t}{\partial d_2} < 0$	$\frac{\partial \Delta \tilde{y}_t}{\partial d_2} = 0$	$\frac{\partial \mathrm{Var}(\Delta y_t - \Delta \tilde{y}_t)}{\partial d_2} > 0$

IV EMPIRICAL EVIDENCE ON CENTRAL BANK INDEPENDENCE

IV.1 Central Bank Independence and the Level of Inflation

According to Alesina (1988, 1989), Alesina and Summers (1993) and Cukierman, Webb and Neyapti (1992) countries with an independent central bank will have a lower rate of inflation than countries with a dependent central bank. As stated in Section I, this well-known inverse relationship between central bank independence and the level of inflation is particularly sensitive to the numerical values of the various indices of central bank independence.

Furthermore, the negative correlation between central bank independence and inflation does not necessarily imply a causal relation from central bank independence to inflation or the other way around. The correlation could be explained by a third factor, e.g. the culture and tradition of monetary stability in a country, leading both to an independent central bank and a low rate of inflation.[19] As an example could be taken Germany, for which country one could argue that the hyperinflation in the 1920s caused such a culture and tradition of monetary stability.[20]

However, in our opinion the degree of central bank independence is the ultimate cause of the level of inflation. For central bank independence is the ability and willingness to conduct an autonomous monetary policy directed at price stability as the single policy goal. If not seriously hampered by other elements of economic policy, such as wage increases, budget deficits and government debt, it will eventually lead to low sustainable inflation.

Therefore, our regression analysis (OLS method) assumes the various indices of central bank independence to be the explanatory variables of the average inflation (CPI) on an annual base in the twelve countries considered (Australia, Belgium, Canada, France, Germany, Italy, Japan, the Netherlands, Switserland, the UK, the US and Sweden):

$$\text{average inflation} = a_0 + \overset{(-)}{a_{1*}} \text{ central bank independence} + \varepsilon_t \qquad (4.29)$$

We investigated empirically the policy independence index of Bade and Parkin (BP), the index of Alesina (AL),[21] the broad index of political independence of Grilli, Masciandaro and Tabellini (GMT), the LVAU index of Cukierman (1992, p. 382) and a new index of policy independence, which we call the Eijffinger Schaling (ES) index.[22] The ES-index of central bank independence is compared with previous indices (BP, AL and GMT) in Eijffinger and Schaling (1993a). This cross-section analysis of the empirical relation between these indices of central bank independence and the level of inflation should be interpreted carefully because of the limited degrees of freedom.

The relationship between the varios indices and average annual inflation is analysed for the whole post-Bretton-Woods period of twenty years (1972-1991). During the fixed exchange rate system of Bretton-Woods countries were fully committed to an exchange rate target and had no room to conduct and autonomous domestic monetary policy. Thus, before 1972 the empirical relation between central bank independence and inflation was much less straightforward than after 1972.[23]

Furthermore, the post-Bretton-Woods period is divided in two sub-periods of ten years each (1972-1981 and 1982-1991 respectively) in order to distinguish between the EMS countries (Belgium, France, Germany, Italy, the Netherlands and partly the UK) and non-EMS countries (Australia, Canada, Japan, Switzerland, the US and Sweden). Before 1982 the EMS countries participated - some like France, Italy and the UK only partly - in the snake arrangement and - except the UK - in the initial orientation phase of the EMS (1979-1982) which was characterized by frequent and large realisements of central rates. After 1982 a period of consolidation (1982-1987) can be discerned within the EMS. According to Ungever (1990), this period was marked by

> 'a widespread consensus to follow stability-oriented policies, an increasing convergence in the development of costs, prices and monetary aggregates, and by long periods without realignments of central rates'. (p. 338)[24]

Table 4.3 Average annual inflation and the various indices of central bank independence.

Explanatory variables	1972-1991	1972-1981	1982-1991
Constant	11.55	15.03	8.07
	(6.93)	(6.58)	(5.53)
Bade-Parkin (BP)	-1.85	-2.25	-1.45
	(-2.85)**	(-2.53)*	(-2.55)*
Adj. R^2	0.39	0.33	0.33
Constant	11.78	15.36	8.20
	(8.21)	(7.69)	(6.30)
Alesina (AL)	-1.98	-2.43	-1.53
	(-3.50)**	(-3.09)**	(-2.98)**
Adj. R^2	0.51	0.44	0.42
Constant	8.82	12.48	5.16
	(5.69)	(6.32)	(4.01)
Grilli et.al. (GMT)	-0.40	-0.85	-0.24
(Political)	(-1.38)	(-1.68)	(-0.74)
Adj. R^2	0.08	0.16	-0.05
Constant	11.01	14.38	7.65
	(10.00)	(9.14)	(7.60)
Eijffinger-Schaling	-1.43	-1.75	-1.12
(ES)	(-3.96)**	(-3.38)**	(-3.39)**
Adj. R^2	0.57	0.49	0.49
Constant	10.30	14.23	6.37
	(7.03)	(7.98)	(4.53)
Cukierman (CUK)	-8.65	-12.47	-4.83
	(-2.41)*	(-2.86)**	(-1.40)
Adj. R^2	0.31	0.39	0.08

Notes: t-values are in parentheses. One asterisk indicates that the coefficient is significantly different from zero at a 95% confidence level and two asterisks indicate that the coefficient is significant at a 99% confidence level.

Consequently, during the second sub-period (1982-1991) the negative correlation between central bank independence and inflation is expected to be less clear cut than during the first sub-period (1972-1981) because of the consolidation in the EMS countries towards exchange rate stability. From 1982 the domestic monetary policy in these countries - besides Germany as the anchor country - could have become increasingly endogenous by focussing on the exchange rate target.

Table 4.3 shows the estimation result of equation (4.29), which explains average annual inflation by the four indices of central bank independence for the whole period (1972-1991) and for both sub-periods (1972-1981 and 1982-1991) respectively. Except for the GMT index of political independence, the inverse relationship between inflation and central bank independence is very clear, although the Alesina and ES index proved to be more significant (higher t-value) than the BP and CUK indices.[25] For Alesina, ES and BP, central bank independence is less significant (lower t-value) during both sub-periods than during the whole post-Bretton-Woods period.

Except for the GMT and CUK measures, the various indices have approximately the same significance in both the first and second sub-period, while that in the second sub-period was expected to be lower than in the first as a consequence of the six EMS countries within the sample of twelve. These outcomes could be the result of the practice that most EMS countries used fully the bilateral band of $\pm$ 2¼% and, for Italy and since October 1990 the UK, the band of $\pm 6\%$. Only the Netherlands and, from 1986, also France, had an explicit exchange rate target for their currency vis-à-vis the Deutsche Mark.

What may be conluded from the cross-section analysis of these twelve countries regarding the relationship between central bank independence and the level of inflation and the quality of the four indices of central bank independence in particular?

Firstly, the negative relation between central bank independence and inflation proved to be very significant for all indices, except for the GMT index of political independence.[26] Clearly, the more independent a central bank is, the lower rate of inflation in the long run.

Figure 4.4 shows that the BP index of policy independence has a significant, negative relation to average annual inflation despite some positive outliers (Italy and the UK) and some negative (Belgium and the Netherlands). The ranking by Bade and Parkin of the latter two countries is evidently too low.

Furthermore, from Figure 4.5 it can be seen that the Alesina 'index' has a more significant, negative relation to inflation, merely by the ad hoc adjusted ranking of Italy.

However, Figure 4.6 shows that the GMT index bears no clear (negative)

Figure 4.4 The Bade-Parkin index and the level of inflation

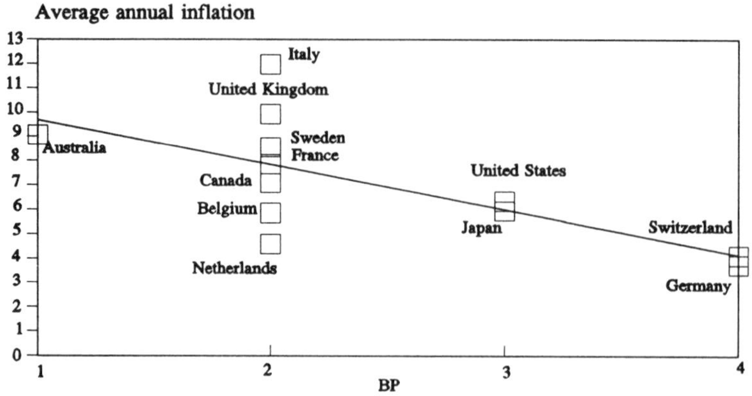

Average inflation = 11.546 - 1.850 * BP (R-square = 0.4482)
t-value (6.931) (2.850)

Figure 4.5 The Alesina index and the level of inflation

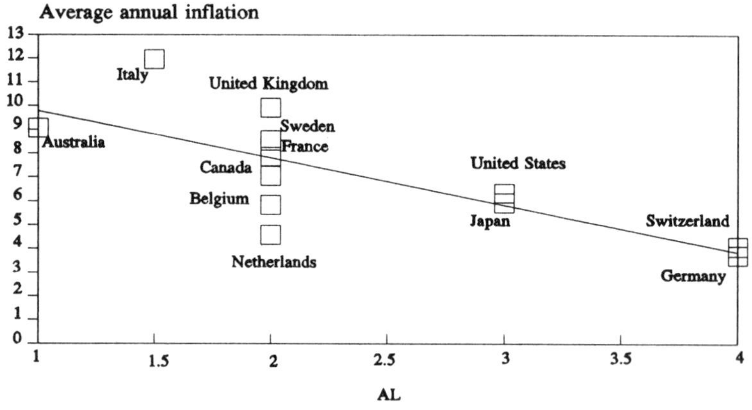

Average inflation = 11.778 - 1.981 * AL (R-square = 0.5507)
t-value (8.205) (3.501)

relation to inflation in most of the eleven countries considered. This could be explained by the broadness of the GMT index comprising many features (see Eijffinger and Schaling (1992)). This index, thereby, waters down the essential features of policy independence, i.e. 1. the procedures for appointing the central bank board, 2. the relationship between, the central bank and government concerning the formulation of monetary policy, and 3. the policy goals of the central bank regarding monetary policy making.

Figure 4.6 The Grilli-Masciandaro-Tabellini index and level of inflation

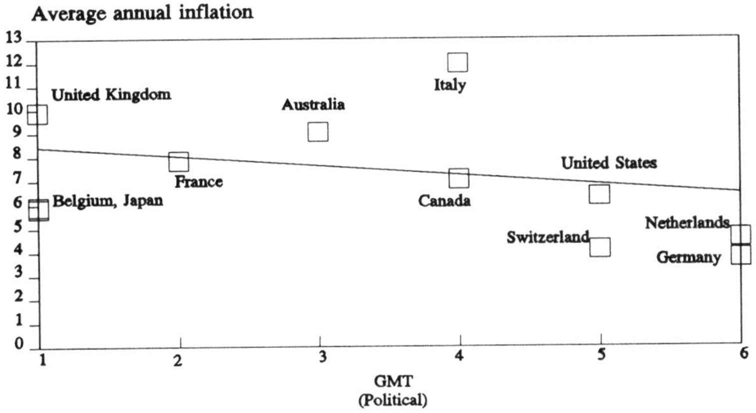

Average inflation = 8.822 - 0.395 * GMT (R-square = 0.1746)
t-value (5.686) (1.380)

Figure 4.7 The Eijffinger-Schaling index and the level of inflation

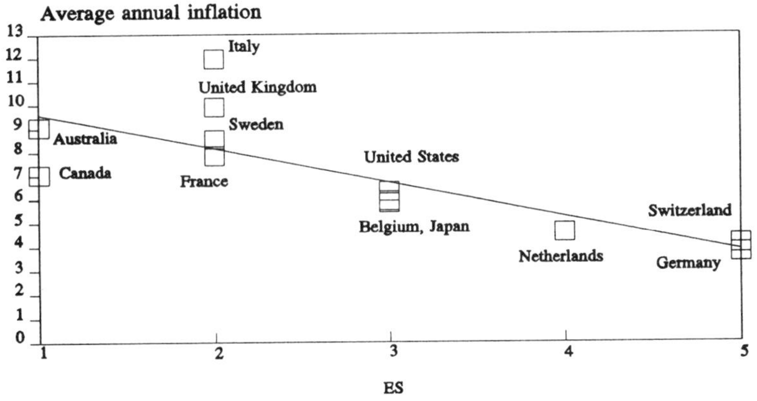

Average inflation = 11.014 - 1.433 * ES (R-square = 0.6100)
t-value (9.998) (3.955)

Figure 4.7 shows that the ES index has an even more significant, negative relation to inflation, although the positive outliers (Italy and the UK) remain.This could, perhaps, be explained by the half-fledged position of these countries with respect to the EMS. Nevertheless, the negative outliers (Belgium and the Netherlands) of the BP and Alesina index disappeared by the more consistent ranking of both countries according to their central bank laws within the context of monetary policy making.

Figure 4.8 The Cukierman index and the level of inflation

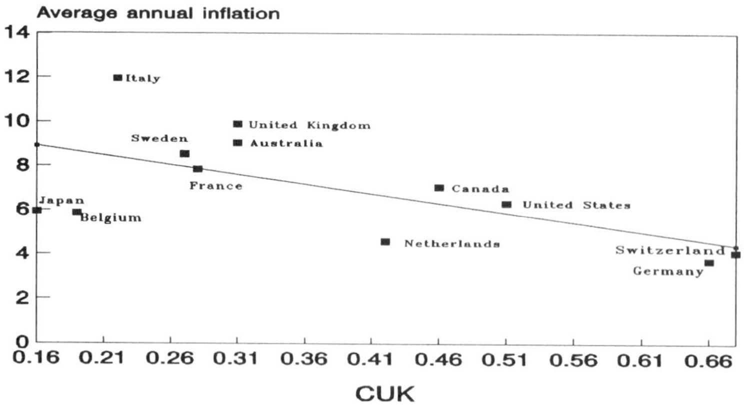

Average inflation = 10.297 - 8.652 * CUK (R-square = 0.3677)
t-value (7.031) (2.412)

Finally, Figure 4.8 shows the CUK index and the level of inflation.

Consequently, empirical evidence on the various indices of central bank independence supports proposition 4.1 (see Section III.3) that the more independent the central bank (the higher d_2), the lower the average inflation rate.[27]

Of course, one should be well aware of the more or less subjective character of the research on central bank independence, which combines both legal-institutional and political-economic criteria and features in constructing indices.

IV.2 Central Bank Independence and the Variability of Inflation

The variability of inflation reflects the degree of monetary and inflationary uncertainty in the economy.

Inflationary uncertainty implies that investers are not sure about the expected (ex ante) future level of inflation and, hence, about expected (ex ante) real interest rates. Therefore, they are less willing to take risks and to invest in either long-term financial assets or physical capital goods. As a consequence lenders demand a higher risk premium on their funds.[28] Thus, higher inflationary uncertainty - measured by the variability of realized inflation - will lead to higher expected real interest rates and to lower levels of investment and output growth.

What is the empirical relationship between central bank independence and the variability of inflation?

First of all, the variability of inflation is positively correlated with the level of inflation and, thereby, with the independence of central banks. Chowdhury (1991) investigated empirically the relation between the level and variability of inflation in 66 countries for the period from 1955 to 1985. He concluded that there is a significant, positive correlation between the level and the variability of inflation during this period. De Haan and Sturm (1992) also examined this relation in 18 industrial countries for the period from 1961 to 1987. They found a clear, positive correlation between both variables for the post-Bretton-Woods sub-periods 1970-1978 and 1979-1987, but not for the sub-period 1961-1969. Consequently, if a high degree of central bank independence results in a low level of inflation, this should also lead to a low variability of inflation. Nevertheless, the negative correlation between independence and inflation variability does not necessarily imply a causal relation from the first to the latter, but could be explained by a third factor. However, our regression analysis assumes the various indices of central bank independence (BP, AL, GMT, CUK and ES) to be the explanatory variables of the variance of monthly inflation (CPI) on an annual base in the twelve countries of our sample:

$$\text{variance inflation} = b_0 + \overset{(-)}{b_{1*}\ \text{central bank independence}} + \eta_t \qquad (4.30)$$

Again, the relationship between the various indices and the variance of monthly inflation is examined for the complete post-Bretton-Woods period of twenty years (1972-1991) and its two sub-periods of ten years (1972-1981 and 1982-1991). During the second sub-period the negative correlation between central bank independence and inflation variability is also expected to be less clear cut than during the first sub-period by the consolidation of EMS countries to exchange rate stability.

Table 4.4 shows the outcomes of equation (4.30) explaining the variance of monthly inflation by the four independence indices. The inverse relationship between inflation variability and central bank independence is only significant for the CUK and GMT indices, for the latter index especially for the second sub-period (!).[29] Generally, the indices do not support, proposition 4.2 that the more independent the central bank (the higher d_2), the lower the variance of the inflation rate.

Table 4.4 Variance monthly inflation and the various indices of central bank independence

Explanatory variables	1972-1991	1972-1981	1982-1991
Constant	0.33	0.29	0.21
	(1.34)	(0.75)	(2.45)
Bade-Parkin (BP)	-0.01	0.03	-0.02
	(-0.07)	(0.23)	(-0.68)
Adj. R^2	-0.10	-0.10	-0.05
Constant	0.33	0.30	0.21
	(1.42)	(0.81)	(2.46)
Alesina (AL)	-0.01	0.03	-0.02
	(-0.09)	(0.21)	(-0.61)
Adj. R^2	-0.10	-0.10	-0.06
Constant	0.58	0.77	0.22
	(3.74)	(3.00)	(5.93)
Grilli et al. (GMT)	-0.08	-0.12	-0.02
(Political)	(-2.04)*	(-1.80)	(-2.48)*
Adj. R^2	0.24	0.18	0.34
Constant	0.39	0.42	0.22
	(2.07)	(1.39)	(3.24)
Eijffinger-Schaling	-0.03	-0.02	-0.02
(ES)	(-0.47)	(-0.18)	(-0.98)
Adj. R^2	-0.08	-0.10	-0.00
Constant	0.63	0.82	0.26
	(3.78)	(2.96)	(4.05)
Cukierman (CUK)	-0.85	-1.20	-0.27
	(-2.10)*	(-1.77)	(-1.74)
Adj. R^2	0.24	0.16	0.16

Notes: t-values are in parentheses. One asterisk indicates that the coefficient is significantly different from zero at a 95% confidence level and two asterisks indicate that the coefficient is significant at a 99% confidence level.

IV.3 Central Bank Independence and the Level of Output Growth

Given the inverse relationship between central bank independence and the level of inflation - see Section IV.1 - one could argue that the expected (ex ante) level of inflation influences expected (ex ante) real interest rates and, thereby, the level of output growth according to the Mundell-Tobin effect. A rise in expected inflation will lead - by Mundell (1963) - to substitution of liquid assets by long-term financial assets and - according to Tobin (1965) - to substitution of liquid assets by physical capital goods, lowering the marginal efficiency of capital, and will result in a decrease of expected real interest rates. Thus, more independent central banks will mitigate inflationary expectations inducing higher expected real interest rates and lower levels of investment and output growth.[30]

However, proposition 4.3 (in Section III.4) states that the mean or average rate of growth of output is independent from the prevailing monetary regime (d_2). Therefore, our regression analysis assumes the four indices of central bank independence (BP, AL, GMT, CUK and ES) to be the explanatory variables of average output growth (volume of GDP) on an annual base, without postulating an expected sign for these variables:

$$\text{average output growth} = c_0 + c_{1*} \text{ central bank independence} + \vartheta_t \quad (4.31)$$

Again, we examined the relationship between the various indices and level of real output growth for the post-Bretton-Woods period (1972-1990) and its two sub-periods (1972-1981 and 1982-1990).

Table 4.5 shows the estimation results of equation (4.31). The relationship between real output growth and central bank independence proves to be insignificant, except for the ES and CUK indices in the first sub-period. The BP and AL index also have higher t-values for the first sub-period than for the second.[31]

These outcomes could be explained by relatively more restrictive monetary policies by independent central banks during the late 1970s - the hey-days of monetary targeting - which resulted in a lower level of economic growth.

In general, empirical evidence on the various indices does support proposition 4.3 stating that there is no relation between central bank independence and average real output growth.[32] In other words, although a high degree of central bank independence is associated with a low level

Table 4.5 Average annual output growth and the various indices of central bank independence

Explanatory variables	1972-1990	1972-1981	1982-1990
Constant	3.04	3.46	2.58
	(4.56)	(4.19)	(4.43)
Bade-Parkin (BP)	-0.16	-0.37	0.06
	(-0.63)	(-1.14)	(0.27)
Adj. R^2	-0.06	0.03	-0.09
Constant	3.06	3.15	2.57
	(4.84)	(4.53)	(4.63)
Alesina (AL)	-0.18	-0.40	0.07
	(-0.71)	(-1.30)	(0.30)
Adj. R^2	-0.05	0.06	-0.09
Constant	3.15	3.11	3.20
	(6.65)	(4.90)	(8.05)
Grilli et.al. (GMT)	-0.13	-0.14	-0.12
(Political)	(-1.07)	(-0.85)	(-1.20)
Adj. R^2	0.02	-0.03	0.04
Constant	3.27	3.63	2.87
	(6.71)	(6.22)	(6.29)
Eijffinger-Schaling	-0.23	-0.38	-0.05
(ES)	(-1.42)	(-2.00)*	(-0.36)
Adj. R^2	0.08	0.21	-0.09
Constant	3.38	3.60	3.14
	(6.83)	(5.76)	(6.87)
Cukierman (CUK)	-1.98	-2.77	-1.12
	(-1.63)	(-1.81)*	(-1.00)
Adj. R^2	0.13	0.17	0.00

Notes: t-values are in parentheses. One asterisk indicates that the coefficient is significantly different from zero at a 95% confidence level and two asterisks indicate that the coefficient is significant at a 99% confidence level.

of inflation in the long run, it has no large costs or benefits in terms of real economic growth. Thus, in countries with an independent central bank no trade off can be found between inflation on the one hand and economic growth on the other hand in the long term.[33]

IV.4 Central Bank Independence and the Variability of Output Growth

What is the relationship between the degree of central bank independence and the variability of real output growth? According to Rogoff (1985) independent central banks purchase a lower level of inflation at the price of a higher variability of real economic growth. By relying more on rules rather than discretion in policy making they tolerate more cyclical variability of economic growth. Consequently, Rogoff's conclusion corresponds very well with our proposition 4.4 (see Section III.4) stating that the more independent the central bank - the higher d_2 - is, the higher the variance of the growth rate of output around the natural rate.

Again, our regression analysis assumes the various independence indices (BP, AL, GMT, CUK and ES) to be the explanatory variables of the variance of monthly output growth (volume of GDP) on an annual base, postulating a positive sign for these variables:

$$\text{variance output growth} = d_0 + \overset{(+)}{d_{1*}} \text{ central bank independence} + \kappa_t \quad (4.32)$$

The coefficient for the BP and AL index do not have the expected, positive sign in any sample period. Besides, none of the coefficients appears to be significantly different from zero. The t-values prove to be the highest for the GMT index.[34] These estimation results imply, of course, that a higher degree of central bank independence does not lead to more variability of real economic growth, rejecting proposition 4.4 quite clearly.

Therefore, having an independent central bank does not result in more variable inflation (see Section IV.2) nor in more variable economic growth in the short term. So, inflation-averse central banks do not trigger off recessions nor do politically sensitive central banks avoid recessions.

Table 4.6 Variance monthly output growth and the various indices of central bank independence

Explanatory variables	1972-1990	1972-1981	1982-1990
Constant	1.81	2.90	0.98
	(2.90)	(2.04)	(2.62)
Bade-Parkin (BP)	-0.23	-0.42	-0.11
	(-0.95)	(-0.76)	(-0.78)
Adj. R^2	-0.01	-0.04	-0.04
Constant	1.73	2.78	0.90
	(2.88)	(2.04)	(2.47)
Alesina (AL)	-0.20	-0.38	-0.08
	(-0.85)	(-0.70)	(-0.56)
Adj. R^2	-0.03	-0.05	-0.07
Constant	0.78	0.89	0.41
	(1.75)	(0.84)	(1.63)
Grilli et.al. (GMT)	0.11	0.27	0.07
(Political)	(0.10)	(0.98)	(1.11)
Adj. R^2	-0.00	-0.00	0.02
Constant	1.20	1.38	0.84
	(2.35)	(1.21)	(2.80)
Eijffinger-Schaling	0.02	0.19	-0.05
(ES)	(0.10)	(0.50)	(-0.50)
Adj. R^2	-0.10	-0.07	-0.07
Constant	1.21	1.84	0.56
	(2.26)	(1.53)	(1.79)
Cukierman (CUK)	0.12	0.13	0.39
	(0.09)	(0.04)	(0.51)
Adj. R^2	-0.10	-0.10	-0.07

Notes: t-values are in parentheses. One asterisk indicates that the coefficient is significantly different from zero at a 95% confidence level and two asterisks indicate that the coefficient is significant at a 99% confidence level.

IV.5 Conclusion

The main conclusions of this theoretical and empirical analysis of central bank independence with respect to the level and variability of inflation and economic growth are the following.

First of all, both our model and estimation results, give further support to the well-known inverse relationship between the degree of central bank independence and the level of inflation found by e.g. Alesina (1988, 1989) and Cukierman, Webb and Neyapti (1992). However, it should be emphasized that these results are particularly sensitive to the numerical values of indices. For example, the CUK and GMT index shows no clear inverse relation to inflation, whereas the ES index proves to have a very significant, negative relation.

Secondly, contrary to CUK, Alesina and Summers (1993) we find no empirical evidence - except for the CUK and GMT indices - supporting our proposition that the more independent the central bank is, the lower the variability of inflation.

Thirdly, according to our proposition that the level of economic growth does not depend on the prevailing monetary regime, no relationship can be found between central bank independence and the level of real output growth in the long run. Our interpretation of this outcome is that the attainment and maintenance of low inflation by an independent central bank is not accompanied by large costs or benefits in terms of sustainable economic growth. The absence of a long-run trade off between inflation and growth implies that the establishment of central bank independence in countries, which did not used to have this, is a free lunch.

Fourthly and finally, our estimation results reject clearly the proposition of a positive relation between independence and the variability of real output growth. An independent central bank does not lead to more variable economic growth in the short run. In other words, inflation-averse central banks do not bear the costs of triggering recessions nor do politically sensitive central banks reap the benefits of avoiding recessions.

NOTES

1. For a survey of the 'state of the art' see Cukierman (1992).
2. This framework is summarized in Alesina and Grilli (1992).
3. For the terminology see Chapter 2, Section VIII.
4. For a variable $\hat{X}$ say, $x \equiv d\ell n\hat{X}$
5. We discuss the impact of demand shocks in Section III.
6. The advantages of this approach will become clear in Section III.2.

7. Alternatively, the loss-function could be assumed quadratic in both the deviations of employment and the real wage from certain target levels. For an analysis along these lines see Funke (1994).
8. Actual output and employment will equal their natural rates when all expectations are fulfilled. Hence, the natural rate of employment equals $\tilde{l}$ and the natural rate of output is $\beta \tilde{\ell} + \mu_t$.
9. Depending on operating procedures the policymaker sets the money stock or the interest rate. However, it is simpler to think of the central bank to choose inflation directly. For a lucid exposition of monetary policy games with the money stock as policy instrument see Canzoneri and Henderson (1991).
10. Remember from Chapter 3 that central banks in which the only or main policy goal (as specified in the law) is price stability are classified as more independent than central banks with a number of objectives in addition to price stability or banks in whose law price stability is not mentioned as an objective at all.
11. For models with reputational effects see chapter 2 Sections VII.3 and VIII.
12. For a review of some important concepts of game theory see Blackburn and Christensen (1989).
13. Demand shocks can be included in the analysis by extending the model with an aggregate-demand curve. This would complicate the algebra without affecting our results.
14. This figure is based on a similar one in Blanchard and Fischer (1989, p. 597).
15. See also Cukierman (1992), Chapter 18.
16. The value of β is taken from Alogoskoufis (1994, p. 211).
17. For instance, introducing multiperiod wage contracts (Fischer (1977b)), would imply policy non-neutrality. In the latter case the degree of central bank independence would show an inverse relation with the level of output.
18. Strictly speaking we are computing Var $(\Delta y_t - \Delta \tilde{y}_t)/\sigma^2_{\Delta\mu}$ where $\sigma^2_{\Delta\mu} = \text{Var } \Delta v_t^{\mu} = \sigma_\mu^2 + \sigma^2_{\mu_{t-1}}$. With $\sigma_\mu^2 = \sigma^2_{\mu_{t-1}} = 1$ we get (4.26).
19. According to the Commission of the European Communities (1990 p. 98) the causal relation implied by their regression analysis runs from inflation to central bank independence. This is certainly incorrect.
20. See Bresciani-Turroni (1953).
21. In Eijffinger and Schaling (1993a) we show that the Alesina (1988, 1989) synthetic indicator of central bank independence is internally inconsistent and does not qualify as an index.
22. In the case of the GMT index, there is no ranking for Sweden and so the sample is only made up of eleven countries.
23. Regression analysis by de Haan and Sturm (1992, pp.308-309) empirically supports this view.
24. Ungerer (1990) makes a distinction between three phases of development of the EMS: the first phase (1979-1982) as a period of initial orientation, the second phase (1982-1987) as a period of consolidation and the third phase (1987-present) as a period of re-examination, in the light of uneasiness about the 'asymmetry' of the system.
25. De Haan and Sturm (1992) find different empirical results for a modified GMT index, measuring both political and economic independence 'except for the entries which are related to supervision of the banking system. Whether or not a central bank has any responsibility for bank supervision provides, in our view, no information as to its independence' (p. 323).
26. This is a consequence of the 'broadness' of the GMT-index. Because GMT use eight criteria in determining the degree of political independence, the essential characteristics of central bank independence are watered down. See Eijffinger and Schaling (1992, pp. 11-12).
27. Cukierman (1993, p. 278) points out that no similar relationship between inflation and

legal independence emerges in LDC's. However in LDC's there is a strong positive association between inflation and the turnover rate (inverse of tenure) of the central bank governor. See Cukierman (1992) Chapter 19 and Cukierman, Webb and Neyapti (1992).

28. Empirical research with respect to the influence of monetary and inflationary uncertainty on real interest rates in the United States is conducted by Mascaro and Meltzer (1983). They conclude that monetary uncertainty - measured by the variability of money growth - resulted in a risk premium for both the money and capital market interest rate in the period from October 1979.

29. Our estimation results for the BP index are according with Bade and Parkin (1988). However, they contradict the findings of Alesina and Summers (1993) who averaged the Alesina index and the GMT index of political and economic independence.

30. Nevertheless, in theory it could be argued that a higher degree of central bank independence results in lower inflationary uncertainty leading to a decrease of expected real interest rates and, thereby, to an increase of investment and output growth. Empirical evidence in sub-section 4.2 rejects the first link of this transmission mechanism.

31. These estimation results for the AL and ES index correspond with de Haan and Sturm. They are also in accordance with Alesina and Summers (1993) and de Long and Summers (1992) for their 'single overall index' based on an average of the Alesina and GMT political and economic independence index. It should be noticed that de Long and Summers (1992) find, however, a positive relationship between central bank independence and economic growth, controlling for initial GDP per worker levels (see in this respect their chart 6 on p. 16).

32. Cukierman (1993, p. 284) points out that since equation (4.31) does not control for other determinants of growth, this finding may reflect an omitted variables bias rather than a lack of association between growth and central bank independence.

33. Cukierman (1993, p. 284) reports that when similar experiments are repeated for LDC's, again, no association is found between *legal* independence and growth. Using several behavioural measures of central bank independence like the turnover rate and controlling for other determinants of growth Cukierman, Kalaitzidakis, Summers, and Webb (1993) find a *ceteris paribus* positive association between growth and central bank independence.

34. Our empirical evidence for the AL and ES index is in accordance with that of De Haan and Sturm (1992). Alesina and Summers (1993) and de Long and Summers (1992) also find for their averaged Alesina-GMT index no support with respect to the relation between independence and the variability of output growth. The same holds for its relationship regarding the average and variance of unemployment rates.

5. Central Bank Independence, Monetary Accommodation and Inflation Persistence

I INTRODUCTION

According to Cukierman (1992) for a closed economy the inflationary bias of discretionary monetary policy may be explained by two arguments. The first argument, the employment motivation for monetary expansion, is based on the assumption that political forces in democratic societies may be tempted to trade price stability for temporary decreases in unemployment. This motive underlies the model of Chapter 4. The second argument, the revenue motive for monetary expansion, focuses on the risk of the government exploiting the central bank's capacity to create seigniorage to finance expenditure that the government is unwilling to finance out of current or future taxation.

In a recent study Grilli, Masciandaro and Tabellini (1991) (GMT) associate the employment and revenue motives for monetary expansion with separate components of central bank independence.

They compare the monetary regimes of eighteen industrial countries (Australia, Austria, Belgium, Canada, Denmark, France, Greece, Ireland, Italy, Japan, the Netherlands, New Zealand, Portugal, Spain, Switzerland, the United Kingdom and the United States) during the post-war period by focusing on political and economic independence of the central bank.

According to GMT, *political independence* is the capacity to choose the final goals of monetary policy, such as inflation or the level of economic activity. Hence this concept is associated with the subjective tradeoffs of the central bank and of political authorities between price stability and other goals such as high employment.[1]

On the other hand, GMT identify *economic independence* with the nature of the monetary instruments under the control of the central bank (such as the discount rate or the ability to conduct open market operations) and with the influence of the government in determining how much to borrow from the central bank. They point out that if the government can influence the quantity and the conditions at which it borrows from the central bank, it also influences the creation of the monetary base.

Hence, the greater the government influence on the monetary financing of the budget deficit, the smaller the economic independence of the central bank.[2]

This latter aspect of the domestic monetary regime seems particularly relevant for less developed countries with poorly developed financial markets. For instance, in the 1980s monetary financing of budget deficits was common practice in Southern-European countries like Italy, Greece, Portugal and Spain. This had much to do with the less-developed financial markets in the 'olive-belt'. See de Grauwe and Papademos (1990) and Eijffinger and Gerards (1991). For an up to date survey on the practice of central bank credit to the government see Cottarelli (1993).

GMT establish an index of economic independence which is then compared with the average inflation rate over the period 1950–1989. For the period of the study e.g. West Germany, Switzerland, the U.S. and Austria were associated with high economic independence whilst the central banks of Italy, Greece, Portugal and Spain indeed had very little economic independence. By and large, the greater the economic independence of the central bank the lower the average inflation rate. Thus GMT find empirical evidence that the *domestic monetary regime* matters for the average inflation rate.

Moreover, as noted by Cukierman (1992, p. 273) inflation is usually a fairly persistent process, i.e. if inflation becomes unusually high, it does not quickly revert to its earlier level, and the same is true if it becomes abnormally low. Recent research by Alogoskoufis and Smith (1991) and by Alogoskoufis (1992) demonstrates that fixed exchange-rate regimes like the international gold standard and the Bretton–Woods gold dollar standard appear to be associated with negligible persistence of inflation, while regimes of managed exchange rates are associated with very high inflation persistence. They propose that the higher inflation persistence is the result of the higher monetary and exchange-rate accommodation of price changes in flexible exchange-rate regimes. Hence, Alogoskoufis and Smith find empirical evidence that *exchange-rate regimes* matter for the persistence of inflation.

In this Chapter we demonstrate that low inflation persistence may also be achieved by setting up central banks that are independent from government influence on monetary financing of budget deficits. Hence we provide theoretical arguments that the *domestic monetary regime* matters for the persistence of inflation. We use an expectations-augmented Phillips curve model with a government budget constraint to suggest that the lower inflation persistence is the result of lower monetary accommodation of government budget deficits.

The Chapter is organized into four remaining sections, followed by an appendix. In Section II we introduce the government budget constraint. In Section III we incorporate this constraint into a simple IS–LM based macromodel with a Lucas surprise supply function. By equating the aggregate demand and supply schedules, in Section IV we derive a closed form solution for expected inflation. From this solution we derive an inverse relationship between the degree of economic independence and the persistence of inflation. That is, an increase in the degree of economic independence of the central bank will result in a decrease in the degree of persistence of inflation. A summary and questions for further research can be found in Section V. The appendix provides the intuition behind the stability properties of the model.

II THE DYNAMICS OF THE GOVERNMENT BUDGET CONSTRAINT

In this section we introduce the government budget constraint that links monetary and fiscal policy. We show that the fraction of the budget deficit financed by money is identical to the degree of fiscal dominance, i.e. the extent to which the burden of satisfying the government's budget constraint falls on the central bank. Conversely, it is shown that the degree of monetary dominance, i.e the extent to which the burden of satisfying the government budget constraint falls on the treasury, may be interpreted as the economic independence of the central bank.

II.1 Monetary versus Bond Financing

In order to simplify the algebra at a later stage of the analysis we abstract from interest payments on government bonds.[3] Under these assumptions the consolidated government-central bank period-by-period (flow) budget constraint is

$$\Delta M_t + \left(\frac{\Delta B}{i}\right)_t = G_t \qquad (5.1)$$

This difference equation asserts that the primary nominal budget deficit G must be financed either by creating money ΔM, or by selling bonds to the private sector. B is the number of outstanding bonds which have infinite lives (perpetuities) paying one-unit coupon.[4] Hence the market value of the stock of bonds will be $(B/i)_t$, where i is the interest rate.

Note that the bond term on the left-hand side of the government budget constraint is the change in the market value of the stock of bonds including capital gains or losses on pre-existing bonds. As shown by e.g. Stevenson et al. (1988, pp. 7-8) such interest rate valuation effects on the bond stock can be argued to have a certain macroeconomic significance. However, in this paper such valuation effects have no critical role to play and for the remainder of the analysis, we shall assume, for simplicity, that the value of the bond stock is unaffected by interest rate changes, and can be measured by B_t/i_0, that is, the number of bonds evaluated at a constant interest rate.

Taking account of these considerations we can rewrite the government budget constraint as

$$\Delta M_t + \frac{\Delta B_t}{i_0} = G_t \tag{5.2}$$

Equation (5.2) is similar to Turnovsky's (1977, p. 70) treatment of the early theory of the government budget constraint. This theory was pioneered by Christ (1967, 1968) and subsequently developed by e.g. Blinder and Solow (1973), Sargent and Wallace (1981) and Buiter (1988).[5]

Introducing F for nominal financial wealth and normalizing i_0 at unity, (5.2) can be rewritten as the system[6]

$$\Delta F_t = G_t \tag{5.3}$$

$$F_t = M_t + B_t \tag{5.4}$$

Log-linearizing (5.3) and (5.4) around a path of steady growth yields

$$\hat{\Delta} f_t = \gamma(g_t + p_t) \tag{5.5}$$

$$f_t = (1 - \phi_0)m_t + \phi_0 b_t \qquad 0 < \phi_0 < 1 \tag{5.6}$$

where lower-case letters refer to logarithmic deviations from steady growth values,[7] γ is the steady growth rate (of all variables) on the reference path and ϕ_0 is the initial share of bonds in financial wealth (B_0/F_0).

Thus f is nominal financial wealth, g the real primary deficit (net of interest payments), p the price level, m the nominal money stock, and b the nominal stock of private bonds (all measured as logarithmic deviations from steady growth values). $\hat{\Delta}$ is the quasi first difference operator $((1 + \gamma) - L)$ and L is the backward shift (lag) operator.[8]

Upon substituting (5.6) in (5.5) and some rearrangement we get the log-linear version of the government budget flow constraint (i.e. equation (5.2))

$$\hat{\Delta} m_t - \gamma p_t = \frac{\gamma}{1 - \varphi_0} g_t - \frac{\varphi_0}{1 - \varphi_0} (\hat{\Delta} b_t - \gamma p_t) \tag{5.7}$$

According to (5.7) given the price level (p), the authorities (i.e. the treasury and the central bank) have three policy variables private bond sales ($\hat{\Delta} b$), monetary policy ($\hat{\Delta} m$) and fiscal policy (g). Any two of these policy variables can be chosen independently. Thus, given the price level and bond sales to the public, $\hat{\Delta} m$ and g are interdependent. The extent to which (5.7) binds $\hat{\Delta} m$ given g or vice versa, depends on the way fiscal and monetary policies are coordinated.

In order to make this more transparent we introduce the concept of monetary seigniorage (e.g. Klein and Neumann 1990, p. 211).

$$S_t = \frac{\Delta M_t}{P_t} \tag{5.8}$$

This concept is widely used in empirical research and measures the wealth transfer which the private sector has to make in order to receive base money from the central bank.[9]

Likewise log-linearizing (5.8) yields

$$s_t = \frac{1}{\gamma} \hat{\Delta} m_t - p_t \tag{5.9}$$

Substituting (5.9) in the government budget constraint (5.7) we end up with

$$s_t = \frac{1}{1 - \varphi_0} g_t - \frac{\varphi_0}{1 - \varphi_0} (\frac{1}{\gamma} \hat{\Delta} b_t - p_t) \tag{5.10}$$

Equation (5.10) emphasizes the interdependence of seigniorage revenues (s) and the fiscal deficit (g) given real private bond sales.

II.2 Coordination of Monetary and Fiscal Policy

Following Sargent and Wallace (1984, p. 16)[10] we consider two forms of monetary and fiscal policy coordination. On the one hand, imagine that monetary policy dominates fiscal policy. Under this coordination scheme, at time t say, the central bank sets monetary policy by choosing m_t. By doing this - given the predetermined money supply at t - 1 and the price level at time t - the central bank determines the amount of revenue it will supply the treasury through monetary seigniorage s_t. Hence if monetary policy dominates fiscal policy, the central bank determines the left hand side of equation (5.10). The treasury then faces the constraints imposed by the private sector demand for bonds b_t, since it must set its deficit g_t so that it can be financed by a combination of the seigniorage determined by the central bank and bond sales to the public[11].

On the other hand, imagine that fiscal policy dominates monetary policy. The treasury sets its deficit g_t. Under this second coordination scheme the central bank faces the constraints imposed by the private sector demand for government bonds for it must finance with seigniorage any discrepancy between the revenue demanded by the treasury and the amount of bonds b_t that can be sold to the public. Sargent and Wallace point out that although a central bank might still be able to control inflation permanently, it is less powerfull than a central bank under the first coordination scheme. For if the treasury's deficit cannot be financed solely by new private bond sales, then the central bank is forced towards monetary accommodation of the government budget deficit. That is, the central bank has to absorb the excess supply of treasury bills in exchange for high-powered money.

Suppose that private bond sales are governed by

$$\Delta B_t = d_3 G_t \qquad 0 \leq d_3 \leq 1 \tag{5.11}$$

Equation (5.11) asserts that a fraction d_3 of the nominal budget deficit is financed by private bond sales, and that the remaining $(1 - d_3)$ is financed by 'printing' money.[12]

Likewise log-linearizing (5.11) yields

$$\hat{\Delta} b_t = \frac{d_3 \gamma}{\varphi_0}(g_t + p_t) \tag{5.12}$$

Substitution of (5.12) into (5.7) yields

$$\hat{\Delta} m_t = \frac{(1 - d_3)\gamma}{1 - \varphi_0}(g_t + p_t) \tag{5.13}$$

Equation (5.13) consists of the lagged money supply, and an accommodation coefficient $(1 - d_3)$ describing the extent to which the money supply accommodates changes in nominal budget deficits. This equation is analogous to Alogoskoufis' (1992, p. 463) parametrization of the international reserve regime.[13]

Hence, the greater the economic independence of the central bank the lower the degree of monetary accommodation $(1 - d_3)$. Conversely, d_3 may be interpreted as an institutional parameter reflecting the degree of monetary dominance, i.e. the extent to which the burden of satisfying the government's budget constraint falls on the fiscal authorities (see Tabellini (1988a), Masciandaro and Tabellini (1988)).

From equation (5.13) it can be seen that if the central bank is completely dependent (if $d_3 = 0$) money growth is completely determined by the nominal deficit. Hence, fiscal policy completely dominates monetary policy. On the other hand, if the central bank is completely independent (if $d_3 = 1$) money growth is equal to zero. Hence, monetary policy completely dominates fiscal policy.

To summarize, in equation (5.11) the fraction of the budget deficit that is financed by private bond sales d_3 is identical to the degree of monetary dominance, which in turn reflects GMT's concept of the economic independence of the central bank.[14] The greater d_3, the greater the economic independence of the central bank. This concludes the section on the governement buget constraint. We turn next to the description of the macromodel.

III A SIMPLE MACROECONOMIC MODEL

In this Section we introduce the government budget constraint (GBC) into a simple IS-LM based macromodel.

III.1 The Demand Side

The IS and LM schedules are given by (5.14) and (5.15)

$$y_t = g_t - \alpha_1(i_t - E_t p_{t+1} + p_t) \qquad \alpha_1 > 0 \qquad (5.14)$$

$$m_t - p_t = y_t - \alpha_2 i_t \qquad \alpha_2 > 0 \qquad (5.15)$$

Equation (5.14) is the savings-investment balance condition. y is the log of aggregate demand, i is the nominal interest rate and E(.) is the operator of rational expectations. Equation (5.15) is the money market equilibrium condition (LM curve).[15] α_2 is the interest rate semi-elasticity of money demand.

The IS-LM model is essentially a two-asset portfolio model comprising money and bonds. From Walras' law the bonds market equilibrium condition is redundant. However, by substituting equation (5.15) in the definition of financial wealth, i.e. equation (5.6), and after some rearrangement we obtain the following expression for the real private sector demand for bonds.[16]

$$b_t - p_t = \frac{\alpha_2(1-\varphi_0)}{\varphi_0} i_t - \frac{1-\varphi_0}{\varphi_0} y_t + \frac{1}{\varphi_0}(f_t - p_t) \quad 0 < \phi_0 < 1 \tag{5.16}$$

Hence, the real private sector demand for bonds depends positively on the nominal interest rate and on real financial wealth and negatively on aggregate demand. Note that by vitue of the derivation of the demand for bonds equation, the elasticities of the asset demand system (5.15) - (5.16) satisfy the familiar adding-up constraints.

Elimination of the nominal interest rate from (5.14) and (5.15) and setting $E_t\Delta p_{t+1} = 0$ gives[17]

$$y_t \equiv \sigma_1(m_t - p_t) + \sigma_2 g_t \text{ where } \sigma_1 \equiv \frac{\alpha_1}{\alpha_1+\alpha_2} \text{ and } \sigma_2 \equiv \frac{\alpha_2}{\alpha_1+\alpha_2} \tag{5.17}$$

From (5.18) it can be seen that the relative effectiveness of monetary and fiscal policy depends on the ratio[18]

$$\frac{\sigma_1}{\sigma_2} = \frac{\alpha_1}{\alpha_2}$$

Combining the GBC, i.e. equation (5.13) with (5.16) yields the aggregate demand schedule:

$$\hat{\Delta} y_t = \frac{(1-d_3)\sigma_1\gamma}{1-\varphi_0}(g_t + p_t) + \sigma_2 \hat{\Delta} g_t - \sigma_1 \hat{\Delta} p_t \tag{5.18}$$

This is a first order difference equation. Hence if we compare equations (5.18) and (5.17) it becomes immediately clear that the GBC imposes a dynamic structure on the static IS-LM framework. This completes the description of the demand side of the model.

III.2 The Supply Side

So far the price level was assumed to be exogenous. Now we introduce a simple supply block. Output is being explained by a Lucas surprise supply function. Since we employ one-period wage contracts policy invariance holds; i.e. output and unemployment never systematically deviate from their natural rates.

Alternatively, we could adopt a staggered contracts specification (Fischer (1977b), Calvo (1983)). However a short-run Phillips curve trade-off - i.e. destruction of the Sargent and Wallace (1975) policy invariance result - is not a necessary condition for the results of this paper. Therefore we abstract from overlapping wage contracts. Again, this has the additional advantage of simplifying expectational dynamics in a later stage of the analysis.[19]

Denoting the average output level by $\tilde{y}$, we assume[20]

$$y_t = \tilde{y} + \frac{\beta}{1 - \beta}(p_t - E_{t-1}p_t) \qquad 0 < \beta < 1 \qquad (5.19)$$

Equation (5.19) is the famous Lucas (1973) surprise supply function. Unanticipated rises in inflation causes output to exhibit transitory deviations from its equilibrium or natural rate $\tilde{y}$. β is the production elasticity of labour.[21] This completes the description of the model.

IV CENTRAL BANK INDEPENDENCE AND INFLATION PERSISTENCE

In this section by equating the aggregate demand and supply schedules we derive a closed form solution for expected inflation. From this solution we derive an inverse relationship between the degree of economic independence and the persistence of inflation. That is, an increase in the degree of economic independence of the central bank reduces inflation persistence.

IV.1 A Closed Form Solution for Expected Inflation

In order to derive an expression for the price level we eliminate y_t from equations (5.18) and (5.19) By using the lag operator (L) on (5.19) and noting that $L\,E_{t-1}\,p_t = p_{t-1}$ we get[22]

$$y_{t-1} = \tilde{y} \qquad (5.20)$$

Substituting (5.19) and (5.20) in (5.18) yields

$$p_t = a_2\,p_{t-1} + a_3\,E_{t-1}\,p_t + a_4\,z_t \qquad (5.21)$$

where the reduced form parameters a_2, a_3 and a_4 obtained from the structural parameters are defined as

$$a_2 \equiv [(1 - \beta)(1 - \varphi_0)\sigma_1\gamma^{-1}]\,a_4$$

$$a_3 \equiv [\beta(1-\varphi_0)(1+\gamma)\gamma^{-1}]a_4$$

$$a_4 \equiv \left[\beta(1-\varphi_0)(1+\gamma)\gamma^{-1} + (1-\beta)\sigma_1\{(1-\varphi_0)(1+\gamma)\gamma^{-1} - (1-d_3)\}\right]$$

and

$$z_t \equiv (1-\beta)[\sigma_1(1-d_3)g_t + (1-\varphi_0)\ \{\sigma_2\gamma^{-1}\hat{\Delta}g_t - \tilde{y}\}]$$

The latter expression only consists of exogenous variables and shocks.

Equation (5.21) is a first-order expectational difference equation which can be solved rather easily. Taking expectations conditional on information at the end of t − 1 of (5.21) we get

$$E_{t-1}p_t = \frac{a_2}{1-a_3}p_{t-1} + \frac{a_4}{1-a_3}E_{t-1}z_t \qquad (5.22)$$

Using λ as short-hand for $a_2/(1-a_3)$, using the definition of λ and taking first differences equation (5.22) can be rewritten as

$$E_{t-1}\Delta p_t - \lambda\ \Delta p_{t-1} = \frac{\lambda\gamma}{(1-\beta)(1-\varphi_0)\sigma_1}E_{t-1}\Delta z_t \qquad (5.23)$$

In order to obtain a closed form solution for expected inflation we need to make assumptions about the exogenous components that make up z.

Following Alogoskoufis and Smith (1991, p. 1266) we assume that this component, i.e. the budget deficit g, is a random walk with drift

$$g_t = \tilde{g} + g_{t-1} + v_t^g \qquad v_t^g \sim N(0, \sigma_g^2) \qquad (5.24)$$

where $\tilde{g}$ is the average (or expected) rate of growth of the real deficit, and v_t^g is a white-noise shock.

From equation (5.24) it follows that

$$\Delta g_t = \tilde{g} + v_t^g \qquad (5.25)$$

and

$$\Delta g_{t-1} = \tilde{g} + v_{t-1}^g \qquad (5.26)$$

Using (5.25) and (5.26) and noting that $\Delta\tilde{y} = 0$ expectations of changes in z are given by

$$E_{t-1}\Delta z_t = (1 - \beta)[\{\sigma_1(1-d_3) + (1-\varphi_0)\,\sigma_2\}\tilde{g} - \gamma^{-1}(1-\varphi_0)\sigma_2\, v_{t-1}^g \quad (5.27)$$

Substituting (5.27) in (5.23) we obtain the following closed form solution for expected inflation

$$E_{t-1}\Delta p_t = \lambda\ \Delta p_{t-1} + \frac{\lambda}{\sigma_1}(\tilde{z} + \xi_{zt-1}) \quad (5.28)$$

where $\tilde{z} \equiv \tilde{g}\gamma[\sigma_1(1 - d_3) + (1 - \varphi_0)\sigma_2]/(1 - \varphi_0)$ is the drift of the composite z process, and $\xi_z \equiv -\sigma_2 v_t^g$ is the white-noise process driving it.

One can see that the persistence of inflation λ, is equal to the root of difference equation (5.22).

IV.2 Monetary Accommodation and The Lucas Critique

By using the definitions of the reduced form parameters a_2 and a_3 (see equation (5.21)), the root can be expressed in terms of the structural parameters

$$\lambda = \frac{1 - \phi_0}{(1 - \varphi_0)(1 + \gamma) - \gamma(1 - d_3)} \quad (5.29)$$

From this expression it can be seen that if $d_3 > \phi_0$ the root is less than unity, and the difference equation for expected inflation – i.e. equation (5.22) – is saddlepath stable. In the appendix we provide the intuition behind this condition.

Taking the first derivative of λ with respect to the degree of economic independence d_3 we find that it is given by

$$\frac{\partial\lambda}{\partial d_3} = \frac{\varphi_0 - 1}{\gamma[(1 - \varphi_0)(1 + \gamma)\gamma^{-1} - (1 - d_3)]^2} < 0 \quad (5.30)$$

From (5.30) we derive proposition 5.1.

Proposition 5.1: The greater the economic independence of the central bank (the higher d_3) the lower the persistence of inflation.

The intuition behind this proposition may be explained as follows. Consider an exogenous increase in the real deficit. This is an aggregate demand shock that raises the price level. Because of both the higher real deficit and the higher price level, the nominal budget deficit goes up. Under the assumptions of the paper (see equation (5.13)) the higher nominal deficit raises the money supply, thereby giving another inflationary impulse. The additional inflationary impulse raises the nominal deficit even further, thereby triggering additional monetary accommodation. Hence inflation persists.

Consider now the role of the central bank. The greater the economic independence of the central bank d_3 , the lower the degree of monetary accommodation $(1 - d_3)$ of nominal budget deficits. Since our model features rational expectations, the rule for the evolution of the money supply, i.e. equation (5.13), is known. Thus, wage setters form their expectations of the price level at time t by taking into account equation (5.13). Suppose the central bank gains more economic independence, i.e. d_3 increases. Wage setters realize that monetary policy becomes less accommodative. With rational wage setters anticipating lower monetary accommodation of government budget deficits expected inflation will be lower. Since future prices are expected to be lower than in the case of high accommodation, wage contracts will reflect these expectations, and wages will be set lower than otherwise. The lower wages are reflected through the path of prices, with the net outcome being lower inflation persistence.

Note that this result is an example of the Lucas (1976) critique of econometric policy evaluation. Given that the structure of an econometric model consists of optimal decision rules of economic agents, and that optimal decision rules vary systematically with changes in the structure of series relevant to the decision maker, it follows that any change in policy (i.e. a shift in the d_3 parameter) will systematically alter the structure of the econometric model (i.e. the persistence of inflation λ).

By again differentiating (5.30) with respect to d_3 we find that

$$\frac{\partial^2\lambda}{\partial d_3^2} = \frac{2(1 - \varphi_0)}{\gamma[(1 - \varphi_0)(1 + \gamma)\gamma^{-1} - (1 - d_3)]^3} > 0 \qquad (5.31)$$

Since $2\gamma^{-1}(1 - \phi) \neq 0$ we have no points of inflection. Using (5.30) and (5.31) we obtain Figure 5.1.

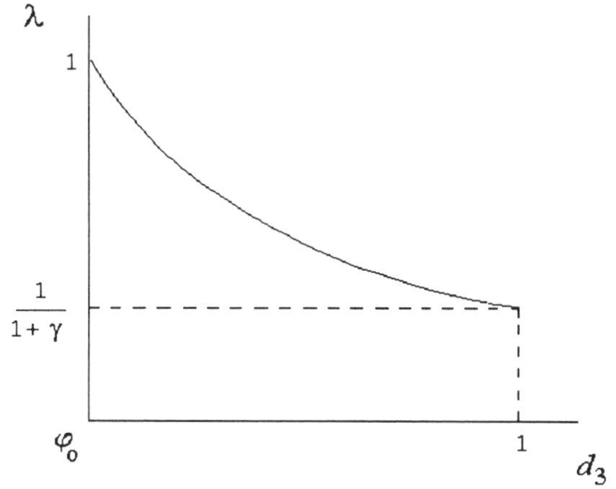

Figure 5.1 Central bank independence and inflation persistence

From the left hand side of the horizontal axis it can be seen that if the degree of economic independence of the central bank (d_3), is equal to the initial share of bonds in financial wealth (ϕ_0), inflation has a unit root.

If the central bank enjoys full economic independence - i.e. if $d_3 = 1$ - the persistence of inflation λ is at its minimum level $1/(1 + \gamma)$. This level is solely determined by the monetary growth rate on the reference path.

In the intermediate case ($\phi_0 < d_3 < 1$), Figure 5.1 pictures an inverse relationship between the degree of economic independence and the persistence of inflation. An increase in the degree of economic independence will result in a decrease of the persistence of inflation. This result is an example of the famous Lucas critique of econometric policy evaluation.

V SUMMARY AND QUESTIONS FOR FURTHER RESEARCH

Using an expectations-augmented Phillips curve model with a government budget constraint we demonstrate that greater economic independence of the central bank reduces inflation persistence.

The intuition behind this result can be summarized as follows. The economic independence of the central bank is identical to the degree of monetary dominance, which in turn reflects the fraction of the nominal budget deficit financed by private bond sales. The greater this fraction the lower the implied monetary accommodation of government budget deficits. With rational wage setters anticipating lower monetary accommodation, expected inflation will be lower. The lower expected inflation results in lower wages and prices, with the net outcome being lower inflation persistence.

Thus lower inflation persistence may not only be caused by the *exchange-rate regime* as shown by Alogoskoufis and Smith (1991) and Alogoskoufis (1992), but also by the way monetary and fiscal policies are coordinated, i.e. by the *domestic monetary regime*. Also our result can be viewed as a dynamic extension of the inverse relationship between economic independence and the level of inflation found by Grilli, Masciandaro and Tabellini (1991).

We ignored the fact that interest paid on bonds is an expense item in the government's budgetary accounts. Hence, an important extension of the model would be to allow for this effect. In the presence of interest payments the total budget deficit equals the sum of the primary deficit and the interest paid on bonds. According to the government's budget constraint this total deficit then needs to be financed by a combination of seigniorage and private bond sales.

Using the same parametrization of central bank independence - i.e. bond financing of the primary budget deficit - it can be shown that due to the inclusion of interest payments equation (5.21) becomes a second-order rather than a first-order expectational difference equation.[23] This means that it would have two backward roots instead of one. This complicates the analytical tractability of persistence. Assuming that the relevant stability conditions are met this leaves a wide variety of possible time paths for inflation, i.e. monotonic convergence, fluctuations or oscillations. It is interesting to note that in the latter case we get a 'new political economy' theory of inflation cyclicality in the tradition of Cukierman (1992, pp. 290-295). However we leave a formal proof for further research.

Finally we sidestepped issues concerning the optimal size of the public sector and the optimal revenue mix for treasuries and central banks. This is discussed in de Jong and van der Ploeg (1991) and van der Ploeg (1991). The conclusion of the latter paper is that in order to assess the case for an independent central bank one should trade-off the welfare gains associated with enhanced monetary discipline and lower inflation against the welfare losses associated with a sub-optimal government revenue mix.

APPENDIX A5: SADDLEPATH STABILITY OF EXPECTED INFLATION

In Section IV.2 it was shown that if

$$d_3 > \phi_0 \qquad \text{(A5.1)}$$

the difference equation for expected inflation - i.e. equation (4.9) - is saddlepath stable. In this appendix we provide the intuition behind this condition.[24] We show that expected inflation converges if the wealth elasticity of the private sector demand for bonds is greater than unity.

In Section II private bond sales were assumed to be governed by

$$\Delta B_t = d_3 G_t \qquad 0 \leq d_3 \leq 1 \qquad \text{(5.11)}$$

Equation (5.11) asserts that a fraction d_3 of the nominal budget deficit is financed by private bond sales.

By using

$$\Delta F_t = G_t \qquad \text{(5.3)}$$

and rearranging (5.11) we obtain

$$d_3 = \frac{\Delta B_t}{\Delta F_t} \qquad \text{(A5.2)}$$

Also in Section II we introduced ϕ_0 for the initial share of bonds in financial wealth B_0/F_0. Hence

$$\phi_0 = \frac{B_0}{F_0} \qquad \text{(A5.3)}$$

Substituting (A.5.2) and (A.5.3) in (A.5.1) yields

$$\frac{\Delta B_t}{\Delta F_t} > \frac{B_0}{F_0} \qquad \text{(A5.4)}$$

or

$$\frac{\Delta B_t}{\Delta F_t} \cdot \frac{F_0}{B_0} > 1 \qquad \text{(A5.5)}$$

Hence the difference equation for expected inflation - i.e. equation (5.28) - is saddlepath stable if the wealth elasticity of the private sector demand for bonds is greater than unity.

NOTES

1. For an in-depth discussion of political independence and the various associated indices of central bank independence see Eijffinger and Schaling (1993a) and de Haan and Sturm (1992).
2. In Section V we explain how the inclusion of interest payments bears on the substance of our results.
3. In Section V we explain how the inclusion of interest payments bears on the substance of our results.
4. The government (the treasury) finances its deficit by bond sales. The difference between total bonds sold and private bond sales consists of bonds sold to the central bank. The central bank pays for its bonds purchases by creating money which ends up in the private sector. For a lucid exposition see Miller (1983).
5. For an excellent study on the dynamics of growth and government debt including criticism of Blinder and Solow (1973) see van Ewijk (1991).
6. This paper does not deal with rational intertemporal consumer behaviour in the sense put forward by Barro (1974). Hence government bonds are viewed as net wealth and the '*Ricardian doctrine*' does not hold.
7. On the reference path of steady growth for a variable X say, $\Delta X_{t+1}/X_t = \gamma$ and $x \equiv d \ell n X$.
8. The quasi first difference operator reduces to the ordinary first difference operator ($\Delta \equiv 1 - L$) if the growth rate (γ) is zero.
9. For instance, using (5.4) it can be shown that $S_t = -\Delta B_t/P_t$, i.e. for a given stock of real financial wealth increases in real base money require the private sector to sell its government securities to the central bank.
10. Of course the original paper is Sargent and Wallace (1981), we cite the 1984 reprint because it is more easy to obtain.
11. The real private sector demand for bonds depends on the nominal interest rate, on real output, and on real financial wealth. An explicit expression will be derived in Section III.
12. In the Sargent and Wallace (1984) analysis because of real interest payments on bonds large deficits eventually require monetary accommodation. Hence - using the notation of this paper - the parameter d_3 would be equipped endogenously, i.e. in dependence of the level of the public debt.
13. Using the notation of this paper Alogoskoufis' equation is $m_t = (1 - d_3)\, p_t + \mu_t$ where $\mu_t \sim N(0, \sigma^2_\mu)$. Alogoskoufis characterizes the classical gold standard, and the gold exchange standards of the interwar period and of Bretton-Woods as low monetary accomodation regimes, and the rest as high accomodation regimes.
14. The fraction d_3 in itself does not say very much about the nature of the monetary instruments under the control of the central bank. However, abstracting from open market policy (i.e. exogenous changes in b), in the context of the model this fraction reflects the public finance aspect of GMT's concept of economic independence.
15. Note that nominal money demand does not depend on expected inflation. Hence, unlike Sargent and Wallace (1981), we do not require the Cagan (1956) money demand function to obtain our results.
16. We are grateful to an anonymous referee for drawing our attention to this point.
17. Abstracting from a wedge between the real and the nominal interest rate has the advantage of simplifying the dynamics of expected inflation in a latter stage of the analysis. More specific, taking account of this effect implies that equation (5.21) would be a second-order rather than a first-order expectational difference equation, meaning that it would have one backward and one forward root.
18. For recent evidence on the associated Monetarist-Keynesian debate of the 1960s and

early 1970s featuring amongst others Friedman and Meiselman (1963), Ando and Modigliani (1965), Andersen and Jordan (1968) and Blinder and Solow (1974) see Kretzmer (1992).

19. Taking account of overlapping wage contracts implies that equation (5.21) would be a second-order rather than a first-order expectational difference equation, meaning that it would have two backward roots instead of one. The latter phenomenon complicates analytical tractability of persistence.
20. For simplicity in this model we abstract from stochastic productivity shocks.
21. In Schaling (1993) we derive (5.19) from the insider-outsider approach to the labour market.
22. For a lucid exposition on the solution of expectational difference equations (including technical details on lag and forward operators in rational expectations models) see Blanchard and Fischer (1989, pp. 261-266).
23. Bond financing of the total budget deficit (including interest payments) obviously leads to instability in the model.
24. This intuition was suggested to us by Lans Bovenberg.

6. Inflation, Growth and the Optimal Degree of Central Bank Independence

I INTRODUCTION

It is a widely held belief that low or zero inflation is an essential or at least a very important condition for high and sustained growth, and that its attainment should be a main aim of government economic policy. For instance, in a recent paper, Andrew Crockett, at the time Executive Director of the Bank of England, states that 'it is generally accepted that price stability not only contributes to social equity, but is central to the goal of improving resource allocation and strengthening the basis of economic growth.'[1]

A similar view is held by the former Vice Chairman of the Federal Reserve Board, David Mullins Jr: 'The elimination of inflation should minimize real interest rates across the maturity spectrum by minimizing risk or uncertainty premia. And, low real interest rates and low effective tax rates encourage investment-producing *growth in productivity* (emphasis mine)'[2] Thus policymakers typically believe that inflation has important adverse effects on long-run economic performance.

There is now a considerable and mounting body of empirical evidence supporting the hypothesis that inflation reduces an economy's rate of growth (Kormendi and Meguire (1985), Grier and Tullock (1989), Fischer (1991), Grimes (1991) and Smyth (1994)) and that the effect is substantial.

This Chapter integrates inflationary foundations for the natural rate of output growth into the literature on central bank independence (Rogoff (1985), Cukierman (1992), Alesina and Summers (1993), Eijffinger and Schaling (1993a, 1993b)). It parametrizes Mullins' view by combining an inflation sensitive growth rate in productivity with the model of Chapter 4.

Following the latter model we define central bank independence as the degree of conservativeness rather than as the political cost of overriding the central bank (Lohmann (1992)). Using a graphical method we develop a new way of determining the optimal degree of conservativeness. As in Lohmann, this degree depends on the balance between *credibility* and *flexibility*. However, unlike Lohmann and Rogoff (1985), we are able to express the upper and lower bounds of the interval containing the optimal degree of independence in terms of the structural parameters of the model.

We find that due to the supply side effect of inflation the extent of macroeconomic instability, measured by the variances of output and inflation, is increased. Also, we show that society's preferred monetary regime need not coincide with central bank independence. If it does however, we show that a higher supply side effect of inflation *lowers* the optimal degree of central bank independence. Thus this paper provides theoretical rationale for Goodhart's (1993, p. 5) claim that:

> 'The case in favour of (a more autonomous Central Bank) is a highly fashionable argument, very much the flavour of the month. Some even regard it as a painless panacea, the obvious way to restore price stability in our countries, without any offsetting loss to growth or output over the medium term.'

The Chapter is organized into six remaining Sections, followed by an appendix. Section II briefly outlines the empirical evidence supporting a negative relationship between inflation and output. Section III extends the Alogoskoufis (1994) version of the Rogoff (1985) model to allow for an inflation sensitive growth rate in productivity. Section IV deals with discretionary policy whilst in Section V and VI central bank independence is discussed. Our conclusions are given in Section VII. The appendix provides the derivation of equation (6.26), of macroeconomic outcomes under any arbitrary monetary regime and of the properties of the function $F(d_2)$ in equation (6.45).

II EMPIRICAL EVIDENCE ON THE SUPPLY SIDE EFFECTS OF INFLATION

Previous work provides support for a significant and substantial negative relationship between inflation or the change in the rate of inflation or both on output growth. The studies can be classified into two types, cross-country analyses and time series analyses for individual countries.

Using post-war data from forty-seven countries Kormendi and Meguire (1985) examined the cross-sectional relationship between output growth and a number of variables. They found a strong negative effect of change between the rate of inflation and output growth.

Kormendi and Meguire's work was extended by Grier and Tullock (1989) who used pooled cross-section and five-year average time series data for 113 countries, the Summers and Heston data set. Three inflation variables were used in the analysis, the rate of inflation, its first difference and the standard deviation of inflation. Grier and Tullock reported results for a number of country classifications and found that in some, but not all, of the cases there was a negative relationship between one or more of the inflation variables and economic growth.

In addition to these published studies there are some unpublished analyses. Shigerhara (1992, p. 37) reports that

> 'a preliminary empirical study by OECD staff that found a 10-percentage-point increase in inflation is associated with about a one-percentage-point slowing of productivity growth for a sample of 18 OECD countries over three periods (1960—73, 1973—79 and 1980—90). These estimated effects are larger than those found in studies, such as Fischer (1992) and Corbo and Rojas (1992), that include developing countries.'

For criticism on cross-section studies see Levine and Renelt (1992) who argue that the growth equation is sensitive to regressor set specification.

All mentioned cross-country studies include a number of variables other than the inflation variables. This is not so in Stanners (1993). Using mainly graphical analysis, Stanners compared growth rates and inflation across a variety of groupings for 14 countries for the period 1980 to 1988 and found no connection between growth rates and inflation. He reached the same conclusion with time series data for individual countries. However, Stanners' study is fatally flawed because no explanatory variables, other than inflation, are included in either his cross-section or his time series analyses.

In an early time series study Jarrett and Selody (1982) used a causality approach to Canadian data and found that a permanent one percentage rate increase in inflation reduced productivity by more than three-tenths of a percentage point.

Grimes (1991) applied regression analysis to data for 21 countries and concluded that 'the costs of even a low inflation rate are estimated to be large given that it is the growth rate, not just the level of output, which is affected by inflation' (Grimes 1991, p.641). Surprisingly, Fischer (1993), shows in linear equations that the statistical significance of the negative association between inflation and growth is stronger for inflation below 15 percent than for higher inflation rates.

A series of time series analyses for the United States strongly support a negative relationship between inflation and output growth. Smyth

(1992) embedded an inflation sensitive natural rate of output in an expectations augmented Phillips curve relationship. He found that each one percentage point increase in inflation reduced output growth by 0.22 percentage points. Estimates of similar magnitudes are obtained using two alternative production function models in Smyth (1993, 1994b). Smyth (1994a) found that inflation significantly and substantially reduced the rate of multifactor productivity growth for the United States; Smyth (1994c) obtained a similar result for German GDP. McMillin and Smyth (forthcoming) found a negative relationship between inflation and growth in VAR model of the U.S. economy. Finally, Rudebusch and Wilcox (1994) using United States data found that an increase in inflation of 1 percent is associated with a 0.35 percent decline in productivity growth, an even bigger coefficient than in the Canadian case. In summary, there is a strong and suggestive negative relation between longer-term growth and inflation and productivity growth and inflation.

In the next section we assume that there exists an inverse relationship between inflation and productivity growth and combine this relationship with the Rogoff (1985) model.

III A SIMPLE CLOSED ECONOMY MODEL

The main purpose of this Section is to combine the Alogoskoufis (1994) version of the Rogoff (1985) model with supply side effects of inflation along the lines of Schaling and Smyth (1994). We assume that there are two types of agents, wage setters (the union) and the central bank. Wage setters unilaterally choose the nominal wage every time period, and the central bank controls monetary policy. The timing of events is as follows. Wage setters sign annual nominal contracts before monetary policy is chosen for that year. Finally, employment is determined by competitive firms. We now move on to the supply side of the model.

Consider the following supply block which is an extension of Chapter 4. Capital will be assumed fixed, and output is given by a short-run production function of the following type

$$y_t = \beta \ell_t + \mu_t \qquad 0 < \beta < 1 \qquad (6.1)$$

where lower-case letters refer to logarithmic deviations from steady state values. Thus, y is the log of output, ℓ the log of employment, and μ_t a measure of productivity. β is the exponent of labour and is less than unity. Having described the level of output, it remains to specify how productivity evolves over time. We assume that the growth rate of productivity, $\Delta\mu_t$, is governed by

$$\Delta\mu_t = g - a_1\Delta p_t + v_t^{\mu} \qquad 0 < a_1 < 1 \tag{6.2}$$

The inflation term results from the supply side effect of inflation. The higher the rate of inflation, the slower the rate of growth of productivity. The variable v_t^{μ} is a random variable. It has mean zero, is serially uncorrelated, and has finite variance σ_{μ}^2. Without loss of generality we normalize σ_{μ}^2 at 1. Note that if $a_1 = 0$ for the *level* of productivity we have a simple stochastic trend specification discussed in Chapter 4. This specification says that over the long run productivity will grow at some average rate, labelled g. However, shocks to productivity, v_t^{μ}, can cause productivity growth to deviate from its mean. Moreover, these shocks are persistent with respect to the *level* of productivity: once perturbed by a v_t^{μ} shock, μ will show no tendency to return to its trendline. Hence, the supply shocks are assumed to have permanent effects on the economy's productivity capacity.

Firms determine employment by equalizing the marginal product of labour to the real wage $w_t - p_t$. This yields the following employment function.

$$\ell_t = -\frac{1}{1-\beta}(w_t - p_t - \mu_t) \tag{6.3}$$

where w is the log of the nominal wage and p the log of the price level. The nominal wage is set at the beginning of each time period and remains fixed for one period. The objective of wage setters is to stabilize employment around a target employment level $\ell_i^s \equiv \tilde{\ell}$. Denoting the log of the labour force by ℓ^s, we assume $\ell_i^s < \ell^s$. Thus we employ the insider-outsider approach to the labour market (Blanchard and Summers (1986), Lindbeck and Snower (1986)).

Thus wages in each period are set to minimize

$$E_{t-1}(\ell_t - \tilde{\ell})^2 \tag{6.4}$$

where E_{t-1} is the operator of rational expectations, conditional on information available at the end of period $t - 1$. The minimization of (2.4) is subject to the labour demand function (6.3).[3] From the first-order conditions for a minimum of (6.4) subject to (6.3) the nominal wage is given by

$$w_t = E_{t-1}p_t + E_{t-1}\mu_t - (1-\beta)\,\tilde{\ell} \tag{6.5}$$

Substituting (6.5) in the labour demand function (6.3), and the resulting equation in the production function, we get the following relation between employment, output and unanticipated shocks

$$\ell_t = \tilde{\ell} + \frac{1}{1-\beta}\left[(1-a_1)(p_t - E_{t-1}p_t) + v_t^{\mu}\right] \tag{6.6}$$

$$y_t = \beta\tilde{\ell} + \mu_t + \frac{\beta}{1-\beta}\left[(1-a_1)(p_t - E_{t-1}p_t) + v_t^{\mu}\right] \tag{6.7}$$

An unanticipated rise in prices $p_t - E_{t-1}p_t$ reduces the real wage, and causes firms to employ more labour. Thus, both aggregate employment and output exhibit a transitory deviation from their respective equilibrium or 'natural' rates $\tilde{\ell}$ and $\beta\tilde{\ell} + \mu_t$.[4] On the other hand, an unanticipated shock to productivity v_t^{μ} increases the marginal product of labour, and given the real wage causes firms to employ more labour. Thus employment rises above $\tilde{\ell}$, and output rises on account of both the higher employment (transitory effect) and the higher productivity (permanent effect).

Subtracting (6.6) from the labour force ℓ^s, using the approximation that the rate of unemployment $u \approx \ell^s - \ell$, and adding and subtracting $(1-a_1)/(1-\beta)p_{t-1}$, we get the following expression for the short-run determination of unemployment.

$$u_t = \tilde{u} - \frac{1}{1-\beta}\left[(1-a_1)(\Delta p_t - E_{t-1}\Delta p_t) + v_t^{\mu}\right] \tag{6.8}$$

where $\tilde{u} = \ell^s - \tilde{\ell}$ can be thought of as the equilibrium or 'natural' rate of unemployment in this model. Thus, (6.8) is the well known expectations augmented 'Phillips curve'. Unemployment deviates from its equilibrium rate only to the extent that there are unanticipated shocks to inflation or productivity.

Note that the reduction in unemployment from unanticipated inflation is smaller than in the case without the supply side effect of inflation $(1 - a_1)/(1 - \beta) < 1/(1 - \beta)$. The reason is that if $a_1 \neq 0$ an unanticipated rise in inflation on the one hand reduces the real wage, and causes firms to employ *more* labour $1/(1 - \beta)$, however it also reduces productivity and this causes firms to employ *less* labour.

Which of the two effects dominates depends on whether $a_1 \gtreqless 1$. In the extreme case that $a_1 = 1$ both effects cancel out and unanticipated inflation has no effect on unemployment. However, with plausible parameter values ($a_1 < 1$) the positive effect will dominate. To give a numerical example, with β being about 0.7 and a_1 equal to 0.2[5] we get $(1 - a_1)/(1 - \beta) = 2.67$. If there is no supply side effect of inflation ($a_1 = 0$) then the gain from unanticipated inflation is 3.34.

Of course, anticipated shocks to inflation and productivity are reflected in wages (equation (6.5)) and do not affect unemployment. We can now incorporate the Phillips curve in a monetary policy game. This is the subject of the next Section.

IV A STATIC GAME BETWEEN WAGE-SETTERS AND THE CENTRAL BANK

IV.1 The Social Welfare versus the Political Approach to Central Bank Behaviour

In order to investigate optimal monetary policy consider a central bank that is concerned with both price stability and unemployment. More specifically we use

$$L_t = \frac{1}{2}(\Delta p_t - \Delta p^*) + \frac{\varepsilon}{2}(u_t - u^*)^2 \tag{6.9}$$

where $0 < \varepsilon < \infty$ and Δp^* and u^* are the inflation and unemployment targets of the central bank. The parameter ε measures the weight of unemployment stabilization relative to inflation stabilization in the preferences of the central bank. Normalizing Δp^* and u^* at zero we get

$$L_t = \frac{1}{2}\Delta p_t^2 + \frac{\varepsilon}{2}u_t^2 \tag{6.10}$$

As pointed out in Chapter 4 the recent literature on monetary policy games has given two competing interpretations to the loss function of the monetary policymaker in equation (6.10). One part of the literature (Havrilesky (1987), Mayer (1990) and Eijffinger and Schaling (1993b)) views the central bank as a mediator between different interest groups that try to steer monetary policy in various directions. On this view, the loss function (6.10) reflects a distributionally motivated political compromise mediated through the central bank between the advocates of employment stimulation and the advocates of price stability. The coefficient ε then measures the relative political clout of the two groups. The other part regards equation (6.10) as a social welfare function and the central bank as a benevolent social planner. (Kydland and Prescott (1977), Barro and Gordon (1983a, 1983b), Rogoff (1985) and Canzoneri (1985)). Since one of the main purposes of this Chapter is to combine the Rogoff (1985) model with supply side effects of inflation along the lines of Schaling and Smyth (1994) we follow Rogoff's analysis and choose the social welfare approach to central bank behaviour.

IV.2 Time Consistent Equilibrium under Fully Discretionary Monetary Policy

Following Alogoskoufis (1994, p. 204) we start with a cooperative game, that is we assume that the natural rate of unemployment is efficient. In the context of the model of Section III this can be represented by the assumption that $\tilde{\ell}$, the target employment level of wage-setters is equal to ℓ^s the effective labour force.

In the latter case the central bank has no incentive to try and reduce unemployment below its equilibrium rate. As there is no conflict between the unemployment targets of wage setters and the central bank, the policy game can be seen as a cooperative one.[6]

We now turn to the case relevant for this Chapter, i.e. the situation where the equilibrium unemployment rate is inefficiently high due to the presence of insiders. In what follows we show that then the equilibrium inflation rate becomes proportional to the natural rate of unemployment. In this case discretionary monetary policy is no longer a Pareto-equilibrium, due to the time-inconsistency of optimal monetary policy.

Assuming that $\tilde{\ell} < \ell^s$, i.e. that $\tilde{u} > 0$ the central bank has incentives to systematically create inflation in order to reduce unemployment below its natural rate.

Substituting the Phillips curve (6.8) in the loss function (6.10) yields

$$L_t = 1/2(\Delta p_t)^2 + \frac{\varepsilon}{2}[\tilde{u} - \frac{(1-a_1)}{1-\beta}\Delta p_t + \frac{(1-a_1)}{1-\beta}E_{t-1}\Delta p_t - \frac{1}{1-\beta}v_t^{\mu}]^2 \qquad (6.11)$$

From the first-order conditions for a minimum of (6.11), i.e. $\partial L_t/\partial \Delta p_t = 0$, we obtain the central bank's reaction function to wage-setters expectations

$$\Delta p_t^D = \frac{\varepsilon(1-\beta)(1-a_1)}{(1-\beta)^2 + \varepsilon(1-a_1)^2}\tilde{u} + \frac{\varepsilon(1-a_1)^2}{(1-\beta)^2 + \varepsilon(1-a_1)^2}E_{t-1}\Delta p_t^D - \frac{\varepsilon(1-a_1)}{(1-\beta)^2 + \varepsilon(1-a_1)^2}v_t^{\mu} \qquad (6.12)$$

where superscript D stands for 'fully discretionary regime'. Taking expectations conditional on information at t−1 of (6.12) gives

$$E_{t-1}\Delta p_t^D = \frac{\varepsilon(1-a_1)}{1-\beta}\tilde{u} \qquad (6.13)$$

Equation (6.13) is the reaction function of wage-setters. Substituting (6.13) in (6.12) we get

$$\Delta p_t^D = \frac{\varepsilon(1-a_1)}{1-\beta}\tilde{u} - \frac{\varepsilon(1-a_1)}{(1-\beta)^2 + \varepsilon(1-a_1)^2} v_t^\mu \tag{6.14}$$

Figure 6.1 shows the central bank's reaction function if $v_t^\mu = 0$, that is the (average) time consistent inflation rate as a function of the expected inflation rate.[7] The dotted line gives this relation for the case that there is no supply side effect of inflation ($a_1 = 0$).

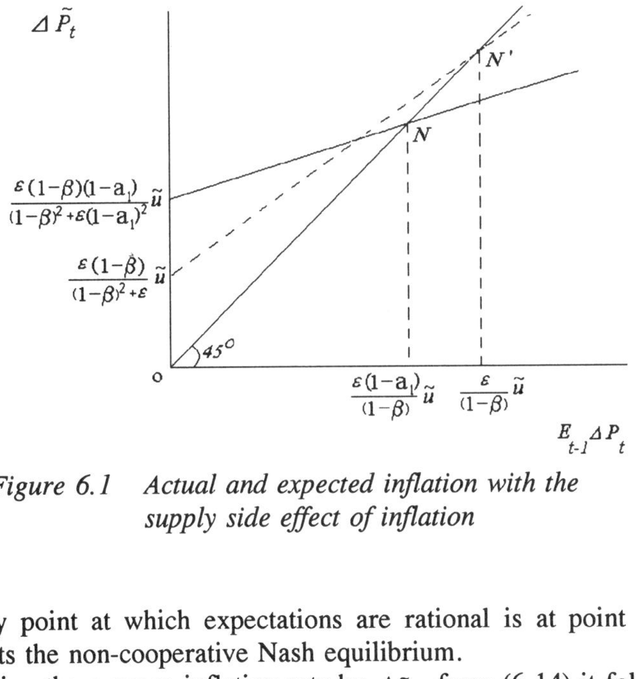

Figure 6.1 *Actual and expected inflation with the supply side effect of inflation*

The only point at which expectations are rational is at point N, which represents the non-cooperative Nash equilibrium.

Denoting the average inflation rate by $\Delta\tilde{p}_t$, from (6.14) it follows that

$$\Delta\tilde{p}_t = \frac{\varepsilon(1-a_1)}{1-\beta}\tilde{u} \tag{6.15}$$

Hence, at point N the inflation rate is above zero (the outcome in the cooperative case). However it is *below* $\varepsilon/(1-\beta)\tilde{u}$ (the outcome in the non-cooperative case when there is no supply side effect of inflation, denoted by N').[8]

Subtracting (6.13) from (6.14) we obtain the following expression for unanticipated inflation

$$\Delta p_t^D - E_{t-1}\Delta p_t^D = \frac{-\varepsilon(1-a_1)}{(1-\beta)^2 + \varepsilon(1-a_1)^2} v_t^{\mu} \tag{6.16}$$

Substituting (6.16) in (6.17) we get

$$u_t^D = \tilde{u} - \frac{(1-\beta)}{[(1-\beta)^2 + \varepsilon(1-a_1)^2]} v_t^{\mu} \tag{6.17}$$

Equations (6.16) and (6.17) highlight the time inconsistency of optimal monetary policy. The monetary policy strategy of the central bank, i.e. equation (6.12) is time-consistent in the sense that at each point in time the inflation rate selected is best, given the current situation. However, as can be seen from equations (6.15) and (6.17), the resulting policy is socially sub-optimal. It is sub-optimal since it results in an excessive level of inflation, i.e. it produces an inflationary bias with no gains in the form of systematic lower unemployment. This completes the description of the non-cooperative Nash equilibrium.

IV.3 Results for Inflation and its Variance

Following Schaling and Smyth (1994, pp. 13–16) in this Section we investigate the consequences of the supply side effect of inflation for the mean and variance of inflation.

Taking the first derivative of (6.15) with respect to a_1, we get

$$\frac{\partial \Delta\tilde{p}_t^D}{\partial a_1} = \frac{-\varepsilon\tilde{u}}{1-\beta} < 0 \tag{6.18}$$

From (6.18) we derive Proposition (6.1)

Proposition 6.1: The higher the supply side effect of inflation (the higher a_1) the lower the average inflation rate.

The intuition behind this result is as follows. In the case of supply side effects of inflation the gains from unexpected inflation are lower than if $a_1 = 0$. The reason is that in addition to decreasing the real wage, unanticipated inflation harms productivity growth and hence employment. Since the central bank cares about both inflation and unemployment it will take this additional effect into account in its policymaking. The result is that the inflationary bias is lower than in the case without supply side effects that is,

$$0 < \frac{\varepsilon(1-a_1)}{1-\beta}\tilde{u} < \frac{\varepsilon}{1-\beta}\tilde{u}$$

We now consider inflation variability. Taking variances of (6.14) we get

$$\text{Var } \Delta p_t = \left[\frac{\varepsilon(1-a_1)}{(1-\beta)^2 + \varepsilon(1-a_1)^2}\right]^2 \tag{6.19}$$

Taking the first derivative of (6.19) with respect to a_1 we get

$$\frac{\partial \text{Var}\,\Delta p_t}{\partial a_1} = \frac{-2\varepsilon^2(1-a_1)[(1-\beta)^2 - \varepsilon(1-a_1)^2]}{[(1-\beta)^2 + \varepsilon(1-a_1)^2]^3} \tag{6.20}$$

By again differentiating (6.20) with respect to a_1, we find that

$$\frac{\partial^2 \text{Var}\,\Delta p_t}{\partial a_1^2} = \frac{2\varepsilon^2[(1-a_1)^4 + (1-\beta)^4 - 10\varepsilon(1-a_1)^2(1-\beta)^2]}{[(1-\beta)^2 + \varepsilon(1-a_1)^2]^4} \tag{6.21}$$

Using (6.20) and (6.21) we obtain Figure 6.2[9]

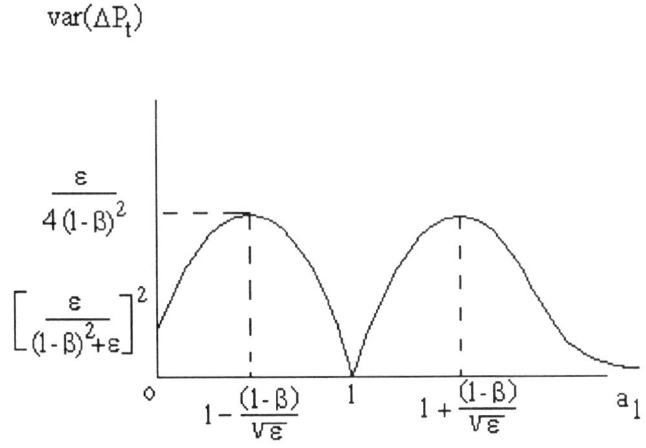

Figure 6.2 The supply side effect of inflation and the variance of inflation

From Figure 6.2 we derive Proposition 6.2.

Proposition 6.2: If the supply side effect of inflation is not too large (if $0 < a_1 < 1 - (1-\beta)/\sqrt{\varepsilon}$) then the higher a_1 the higher the variance of the inflation rate.

To give a numerical example, with the same parameter values as before and ε being equal to 1, we get Var $\Delta p_t = 1.20$. If there is no supply side effect ($a_1 = 0$), then Var $\Delta p_t = 0.84$. Thus the ratio of the variance with the supply side effect to the ratio without the supply side effect is 1.43. This example suggests that the supply side effect of inflation adds considerably to the magnitude of inflationary fluctuations. This completes the description of the results on the mean and variance of inflation.

IV.4 Results for Growth and its Variance

In this section we examine the effects of the supply side effect of inflation on the mean and variance of output growth. Consider

$$\tilde{y}_t = \beta\tilde{\ell} + \mu_t \tag{6.22}$$

Taking first differences and substituting (6.2) we get

$$\Delta\tilde{y}_t = g - a_1\Delta p_t + v_t^{\mu} \tag{6.23}$$

Equation (6.23) is identical to the specification used in Schaling and Smyth (1994, p. 3). The higher the rate of inflation, the slower the rate of growth in the natural level of output. Again if $a_1 = 0$ for the *level* of the natural rate of output we have the simple stochastic trend specification used in Chapter 4.

At this stage, the inflation rate has already been determined by the optimizing behaviour of the central bank. Hence the inflation rate in equation (6.23) is the time-consistent inflation rate under discretion Δp_t^D given by equation (6.14).

Hence we have

$$\Delta\tilde{y}_t = g - a_1\Delta p_t^D(a_1) + v_t^{\mu} \tag{6.24}$$

where the dependence of the inflation rate under discretion on a_1 is stressed by writing Δp_t^D as a function of a_1.

We now consider the effect of changes in a_1 on the natural rate of growth. The first derivative of $\Delta\tilde{y}_t$ with respect to a_1 is given by[10]

$$\frac{\partial \Delta \tilde{y}_t}{\partial a_1} = -[\Delta p_t^D + a_1 \frac{\partial \Delta p_t^D}{\partial a_1}] \tag{6.25}$$

where the first term between brackets is the discretionary inflation rate (which is given by equation (6.14)), and the second term includes the supply side effect of inflation on inflation under discretion.

Since both terms contain the innovation to productivity growth v_t^μ the supply side effect of inflation on the natural rate of growth is *stochastic.*[11]

Denoting the left hand side of (6.25) by M, in appendix A we show that

$$\frac{\partial \Delta \tilde{y}_t}{\partial a_1} = M \qquad M \sim [\frac{\varepsilon(2a_1 - 1)\tilde{u}}{1-\beta},\ \sigma_M^2] \tag{6.26}$$

where $\sigma_M^2 = \varepsilon^2[(1-\beta)^2(1-2a_1)+(1-a_1)^2\varepsilon]^2/[(1-\beta)^2+\varepsilon(1-a_1)^2]^4$. To give a numerical example with the same parameter values as before, $E_{t-1}M$ = $-2\tilde{u}$ and $\sigma_M^2 \equiv 17.0$. From (6.26) we derive Proposition (6.3).

Proposition 6.3: If $a_1 < 0.5$, the higher the supply side effect of inflation (on average) the lower the natural rate of growth.

The intuition behind this proposition is the following. In appendix A we show that

$$E_{t-1} \frac{\partial \Delta \tilde{y}_t}{\partial a_1} = -\Delta\tilde{p}_t^D - a_1 \frac{\partial \Delta \tilde{p}_t^D}{\partial a_1} \tag{A6.4}$$

where the first term on the right hand side of (A6.4) is negative, (because average inflation under discretion is positive) and the second term is positive (because according to proposition 6.1, the supply side effect of inflation on inflation is negative).

Which of the two effects dominates depends on the value of a_1. However, empirical research (Grimes (1991), Smyth (1994a)) suggests that a_1 is close to 0.2 and thus smaller than 0.5. Hence it is plausible that the negative effect dominates.

We now turn to the variability of output growth. Taking first differences of (6.7) and substituting (6.16) in the resulting equation yields

$$\Delta y_t = \Delta \tilde{y}_t + \frac{\beta(1-\beta)}{(1-\beta)^2 + \varepsilon(1-a_1)^2} \Delta v_t^{\mu} \tag{6.27}$$

Taking variances of this expression yields[12]

$$\mathrm{Var}(\Delta y_t - \Delta \tilde{y}_t) = 2\left[\frac{\beta(1-\beta)}{(1-\beta)^2 + \varepsilon(1-a_1)^2}\right]^2 \tag{6.28}$$

Taking the first derivative of (6.28) with respect to a_1 we get

$$\frac{\partial \mathrm{Var}(\Delta y_t - \Delta \tilde{y}_t)}{\partial a_1} = \frac{8\varepsilon(1-a_1)\beta^2(1-\beta)^2}{[(1-\beta)^2 + \varepsilon(1-a_1)^2]^3} > 0 \tag{6.29}$$

By again differentiating (6.29) with respect to a_1, we find that

$$\frac{\partial^2 \mathrm{Var}(\Delta y_t - \Delta \tilde{y}_t)}{\partial a_1^2} = \frac{8\varepsilon\beta^2(1-\beta)^2\ [(1-\beta)^2 - 5\varepsilon\ (1-a_1)^2]}{[(1-\beta)^2 + \varepsilon(1-a_1)^2]^4} \tag{6.30}$$

By setting $(1-\beta)^2 - 5\varepsilon(1 - a_1)^2$ equal to zero we find two points of inflection at $a_1 = 1 \pm (1-\beta)\sqrt{20\varepsilon}\ /-10\varepsilon$. Using (6.29) and (6.30) we obtain Figure 6.3.

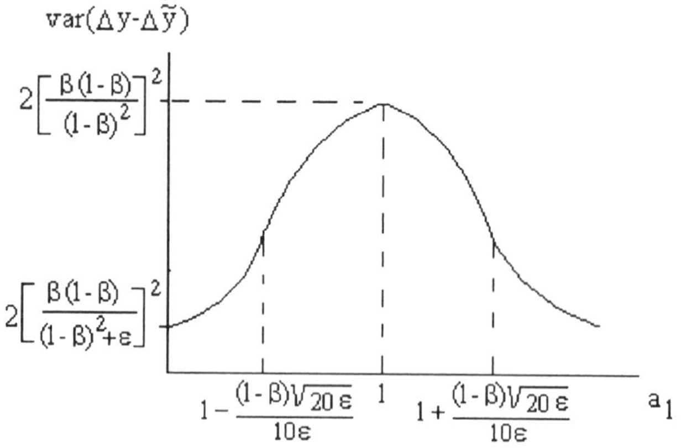

Figure 6.3 The supply side effect of inflation and the variance of output growth

From Figure 6.3 we derive Proposition 6.4.

Proposition 6.4: If $a_1 < 1$ the higher the supply side effect of inflation (the higher a_1) the higher the variance of the growth rate of output around its mean or average rate of growth.

To give a numerical example, with the same parameter values as before, we get $Var(\Delta y_t - \Delta \tilde{y}_t) = 0.16$. If there is no supply side effect, then $Var(\Delta y_t - \Delta \tilde{y}_t) = 0.08$. Thus the ratio of the variance with the supply side effect to the ratio without the supply side effect is 2. This example suggests that the supply side effect of inflation adds considerably to the magnitude of fluctuations in economic growth. Finally we summarise the main propositions from this section in Table 6.1.

Table 6.1 Inflation, growth and fluctuations

Inflation		Growth	
Mean	Variance	Mean	Variance
$\frac{\partial \Delta \tilde{p}_t}{\partial a_1} < 0$	$\frac{\partial Var\ \Delta p_t}{\partial a_1} > 0$	$E_{t-1} \frac{\partial \Delta \tilde{y}_t}{\partial a_1} < 0$	$\frac{\partial [Var(\Delta y_t - \Delta \tilde{y}_t)]}{\partial a_1} > 0$

V CENTRAL BANK INDEPENDENCE

Having analyzed the effects of inflation on growth and fluctuations under discretionary policy, we now turn to a discussion of the supply side effect of inflation under a regime in which society has responded to the time consistency problem by setting up an independent central bank.

V.1 Monetary Policy under a 'Conservative' Central Banker

As stated in Chapter 1 there is a world-wide tendency to establish more independent central banks. Therefore now, following Rogoff (1985, pp. 1177—1180) we consider central bank independence as an institutional response to the time consistency problem. Rogoff demonstrates that society can make itself better off by selecting an agent to head the central bank who is known to place a greater weight on inflation stabilization (relative to unemployment stabilization) than is embodied in the social loss function L_t. He demonstrates that, in choosing among potential candidates, it is never optimal to choose an individual who is known to care 'too little' about unemployment.

Suppose, for example that in period t-1 society selects an agent to head the central bank in period t. The reputation of this individual is such that it is known that if he is appointed to head the central bank, he will maximize the following objective function

$$I_t = \frac{(1+d_2)}{2}\Delta p_t^2 + \frac{\varepsilon}{2}u_t^2 \qquad 0 < d_2 < \infty \qquad (6.31)$$

When d_2 is strictly greater than zero, then this agent places a greater relative weigth on inflation stabilization than society does. Note that if $d_2 = 0$ equation (6.31) reduces to the social loss function (6.10) and we obtain the results under the fully discretionary regime of Section IV.2. Similarly, the case where $d_2 \to \infty$ is formally equivalent to full commitment to a simple zero inflation. Hence, the case of central bank independence can be viewed as intermediate - as a 'balance' — between rules and discretion. The algorithm for deriving the time—consistent equilibrium is exactly the same as in Section IV.2. Equations (6.32) and (6.33) are the 'I' regime counterparts of equations (6.14) and (6.17) respectively:

$$\Delta p_t^I = \frac{\varepsilon(1-a_1)}{(1-\beta)(1+d_2)}\tilde{u} - \frac{\varepsilon(1-a_1)}{(1+d_2)(1-\beta)^2 + \varepsilon(1-a_1)^2}v_t^{\mu} \qquad (6.32)$$

$$u_t^I = \tilde{u} - \frac{(1+d_2)(1-\beta)}{[(1+d_2)(1-\beta)^2 + \varepsilon(1-a_1)^2]}v_t^{\mu} \qquad (6.33)$$

where superscript I denotes the independent central bank regime. A comparison of (6.14) and (6.32) shows that inflation under a fully discretionary regime and under an independent central bank are only only identical if $d_2 = 0$.

Since ex hypothesi $d_2 > 0$, $\Delta\tilde{p}_t^D > \Delta\tilde{p}_t^I$, i.e. average inflation will be higher under the discretionary regime than under an independent central bank. This result confirms our intuition that credibly increasing the central banker's commitment to inflation stabilization reduces the discretionary rate of inflation. This completes the description of the results under an independent central bank. We now move on to compare the expected values of the loss functions of society under the two alternative monetary regimes.

V.2 Evaluation of Central Bank Independence

In this section we evaluate central bank independence as an institutional device to overcome the time-consistency problem. We calculate the expected values of the loss function of society under discretion and under an independent central bank. We show that for society the optimal framework for monetary stability depends on the balance between *credibility* and *flexibility*.

To facilitate expositions in later sections, following Rogoff (1985, pp. 1175—1176), we shall first develop a notation for evaluating the expected value of society's loss function under any arbitrage policy regime 'A', $E_{t-1}L_t^A$.

$$E_{t-1}L_t^A = \frac{1}{2}[\varepsilon\tilde{u}^2] + \Pi^A + \Gamma^A \tag{6.34}$$ [13]

where $\Pi^A \equiv 1/2(\Delta\tilde{p}^A)^2$ and $\Delta\tilde{p}_t^A$ is the mean inflation rate in period t.

$$\Gamma^A \equiv \frac{1}{2}E_{t-1}\Big\{\varepsilon\Big[\frac{v_t^{\mu}}{1-\beta} + \frac{(1-a_1)}{1-\beta}(\Delta p_t^A - E_{t-1}\Delta p_t^A)\Big]^2 + (\Delta p_t^A - E_{t-1}\Delta p_t^A)^2\Big\}$$

The first component of $E_{t-1}L_t^A$, $1/2\,[\varepsilon\tilde{u}^2]$ is nonstochastic and invariant across monetary regimes. It represents the deadweight loss due to the labour market distortion ($\tilde{u} > 0$, see Section IV.2). This loss cannot be reduced through monetary policy in a time—consistent rational expectations equilibrium.

The second term depends on the mean inflation rate. This term is also nonstochastic but does depend on the choice of monetary policy regime.

The final term, Γ^A, represents the 'stabilization' component of the loss function. It measures how succesfully the central bank offsets desturbances to stabilize unemployment and inflation around their mean values.

By substituting the relevant results ((6.14) and (6.17), (6.32) and (6.33)) into society's loss function (6.10) and taking expectations we obtain the D and I regime counterparts of expression (6.34). Abstracting from the (common) deadweight loss, one gets

$$\Pi^D + \Gamma^D = \frac{\varepsilon^2(1-a_1)^2}{2(1-\beta)^2}\tilde{u}^2 + \frac{\varepsilon^2(1-a_1)^2 + \varepsilon(1-\beta)^2}{2[(1-\beta)^2 + \varepsilon(1-a_1)^2]^2} \tag{6.35}$$

$$\Pi^I + \Gamma^I = \frac{\varepsilon^2(1-a_1)^2}{2[(1-\beta)(1+d_2)]^2}\tilde{u}^2 + \frac{\varepsilon^2(1-a_1)^2 + \varepsilon[(1+d_2)(1-\beta)]^2}{2[(1+d_2)(1-\beta)^2 + \varepsilon(1-a_1)^2]^2} \tag{6.36}$$

As long as the natural rate of unemployment is efficient ($\tilde{u} = 0$) $\Pi^A = 0$, the choice of regime only depends on the stabilization component of the loss function. It can then be shown that

$$\Gamma^D < \Gamma^I \tag{6.37}$$

Hence the fully discretionary regime outperforms the independent central bank regime in stabilizing supply shocks.

However, if the natural rate of unemployment is inefficiently high ($\tilde{u} > 0$) results differ significantly. In the absence of shocks society would prefer an independent central bank to the discretionary regime, because

$$\Pi^I < \Pi^D \tag{6.38}$$

From (6.37) it can be seen that the central bank's response to unanticipated supply shocks is best with discretion. This means that discretion gives the central bank the option of reacting optimally to domestic real shocks.

On the other hand from (6.38) it can be seen that an independent central bank out-performs the fully discretionary regime in bringing down the time-consistent rate of wage inflation.

By setting up an independent central bank society reduces its *credibility* problem vis-á-vis the union but loses the option of reacting optimally to domestic real shocks, i.e. it loses *flexibility*. As shown by Lohmann (1992) and Alogoskoufis (1994), which of the two forces dominates depends on the relative strength of the two distortions, namely the inefficiency of the high natural rate of unemployment which produces the high inflation problem, and the inefficiency arising from pre-set nominal contracts that cannot take account of real shocks.

Subtracting (6.36) from (6.35) the per-period difference in welfare losses between the fully discretionary regime and the independent central bank regime is given by

$$E_{t-1}[L_t^D - L_t^I] = \tfrac{1}{2}\Big[\frac{d_2\varepsilon^2(1-a_1)^2(2+d_2)}{(1-\beta)^2(1+d_2)^2}\,\tilde{u}^2 - \frac{d_2\varepsilon^2(1-a_1)^2(1-\beta)^2}{[(1-\beta)^2\varepsilon(1-a_1)^2][(1+d_2)(1-\beta)^2 + \varepsilon(1-a_1)^2]^2}\Big] \tag{6.39}$$

An independent central bank would dominate a fully discretionary regime if

$$\tilde{u} > \frac{(1-\beta)^2(1+d_2)\sqrt{d_2}}{\sqrt{(2+d_2)}\,[(1+d_2)(1-\beta)^2+\varepsilon(1-a_1)^2]\sqrt{[(1-\beta)^2+\varepsilon(1-a_1)^2]}} \qquad (6.40)$$

To give a numerical example, with the same parameter values as before and $d_2 = 4$,[14] if there is no supply side effect of inflation ($a_1 = 0$) the inefficiency in the natural rate of unemployment must exceed about 24.5 percentage points. However, with the supply side effect of inflation ($a_1 = 0.2$) in order for an independent central bank regime to dominate the discretionary regime $\tilde{u}$ must exceed 39.5 percentage points. This example suggests that the supply side effect of inflation — ceteris paribus — weakens the case for central bank independence. This concludes the comparison of monetary regimes. We now move on to an investigation of the factors influencing the optimal degree of central bank independence. This is the subject of Section VI.

VI THE OPTIMAL DEGREE OF CENTRAL BANK INDEPENDENCE

In this Section we show that the optimal degree of central bank independence is contingent on the supply side effect of inflation. More specific we show that the higher the supply side effect of inflation the lower the optimal degree of central bank independence.

VI.1 The Rogoff Theorem

First we reproduce Rogoff's (1985) proof that for society it is optimal to select an agent to head the independent central bank who places a large, but finite weight on inflation. The optimal degree of central bank independence d_2^* is defined as the value of d_2 that minimizes the expected value of the loss function of society $E_{t-1}L_t^I$. Abstracting from the (regime-invariant) deadweight loss the expected value of the social loss function under regime 'I' is

$$\Pi^I + \Gamma^I = \frac{\varepsilon^2(1-a_1)^2}{2[(1-\beta)(1+d_2)]^2}\,\tilde{u}^2 + \frac{\varepsilon^2(1-a_1)^2+\varepsilon[(1+d_2)(1-\beta)]^2}{2[(1+d_2)(1-\beta)^2+\varepsilon(1-a_1)^2]^2} \qquad (6.36)$$

To solve for the value of d_2 that minimizes $E_{t-1}L_t^I$, differentiate (6.36) with respect to d_2

$$\frac{\partial E_{t-1}L_t^I}{\partial d_2} = \frac{\partial \Pi^I}{\partial d_2} + \frac{\partial \Gamma^I}{\partial d_2} \tag{6.41}$$

$$\frac{\partial \Gamma}{\partial d_2} = \frac{\varepsilon^2(1-\beta)^2(1-a_1)^2 d_2}{[(1+d_2)(1-\beta)^2+\varepsilon(1-a_1)^2]^3} \tag{6.42}$$

$$\frac{\partial \Pi^I}{\partial d_2} = \frac{-\varepsilon^2(1-a_1)^2\ \tilde{u}^2}{(1-\beta)^2(1+d_2)^3} \tag{6.43}$$

We are now ready to prove:

Proposition 6.5: For $\tilde{u} > 0,\ 0 < a_1 < 1,\ 0 < d_2^* < \infty$

Proof: note that $d_2 > -1$ by assumption. Thus by inspection of (6.43) $\partial\Pi^I/\partial d_2$ is strictly negative. Note also, by inspection of (6.42), that $\partial\Gamma^I/\partial d_2$ is strictly negative for $-[\varepsilon(1-a_1)^2+(1-\beta)^2]/(1-\beta)^2 < d_2 < 0$, zero when $d_2 = 0$ and positive for $d_2 > 0$. Therefore, $\partial E_{t-1}L_t^I/\partial d_2$ is strictly negative for $d_2 \leq 0$, $\partial E_{t-1} L_t^I/\partial d_2$ must change from negative to positive at some sufficiently large value of d_2, since as d_2 approaches positive infinity, $\partial\Gamma^I/\partial d_2$ converges to zero at rate d_2^{-2}, whereas $\partial\Pi^I/\partial d_2$ converges to zero at rate d_2^{-3}. Therefore $d_2^* < \infty$.[15]

Q.E.D.

VI.2 The Supply Side Effect of Inflation and the Optimal Degree of Central Bank Independence

Proposition 6.5 is Rogoff's theorem extended for the case of supply side effects of inflation. Hence, we have shown that his theorem also holds in the presence of supply side effects of inflation.

In this Section we show that the higher the supply side effect of inflation the lower the optimal degree of central bank independence. First using a graphical method we develop an alternative way of determining the optimal degree of central bank independence. Next, we show how this result is conditioned on the supply side effect of inflation.

By setting (6.41) equal to zero we obtain the first-order condition for a minimum of $E_{t-1}L^I_t$

$$0 = \frac{\partial \Pi^I}{\partial d_2} + \frac{\partial \Gamma^I}{\partial d_2} \tag{6.44}$$

Substituting (6.42) and (6.43) into (6.44) yields

$$\frac{-\varepsilon^2(1-a_1)^2\tilde{u}^2}{(1-\beta)^2(1+d_2)^3} + \frac{\varepsilon^2(1-\beta)^2(1-a_1)^2 d_2}{[(1+d_2)(1-\beta)^2+\varepsilon(1-a_1)^2]^3} = 0 \tag{6.45}$$

Equation (6.45) determines d_2^* as an implicit function of ε, a_1, $\tilde{u}$ and β. A solution for d^*_2 always exists and is unique.

To see this we adapt a graphical method used by Cukierman (1992, pp. 170-172) in the context of a dynamic game.

Rewrite (6.45) as

$$d_2 = \frac{[(1+d_2)(1-\beta)^2+\varepsilon(1-a_1)^2]^3\tilde{u}^2}{(1-\beta)^4(1+d_2)^3} \equiv F(d_2) \tag{6.46}$$

Note that the function $F(d_2)$ on the right-hand side of equation (6.46) is monotonically decreasing in d_2 that

$$F(0) = \frac{[(1-\beta)^2+\varepsilon(1-a_1)^2]^3\tilde{u}^2}{(1-\beta)^4}, \quad \lim_{d_2\to\infty} F(d_2) = (1-\beta)^2\tilde{u}^2$$

and

$$(1-\beta)^2\tilde{u}^2 < F(d_2) < \frac{[(1-\beta)^2+\varepsilon(1-a_1)^2]^3\tilde{u}^2}{(1-\beta)^4}$$

(These statements are demonstrated in appendix C to this chapter.)

We are now ready to prove:

Proposition 6.6: For $0 < a_1 < 1$

$$(1-\beta)^2\,\tilde{u}^2 < d_2^* < \frac{[(1-\beta)^2+\varepsilon(1-a_1)^2]^3\tilde{u}^2}{(1-\beta)^4}$$

Proof: the left-hand side of (6.46) is a 45-degree straight line through the origin. Since $F(0) = [(1-\beta)^2 + \varepsilon(1-a_1)^2]^3\tilde{u}^2/(1-\beta)^4$ and $\partial F/\partial d_2 < 0$, these two functions must intersect at one and only on point. Moreover, since $\tilde{u}^2\,(1-\beta)^2 < F(d_2) < [(1-\beta)^2 + \varepsilon(1-a_1)^2]^3\tilde{u}^2/(1-\beta)^4$, the intersection occurs at a value of d_2 that is bounded between $(1-\beta)^2\tilde{u}^2$ and $[(1-\beta)^2 + \varepsilon(1-a_1)^2]^3\tilde{u}^2/(1-\beta)^4$.

Q.E.D.

Figure 6.4 illustrates the argument graphically. Clearly a solution for d_2 exists and is unique.

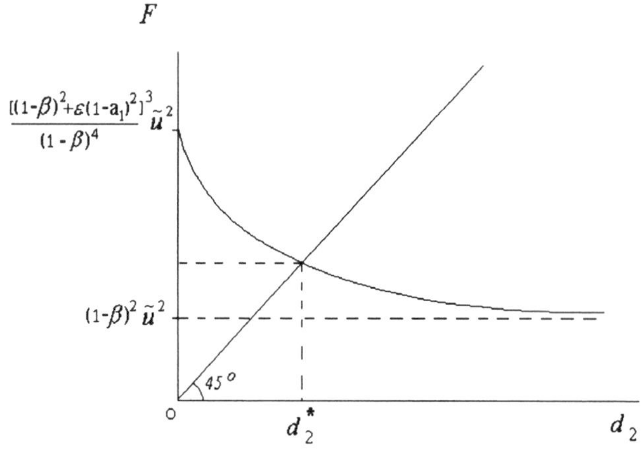

Figure 6.4 The supply side effect of inflation and the optimal degree of central bank independence

We are now ready to prove:

Proposition 6.7: The higher the supply side effect of inflation (the higher a_1) the lower the optimal degree of central bank independence.

Proof: from appendix C, $\partial F/\partial a_1 < 0$, this implies that when a_1 goes up, the curve $F(d_2)$ in Figure 6.4 shifts downward. As a consequence the equilibrium value of d_2 decreases.

Q.E.D.

The intuition underlying this proposition is as follows. A higher supply side effect of inflation implies a lower time consistent rate of inflation (see Proposition 6.1) and consequently a lower Π^I component of the social loss function. This means that society's credibility problem is reduced. Hence, with an unaltered relative weight placed on inflation versus unemployment stabilization the monetary authorities' commitment to fighting inflation is now too high. This establishes the intuition with respect to Proposition 6.7.

VII CONCLUDING REMARKS

Central bankers typically believe that inflation has adverse effects on output growth. This paper has investigated the interdependence of the choice of domestic monetary regime and the supply side effects of inflation.

Unlike in papers by Barro and Gordon (1983a, 1983b), Rogoff (1985) and Lohmann (1992), the rate of growth of productivity here depends on the inflation rate. The main implication of this is that the slope of the Phillips curve, that is the benefits of unanticipated inflation, depend on the supply side effect of inflation. The implication of this mechanism are two-fold.

First, as shown in Section VI society's optimal framework for monetary stability — being contingent on the slope of the Phillips curve — also depends on the supply side effect of inflation. Loosely speaking as inflation becomes more harmful for output growth society moves away from the independent central bank regime (which is first best in terms of *credibility*) towards *discretion* (which is first best in terms of *flexibility*).

This means that in general it need not be optimal for society to have an independent central bank. Secondly, as shown in Proposition 6.7, if society's optimal framework for monetary stability does coincide with central bank independence, a higher supply side effect of inflation lowers *the optimal degree* of central bank independence. This means that society's optimal central banking institution is contingent on the supply side effect of inflation.

APPENDIX A6: THE DERIVATION OF EQUATION (6.26)

In this appendix we derive equation (6.26) from

$$\frac{\partial \Delta \tilde{y}_t}{\partial a_1} = -\Delta p_t^D - a_1 \frac{\partial \Delta p_t^D}{\partial a_1} \tag{6.25}$$

The discretionary rate of inflation can be decomposed as

$$\Delta p_t^D = \Delta \tilde{p}_t^D + (\Delta p_t^D - E_{t-1}\Delta p_t^D) \tag{A6.1}$$

where $\Delta \tilde{p}_t^D$ is the average inflation rate.

Substituting (A6.1) in (6.25) we get

$$\frac{\partial \Delta \tilde{y}_t}{\partial a_1} = -\Delta \tilde{p}_t^D - (\Delta p_t^D - E_{t-1}\Delta p_t^D) - a_1\left[\frac{\partial \Delta \tilde{p}_t^D}{\partial a_1} + \frac{\partial(\Delta p_t^D - E_{t-1}\Delta p_t^D)}{\partial a_1}\right] \tag{A6.2}$$

where the second term on the right hand side is given by

$$\Delta p_t^D - E_{t-1}\Delta p_t^D = \frac{-\varepsilon(1-a_1)}{(1-\beta)^2 + \varepsilon(1-a_1)^2} v_t^\mu \tag{6.16}$$

Taking the first derivative of (6.16) with respect to a_1 yields

$$\frac{\partial(\Delta p_t^D - E_{t-1}\Delta p_t^D)}{\partial a_1} = \frac{\varepsilon v_t^\mu[(1-\beta)^2 - \varepsilon(1-a_1)^2)]}{[(1-\beta)^2 + \varepsilon(1-a_1)^2]^2} \tag{A6.3}$$

Since both (6.16) and (A6.3) contain the innovation to productivity growth v_t^μ, the response of growth with respect to inflation, $\partial\Delta\tilde{y}_t/\partial a_1$ as expressed by the right hand side of (A6.2) is stochastic. Taking expectations conditional on information at the end of t-1 of (A6.2) yields

$$E_{t-1}\frac{\partial \Delta \tilde{y}_t}{\partial a_1} = -\Delta \tilde{p}_t^D - a_1 \frac{\partial \Delta \tilde{p}_t^D}{\partial a_1} \tag{A6.4}$$

where the first term on the right hand side is given by

$$\Delta \tilde{p}_t^D = \frac{\varepsilon(1-a_1)\tilde{u}}{1-\beta} \tag{6.15}$$

and the second term is

$$\frac{\partial \Delta \tilde{p}_t^D}{\partial a_1} = \frac{-\varepsilon \tilde{u}}{1-\beta} \tag{6.18}$$

Substituting (6.15) and (6.18) in (A6.4) we get

$$E_{t-1} \frac{\partial \Delta \tilde{y}_t}{\partial a_1} = \frac{\varepsilon(2a_1 - 1)\tilde{u}}{1-\beta} \tag{A6.5}$$

Subtracting (A6.5) from (A6.2) we obtain

$$\frac{\partial \Delta \tilde{y}_t}{\partial a_1} - E_{t-1} \frac{\partial \Delta \tilde{y}_t}{\partial a_1} = E_{t-1} \Delta p_t^D - \Delta p_t^D \;\; - a_1 \frac{\partial(\Delta p_t^D - E_{t-1} \Delta p_t^D)}{\partial a_1} \tag{A6.6}$$

The definition of the variance of $\partial \Delta \tilde{y}_t / \partial a_1$ is

$$\text{Var} \frac{\partial \Delta \tilde{y}_t}{\partial a_1} = E_{t-1}[\frac{\partial \Delta \tilde{y}_t}{\partial a_1} \; - \; E_{t-1} \frac{\partial \Delta \tilde{y}_t}{\partial a_1}]^2 \tag{A6.7}$$

Substituting (6.16) and (A6.3) into (A6.6) and the resulting expression in (A6.7) noting that $\sigma_\mu^{\;2} = 1$ yields

$$\text{Var} \frac{\partial \Delta \tilde{y}_t}{\partial a_1} = \frac{\varepsilon^2[(1-\beta)^2(1-2a_2) + (1-a_1)^2\varepsilon]^2}{[(1-\beta)^2 + \varepsilon(1-a_1)^2]^4} \tag{A6.8}$$

Denoting $\partial \Delta \tilde{y}_t / \partial a_1$ by M we obtain equation (6.26) of the text.

APPENDIX B6: THE DERIVATION OF THE EXCEPTED VALUE OF SOCIETY'S LOSS FUNCTION UNDER ANY ARBITRARY MONETARY POLICY REGIME

In this Appendix following Rogoff (1985, pp. 1175—1176) we develop a notation for evaluating the expected value of society's loss function under any arbitrary monetary policy regime 'A', $E_{t-1}L_t^A$ (equation 6.34) of the text. Unemployment under regime A is given by

$$u_t^A = \tilde{u} - \frac{(1-a_1)}{1-\beta}(\Delta p_t^A - E_{t-1}\Delta p_t^A) - \frac{1}{1-\beta}v_t^\mu \qquad \text{(B6.1)}$$

Squaring and taking expectations yields

$$E_{t-1}(u_t^A)^2 = \tilde{u}^2 + E_{t-1}[\frac{v_t^\mu}{1-\beta} + \frac{1-a_1}{1-\beta}(\Delta p_t^A - E_{t-1}\Delta p_t^A)]^2 \qquad \text{(B6.2)}$$

The inflation rate under regime A can be expanded as

$$\Delta p_t^A = \Delta\tilde{p}_t^A + (\Delta p_t^A - E_{t-1}\Delta p_t^A) \qquad \text{(B6.3)}$$

where $\Delta\tilde{p}_t^A$ is the mean (expected) inflation rate in period t. Squaring and taking expectations in turn yields

$$E_{t-1}(\Delta p_t^A)^2 = (\Delta\tilde{p}_t^A)^2 + E_{t-1}(\Delta p_t^A - E_{t-1}\Delta p_t^A)^2 \qquad \text{(B6.4)}$$

The expected value of society's loss function under regime A is

$$E_{t-1}L_t^A = \frac{1}{2}E_{t-1}(\Delta\tilde{p}_t^A)^2 + \frac{\varepsilon}{2}E_{t-1}(u_t^A)^2 \qquad \text{(B6.5)}$$

Substituting (B6.2) and (B6.4) into (B6.5) one obtains equation (6.34) of the text.

APPENDIX C6: DERIVATION OF THE PROPERTIES OF THE FUNCTION $F(d_2)$ IN EQUATION (6.45)

1 Demonstration that $\partial F/\partial d_2 < 0$.

The first derivative of F with respect to d_2 is given by

$$\frac{\partial F}{\partial d_2} = \frac{-3\tilde{u}^2\varepsilon(1-a_1)^2[(1+d_2)(1-\beta)^2+\varepsilon(1-a_1)^2]^2}{(1-\beta)^4(1+d_2)^4} \qquad \text{(C6.1)}$$

(C6.1) is negative since $a_1 < 1$

2 Demonstration that $\partial^2 F / \partial d_2^2 > 0$.

The second derivative of F with respect to d_2 is given by

$$\frac{\partial^2 F}{\partial d_2^2} = \frac{6\tilde{u}^2 \varepsilon (1-a_1)^2 \Gamma [\Gamma - \varepsilon(1-a_1^2)]}{(1-\beta)^4 (1+d_2)^5} \tag{C6.2}$$

where $\Gamma \equiv (1+d_2)(1-\beta)^2 + 2\varepsilon(1-a_1)^2$ (C.6.2) is positive since $a_1 < 1$

3 Demonstration that $F(0) = [(1-\beta)^2 + \varepsilon(1-a_1)^2]^3 \tilde{u}^2 / (1-\beta)^4$

This can be shown by direct examination of the right-hand side of (6.46) at $d_2 = 0$.

4 Demonstration that $\tilde{u}^2(1-\beta)^2 < F(d_2) < [(1-\beta)^2 + \varepsilon(1-a_1)^2]^3 \tilde{u}^2 / (1-\beta)^4$

Since $F(0) = [(1-\beta)^2 + \varepsilon(1-a_1^2)]^3 \tilde{u}^2 / (1-\beta)^4$, $\lim_{d_2 \to \infty} F(d_2) = \tilde{u}^2(1-\beta)^2$ and

$\partial F / \partial d_2 < 0$, $F(d_2)$ must be bounded between $\tilde{u}^2(1-\beta^2)$ and F(0).

5 Demonstration that $\partial F / \partial a_1 < 0$

The first derivative of F with respect to a_1 is given by

$$\frac{\partial F}{\partial a_1} = \frac{-6\varepsilon(1-a_1)\tilde{u}^2 [(1+d_2)(1-\beta)^2 + \varepsilon(1-a_1)^2]^2}{(1-\beta)^4 (1+d_2)^3} \tag{C6.3}$$

(C6.3) is negative since $a_1 < 1$.

NOTES

1. See Crockett (1994), p. 167.
2. See Mullins (1994), p. 6.
3. Alternatively, the loss function could be assumed quadratic in both the deviations of

employment and the real wage from certain target values. For an analysis along these lines see Chapter 7.

4. Actual output and employment will equal their natural rates when all expectations are fulfilled. Hence, the natural rate of employment equals $\tilde{\ell}$ and the natural rate of output is $\beta\tilde{\ell} + \mu_t$.
5. For a_1 we have used the estimate in Smyth (1994a). The value of β is taken from Alogoskoufis (1994, p. 211).
6. For more details see Chapter 4, Section III.2.
7. This figure is based on a similar one in Blanchard and Fischer (1989, p. 597). It is drawn assuming that $0 < a_1 < \varepsilon - (1-\beta)^2/\varepsilon$.
8. For a comparison see also Figure 4.1 for the case that $d_2 = 0$.
9. Since the nominator of (4.13) is a fourth-order equation in a_1 we are unable to locate points of inflection.
10. (6.24) is an equation of the form $y = a.x(a)$. Hence the first derivative is $dy/da = x(a) + a.(dx/da)$.
11. We derive an expression for $\partial\Delta p_t^D/\partial a_1$ in appendix A.
12. Strictly speaking we are computing $Var(\Delta y_t - \Delta\tilde{y}_t)/\sigma^2_{\Delta\mu}$ where $\sigma^2_{\Delta\mu} = Var\ \Delta v_t^\mu = \sigma_\mu^2 + \sigma^2_{\mu_{t-1}}$. With $\sigma_\mu^2 = \sigma^2_{\mu_{t-1}}$ we get (6.30).
13. We derive equation (6.34) in the appendix.
14. The value of d_2 is the same as in Chapter 4.
15. As pointed out by Rogoff (1985, p. 1178) it is extremely difficult to write down a closed form solution for d_2^*.

7. Wage Formation, Monetary Targeting, and the Optimal Degree of Central Bank Independence

I INTRODUCTION

In Chapters 3 and 4 we have focused on the quantification of central bank independence using a number of attributes from central bank laws.

These Chapters investigate the *positive* issue of the relation between monetary regimes and economic performance. Broadly speaking, the conclusion is that the more independent the central bank, the lower the inflation rate, while the rate of output growth is unaffected.

However, these Chapters do not explain the observed differences in central bank independence. For instance, no explanation is offered for the very high independence of the Deutsche Bundesbank. It has often been pointed out that this independence may be explained by Germany's underlying aversion to inflation associated with its experience of hyper inflation in the 1920s.[1] This brings us to an important issue in the political economy of central banking; the relation between institutional design and individual and collective beliefs, preferences and strategies. Here the question to de dealt with is the *normative* issue of how independent a central bank should be; i.e. the optimal degree of central bank independence. Recent work in this area is Cukierman (1994) and Eijffinger and Schaling (1995). In addition to these studies in Chapter 6 we develop a theory that predicts that optimal central bank independence will be lower, the more harmful inflation is for economic growth (the higher the supply side effect of inflation).

In this Chapter we combine the model of Chapter 4 with labour union behaviour along the lines of New-Keynesian bargaining theories of unemployment. Building on the work of Funke (1994) we characterize wage setting in a totally unionized economy under a constant money supply rule, GNP targeting, full commitment to a simple zero inflation rule ('inflation targeting') a discretionary regime and an independent central bank.[2] The wage formation strategy of the union can be either cooperative or aggressive. Following Chapters 4 and 6 we define central bank independence as the degree of conservativeness rather than as the political cost of overriding the central bank (Lohmann (1992)). Using the graphical method of Chapter 6 we show that the optimal degree of central bank independence depends on the balance between *credibility* and *flexibility*

Unlike Lohmann (1992) and Rogoff (1985), we are able to express the upper and lower bounds of the interval containing the degree of independence in terms of the structural parameters of the model. We find that society's preferred monetary regime need not coincide with central bank independence. If it does however, we show that the more aggressive the union the higher the optimal degree of central bank independence. This means that society's optimal central banking institution is contingent on the labour market regime.

The Chapter is organized into six remaining sections, followed by two appendices. Section II extends Chapter 4 to allow for cooperative and aggressive wage formation strategies. Section III deals with discretionary policy whilst in Section IV inflation targeting, money supply targeting, GNP targeting and central bank independence is discussed. Sections V and VI extend Funke's analysis to allow for an independent central bank. Our conclusions are given in Section VII. The appendices provide the derivation of macroeconomic outcomes under any arbitrary monetary regime, of the expected loss of the union and of the properties of the function $F(d_2)$ in equation (7.68).

II A SIMPLE CLOSED ECONOMY MACROMODEL

II.1 The Model

The main purpose of this section is to combine the Alogoskoufis (1994) model of wage and employment determination with union behaviour along the lines of Funke (1994), to allow for cooperative and aggressive wage formation strategies. We assume that there are two types of agents, wage setters (the union) and the central bank. Wage setters unilaterally choose the nominal wage every time period, and the central bank controls monetary policy.

The timing of events is as follows. In the first stage wage setters sign annual nominal contracts (Gray (1976), Fischer (1977a)). Wage setters know the domestic monetary regime, that is they know whether the central bank follows a constant money supply rule, a nominal income rule, a price level rule, a discretionary regime or whether it is an independent agent. They take this information into account in forming their expectations. In the second stage stochastic shocks to productivity and velocity of money demand realize. These shocks are random and cannot be observed at the time wage contracts are signed. In the third stage the central bank observes the values of the shocks and — contingent on the chosen regime — reacts to the shocks accordingly. In the fourth and final stage employment is determined by competitive firms. This timing of events can be summarized as follows.

1	2	3	4
Nominal wage contracts signed	Shocks realize	Central bank sets monetary policy	Employment determined

Figure 7.1 The timing of events

We now move to the supply side of the model.

II.2 Wage and Employment Determination

Consider the following supply block which is an extension of Chapter 4. Capital will be assumed fixed, and output is given by a short-run Cobb-Douglas production function

$$y_t = \beta \ell_t + \mu_t \qquad 0 < \beta < 1 \qquad (7.1)$$

where lower-case letters refer to logarithmic deviations from steady state values. Thus, y is the log of output, ℓ the log of employment, and μ_t a measure of productivity. β is the exponent of labour and is less than unity.

Having described the level of output, it remains to specify how productivity evolves over time. For simplicity we assume that shocks to productivity are normally distributed with zero mean and finite variance

$$\mu_t = v^{\mu}_t \qquad v^{\mu}_t \sim N(0, \sigma^2_{\mu}) \qquad (7.2)$$

Firms determine employment by equalizing the marginal product of labour to the real wage $w_t - p_t$. This yields the following employment function

$$\ell_t = -\frac{1}{1-\beta}(w_t - p_t - \mu_t) \qquad (7.3)$$

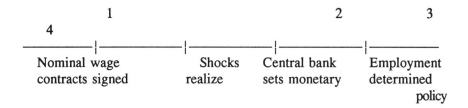

where w is the log of the nominal wage and p the log of the price level.

The nominal wage is set at the beginning of each period and remains fixed for one period. The objective of wage setters is to stabilize real wages and employment around their target levels. Thus wages in each period are set to minimize

$$W_t = E_{t-1}\left[\frac{d_4}{2}(w_t - p_t - \tau)^2 + \frac{1}{2}(\ell - \ell^*)^2\right] \tag{7.4}$$

where E_{t-1} is the operator of rational expectations, conditional on information at the end of period t — 1. τ and ℓ^* are the real wage and employment targets of the union. d_4 is the weight assigned to real wage stabilization relative to employment stabilization in the preferences of the union. We assume that $\ell^* \equiv \ell_i^s$ where ℓ_i^s is the number of insiders. Denoting the log of the labour force by ℓ^s, we assume $\ell_i^s < \ell^s$. Thus we employ a variant of the insider—outsider approach to the labour market (Blanchard and Summers (1986), Lindbeck and Snower (1986)). In the special case that $d_4 = 0$ equation (7.4) reduces to the simple insider-outsider specification used in Chapter 4. The minimization of (7.4) is subject to the labour demand function (7.3).[3]

From the first-order conditions for a minimum of (7.4) subject to (7.3) the nominal wage is given by

$$w_t = E_{t-1}p_t - (1-\beta)\,\tilde{\ell} \tag{7.5}$$

where $\tilde{\ell} \equiv \ell^* - d_4(1-\beta)\tau / d_4(1-\beta)^2 + 1$. Substituting (7.5) in the labour demand function (7.3), and the resulting equation in the production function, we get the following relation between employment, output and unanticipated shocks

$$\ell_t = \tilde{\ell} + \frac{1}{1-\beta}(p_t - E_{t-1}p_t + \mu_t) \tag{7.6}$$

$$y_t = \tilde{y} + \frac{\beta}{1-\beta}(p_t - E_{t-1}p_t) + \frac{\mu_t}{1-\beta} \tag{7.7}$$

where $\tilde{y} \equiv \beta\,\tilde{\ell}$.

An unanticipated rise in prices $p_t - E_{t-1}p_t$ reduces the real wage, and causes firms to employ more labour. Thus, both aggregate employment and output exhibit a transitory deviation from their respective equilibrium or 'natural' rates $\tilde{\ell}$ and $\beta\tilde{\ell}$.[4]

Subtracting (7.6) from the labour force ℓ^s, using the approximation that the rate of unemployment u $\approx \ell^s - \ell$, we get the following expression for the short-run determination of unemployment

$$u_t = \tilde{u} - \frac{1}{1-\beta}(p_t - E_{t-1}p_t + \mu_t) \tag{7.8}$$

where $\tilde{u} = \ell^s - \tilde{\ell}$. $\tilde{u}$ can be thought of as the equilibrium or 'natural' rate of unemployment in this model. Thus, (7.8) is the well known expectations augmented 'Phillips curve'. Unemployment deviates from its equilibrium rate only to the extent that there are unanticipated shocks to inflation or productivity. Anticipated shocks to inflation and productivity are reflected in wages (equation (7.5)) and do not affect unemployment. We now turn to the determinants of the natural rate of unemployment.

II.3 The Natural Rate of Unemployment

In this section we investigate the factors affecting the natural rate of unemployment. In equation (7.5) the permanent or equilibrium level of employment was shown to be equal to

$$\tilde{\ell} \equiv \frac{\ell^* - d_4(1-\beta)\tau}{d_4(1-\beta)^2 + 1}$$

Substituting this expression into the definition of the natural rate of unemployment, $\tilde{u} \equiv \ell^s - \tilde{\ell}$ and normalizing ℓ^s at zero we get

$$\tilde{u} = \frac{d_4(1-\beta)\tau - \ell^*}{d_4(1-\beta)^2 + 1} \tag{7.9}$$

Hence the higher the target value of the real wage (τ) or the smaller the target employment level (ℓ^*) the higher the natural rate of unemployment.

Next consider the relationship between the weight assigned to real wage stabilization relative to employment stabilization in the preferences of the union - i.e. the wage negotiation parameter - and the natural rate of unemployment.

Taking the first derivative of (7.9) with respect to d_4, we get

$$\frac{\partial \tilde{u}}{\partial d_4} = \frac{(1-\beta)[\tau + (1-\beta)\ell^*]}{[d_4(1-\beta)^2 + 1]^2} > 0 \tag{7.10}$$

From (7.10) we derive Lemma 7.1

Lemma 7.1: The greater the weight of real wage stabilization versus employment stabilization in the preferences of the union (the higher d_4) the higher the natural rate of unemployment.

The intuition behind this lemma is the following. The higher the wage negotiation parameter d_4 the higher real wages will be. Higher real wages drive down labour demand (see equation (7.3)) and hence increase unemployment.

By again differentiating (7.10) with respect to d_4 we find that

$$\frac{\partial^2 \tilde{u}}{\partial d_4^2} = \frac{-2(1-\beta)^3\ [\tau + (1-\beta)\ell^*]}{[d_4(1-\beta)^2 + 1]^3} < 0 \qquad (7.11)$$

Using (7.10) and (7.11) we obtain Figure 7.2.

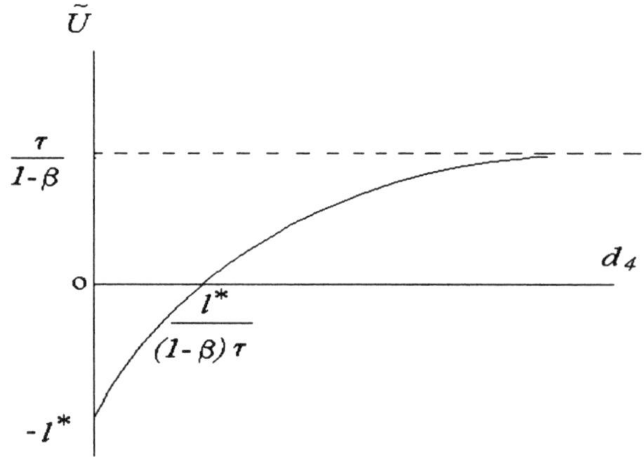

Figure 7.2 Wage negotiation behaviour and the natural rate of unemployment

From Figure 7.2 we derive Lemma 7.2.

Lemma 7.2: If the weight of real wage stabilization versus employment stabilization in the preferences of the union (d_4) equals $\ell^*\ ((1-\beta)\tau)^{-1}$, the natural rate of unemployment is zero.

This follows directly from the nominator of (7.9). In investigating the relationship between d_4 and $\tilde{u}$ in the remainder of this paper we restrict attention to the case where $d_4 \, \varepsilon \, (\ell^* \, ((1 - \beta)\tau)^{-1}; \, \infty \rangle$, i.e. to situations where $\tilde{u} \geq 0$.

This completes the desciption of the factors affecting the natural rate of unemployment. We can now incorporate the Phillips curve in a monetary policy game. This is the subject of the next section.

III A STATIC GAME BETWEEN A UNION AND THE CENTRAL BANK

III.1 The Social Welfare versus the Political Approach to Central Bank Behaviour

In order to investigate optimal monetary policy consider a central bank that is concerned with both price stability and unemployment.

More specifically we use

$$L_t = \frac{1}{2} (\Delta p_t - \Delta p^*) + \frac{\epsilon}{2} (u_t - u^*)^2 \tag{7.12}$$

where $0 < \varepsilon < \infty$ and Δp^* and u^* are the inflation and unemployment targets of the central bank. The parameter ε measures the weight of unemployment stabilization relative to inflation stabilization in the preferences of the central bank. Normalizing Δp^*, u^* and p_{t-1} at zero we get [5]

$$L_t = \frac{1}{2} p_t^2 + \frac{\varepsilon}{2} u_t^2 \tag{7.13}$$

As pointed out in Chapters 4 and 6, the recent literature on monetary policy games has given two competing interpretations to the loss function of the monetary policymaker in equation (7.13).

One part of the literature (Havrilesky (1987), Mayer (1990) and Eijffinger and Schaling (1993b)) views the central bank as a mediator between different interest groups that try to push monetary policy in various directions. On this view, the loss function (7.13) reflects a distributionally motivated political compromise mediated through the central bank between the advocates of employment stimulation and the advocates of price stability. The coefficient ε then measures the relative political clout of the two groups. The other part regards equation (7.13) as a social welfare function and the central bank as a benevolent social planner (Kydland and Prescott (1977), Barro and Gordon (1983a, 1983b), Rogoff (1985) and Canzoneri (1985)).

Since one of the main purposes of this Chapter is to combine the Rogoff (1985) model with union behaviour along the lines of Funke (1994), we follow Rogoff's analysis and choose the social welfare approach to central bank behaviour.

III.2 Union Behaviour and the Natural Rate of Unemployment

Following the analysis in Chapter 4 we start with a cooperative game, i.e. we assume that the natural rate of unemployment is efficient. In the context of the model of sub-section (II.2), this can be represented by the assumption that $\tilde{u}$ the natural rate of unemployment is equal to zero. In the latter case the central bank has no incentive to try and reduce unemployment below its equilibrium rate. As there is no conflict between the unemployment targets of the union and the central bank, the policy game can be seen as a cooperative one.[6] By using Lemma 7.2 it can be seen that the achievement of the central bank's final targets, full employment and price stability, is not jeopardized if $d_4 = d_4^*$ where $d_4^* \equiv \ell^* ((1 - \beta)\tau)^{-1}$.[7]

Hence, for given levels of τ and ℓ^* ($\tau, \ell^* > 0$), a union is considered as *cooperative* if $d_4 = d_4^*$. This state of affairs is summarized in the first column of Table 7.1.

Table 7.1 Union behaviour and the natural rate of unemployment

Central bank	Wage-setters	
	$d_4 = d_4^*$ $\tilde{u} = 0$	$d_4 > d_4^*$ $\tilde{u} > 0$
$u^* = 0$	$u^* = \tilde{u}$	$u^* < \tilde{u}$
Natural rate	Efficient	Inefficient
Union	Cooperative	Aggressive

We now turn to the third column of Table 7.1, i.e. the situation where the equilibrium unemployment rate is inefficiently high. In the latter case discretionary monetary policy is no longer a Pareto-equilibrium, due to the time-inconsistency of optimal monetary policy. From Figure 7.2 it can be seen that $\tilde{u} > 0$ if $d_4 > d_4^*$. Hence, using the terminology of Funke (1994, p. 328), for given levels of τ and ℓ^* ($\tau, \ell^* > 0$), a union is considered as *aggressive* if $d_4 > d_4^*$.

III.3 Time-Consistent Equilibrium Under Fully Discretionary Monetary Policy

Assuming that the union is aggressive i.e., that $d_4 > d_4^*$ the central bank has incentives to systematically create inflation in order to reduce unemployment below its natural rate.

Substituting the Phillips curve (7.8) in the loss function (7.13) yields

$$L_t = \frac{1}{2} p_t^2 + \frac{\varepsilon}{2} [\tilde{u} - \frac{1}{1-\beta} p_t + \frac{1}{1-\beta} E_{t-1} p_t - \frac{1}{1-\beta} \mu_t]^2 \tag{7.14}$$

From the first order conditions for a minimum of (7.14), i.e. $\partial L_t / \partial p_t = 0$, we obtain the central bank's reaction function to the union's inflationary expectations

$$p_t^D = \frac{\epsilon (1-\beta)}{(1-\beta)^2 + \epsilon} \tilde{u} + \frac{\epsilon}{(1-\beta)^2 + \epsilon} E_{t-1} p_t^D - \frac{\epsilon}{(1-\beta)^2 + \epsilon} \mu_t \tag{7.15}$$

where superscript D stands for 'fully discretionary regime'.

Taking expectations conditional on information at t — 1 of (7.15) gives

$$E_{t-1} p_t^D = \frac{\epsilon}{1-\beta} \tilde{u} \tag{7.16}$$

Equation (7.16) is the reaction function of the union. Upon substituting (7.16) in (7.5) and noting that $\tilde{\ell} \equiv -\tilde{u}$ [8] we get the union's nominal wage demands under the discretionary regime

$$w_t^D = [\frac{\epsilon + (1-\beta)^2}{1-\beta}] \tilde{u} \tag{7.17}$$

The more aggressive unions are (see lemma 7.1), or the more concerned the central bank is about unemployment stabilization (larger ϵ), the higher nominal wage settings.

The resulting price level, real wage and unemployment rate are

$$p_t^D = \frac{\epsilon}{(1-\beta)} \tilde{u} - \frac{\epsilon}{(1-\beta)^2 + \epsilon} \mu_t \tag{7.18}$$

$$w_t^D - p_t^D = (1-\beta) \tilde{u} + \frac{\epsilon}{(1-\beta)^2 + \epsilon} \mu_t \tag{7.19}$$

$$u_t^D = \tilde{u} - \frac{(1-\beta)}{(1-\beta)^2 + \epsilon}\,\mu_t \qquad (7.20)$$

The result indicates that under the fully discretionary regime the central bank's targets, full employment and price stability, can only be reached as long as the union is fully cooperative ($\tilde{u} = 0$, i.e. $d_4 = d_4^*$) and there are no shocks ($\mu_t = 0$). Under these circumstances both the union's and the central bank's loss function are minimized ($W_t = L_t = 0$).

However, if the union is aggressive ($d_4 > d_4^*$) the central bank can no longer reach its targets. In the absence of shocks, inflation (the price level) is higher than socially desired and unemployment below its socially optimal rate. This outcome, however reflects the preferences of the union exactly.

If society does not care about employment ($\varepsilon = 0$), the central bank (as a social planner) is only concerned about inflation. Hence, setting $\varepsilon = 0$ in equations (7.18) — (7.20) yields the results associated with inflation targeting. (See Section IV.3).

IV MONETARY TARGETING AND CENTRAL BANK INDEPENDENCE

As stated by Rogoff (1985, p. 1180) the adoption of intermediate monetary targeting and/or central bank independence may be viewed as an institutional response to the time-consistency problem.

Suppose, for example that through a system of rewards and punishments the central bank's incentives are altered so that it places some direct weight on achieving a low rate of growth for a nominal variable such as the price level, nominal GNP, or the money supply.

Although these alternative targets have different stabilization proportions, Rogoff argues that credibly increasing the central bank's commitment to achieving any of them would reduce the discretionary rate of inflation.

Next, Rogoff considers central bank independence. Rogoff demonstrates that society can make itself better off by selecting an agent to head the central bank who is known to place a greater weight on inflation stabilization (relative to unemployment stabilization) than is embodied in the social loss function L_t.

In this section we characterize the wage setting behaviour under a constant money supply rule, a nominal income rule, inflation targeting and central bank independence. Again, the wage formation strategy of the union can be either aggressive or cooperative.

IV.1 Constant Money Supply Rule

For more than two decades target growth rates for one or another measure of money have often played a key role in the formulation and implementation of monetary policy. European central banks, including in particular the Bundesbank have been especially prominent in this regard.[9] Thus monetary stability may be achieved by maintaining steady growth or even a steady level of money. It is the latter regime that is parametrized in this section.

The central bank announces that it will follow a constant money supply rule. Although it is no easy task to impose an external mechanism that effectively ties the hands of the policy-maker, it is assumed that this precommitment is credible and irrevocable.

Under a constant money rule the aggregate demand equation may be described by

$$y_t = \sigma_1 (m_t - p_t) + v_t \tag{7.21}$$

where v is a transitory demand shock, $v \sim N(0, \sigma_v^2)$, which e.g. may be interpreted as a disturbance in the public's demand for money. The disturbances v and μ are assumed to be independent and serially uncorrelated.

The union sets the wage so as to minimize its expected loss from (7.4) under the condition that the central bank follows a constant money rule (4.1) with $m_t = 0$. Since $E_{t-1}\mu_t = E_{t-1}v_t = 0$ wage demands are not influenced by shocks. Therefore the expected loss of the union is minimized if the wage is negotiated at[10]

$$w_t^M = \frac{\hat{\beta}}{\sigma_1} \tilde{u} \tag{7.22}$$

where superscript M denotes the money supply targeting regime and $\hat{\beta} \equiv \beta + \sigma_1 (1 - \beta)$.

The more aggressive unions are (see Lemma 7.1), or the smaller the absolute value of the price elasticity of aggregate demand[11] (σ_1) the higher nominal wage settings.

The intuition behind this effect is the following. The nominal wage depends on both *real* and *monetary* components. This is shown in equation (7.5).

$$w_t = E_{t-1}p_t - (1 - \beta)\tilde{\ell} \tag{7.5}$$

As can be seen from the first term on the right hand side, the monetary component is identical with the expected price level. Under a constant money supply rule the expected price level is higher the lower σ_1 (this can be seen from equation (A7.2) from appendix A). Hence, the lower σ_1 the higher nominal wage settings. The resulting price level, real wage and unemployment rate are

$$p_t^M = \frac{\beta}{\sigma_1}\tilde{u} + \frac{1}{\hat{\beta}}[(1-\beta)v_t - \mu_t] \tag{7.23}$$

$$w_t^M - p_t^M = (1-\beta)\tilde{u} - \frac{1}{\hat{\beta}}[(1-\beta)v_t - \mu_t] \tag{7.24}$$

$$u_t^M = \tilde{u} - \frac{1}{\hat{\beta}}[(1-\beta)v_t - \mu_t] \tag{7.25}$$

A comparison of (7.17) and (7.22) shows that nominal wage claims under the fully discretionary regime and under a money supply targeting regime are only identical if $\sigma_1 = \beta(1-\beta)/\varepsilon$.

Hence, if $\sigma_1 > \beta(1-\beta)/\varepsilon$ nominal wage demands will be higher under the discretionary regime than under a constant money supply rule. The intuition behind this result is the following. Again using equation (7.5) and noting that the real component of wage setting — $(1-\beta)\tilde{\ell}$, is the same under all monetary regimes, differences in nominal wage claims reflect differences in expected inflation. From equation (7.16) it can be seen that the more concerned the central bank is with unemployment stabilization (the higher ε) the higher expected inflation. Also from equation (A7.2) we know that the higher σ_1 the lower expected inflation under a constant money supply rule. Hence if σ_1 is relatively high (as determined by the inequality above), nominal wage demands will be higher under the discretionary regime than under a constant money supply rule. It is the latter case which is assumed to hold throughout the paper, that is we assume that committing to a constant money supply rule reduces the rate of inflation.[12]

IV.2 Nominal Income Rule

In the eighties economists like Tobin (1983), Bean (1983), and Taylor (1985) discussed nominal GNP as an intermediate target for monetary policy. Therefore now we will analyze the case where the central bank follows a nominal income rule and is supposed to be able to target nominal income accurately, which implies that[13]

$$y_t + p_t = c \tag{7.26}$$

where c denotes the policy determined level of nominal income.

Assuming that the central bank wants to keep nominal income at its equilibrium level c = 0, the union sets the wage under the condition

$$w_t^N = \tilde{u} \tag{7.27}$$

where superscript N stands for nominal income rule.

A comparison of (7.22) and (7.27) shows that nominal wage claims under a money supply rule and under a nominal income rule are only identical if $\sigma_1 = 1$. As pointed out by Funke (1994), p. 7 this reflects that the slope of both aggregate demand curves (see (7.21) and (7.26)) are identical if $\sigma_1 = 1$. However, empirical results suggest that under a money supply rule the absolute value of the price elasticity of aggregate demand is in the short run smaller than 1 ($\sigma_1 < 1$). This implies that nominal wage demands will be higher under a money supply rule than under a nominal income rule. We already know that nominal wage demands are highest under the discretionary regime. Thus, we have $w_t^D > w_t^M > w_t^N$.

Under a nominal income rule the resulting price level, real wage and unemployment rate are:

$$p_t^N = \beta\,\tilde{u} - \mu_t \tag{7.28}$$

$$w_t^N - p_t^N = (1 - \beta)\tilde{u} + \mu_t \tag{7.29}$$

$$u_t^N = \tilde{u} \tag{7.30}$$

As is known, a nominal income rule fully absorbs all demand shocks. Furthermore, in the absence of shocks the inflation rate under a nominal income rule (7.28) is lower than under a money supply rule (7.23) under the assumption that $\sigma_1 < 1$. However, the real wage increase and the unemployment loss are identical in both regimes.

IV.3 Inflation Targeting

Now, the above results will be compared to the case where the central bank targets the inflation rate directly. This case is relevant since in some Anglo-Saxon countries, e.g. Canada, New Zealand and the United Kingdom, monetary authorities are trying to achieve monetary stability by an inflation target. Again, it is assumed that the central bank can target the inflation rate accurately, which in fact, implies that money supply changes transmit quickly and forseeably into price level changes.[14]

Since p_{t-1} is known at the time the central bank commits itself to achieving a target for $p_t - p_{t-1}$ (the inflation rate), price—level targeting and inflation-rate targeting are equivalent in this paper. Therefore from now on we will use the phrases 'price level rule' and 'inflation targeting' to denote the same regime.[15] As stated by Fischer (1994a, pp. 33-34), once monetary control errors are taken into account it becomes important to make the distinction between a *zero inflation target* and a target of *price stability*.

We assume the target inflation rate Δp^* to be zero. By setting $p_t = 0$ in equation (7.21) and rearranging, we obtain the implied evolution of the money supply.[16] An alternative way of deriving the results in this subsection is to set $\varepsilon = 0$ in equations (7.18) — (7.20).

If the central bank follows a strict price level rule, the nominal wage which minimizes the expected loss from (7.3) is given by:

$$w_t^P = (1 - \beta)\tilde{u} \tag{7.31}$$

where superscript P denotes price level targeting. Obviously, nominal wage demands are lower under a price level rule than under nominal income targeting, a constant money supply rule or the discretionary regime. Hence, $w_t^D > w_t^M > w_t^N > w_t^P$. Since the central bank adjusts the money supply so as to keep the price level constant

$$p_t^P = 0 \tag{7.32}$$

$$w_t^P - p_t^P = (1 - \beta)\tilde{u} \tag{7.33}$$

$$u_t^P = \tilde{u} - \frac{\mu_t}{1-\beta} \tag{7.34}$$

Independent of the size of shocks the union can reach its (ex ante) preferred real wage (see (7.4)). However, a supply shock is fully transmitted to unemployment.[17]

IV.4 Central Bank Independence

As stated by Eijffinger (1994, p. 309) in Western Europe there is a clear tendency to establish (more) independent central banks and to foster, thereby, monetary stability. According to the Maastricht Treaty, the independent European Central Bank is fully committed to the goal of price stability in the final stage of EMU by 1997 or later. France and Spain reformed their central bank laws in order to make the Banque de France and the Banco de España more independent of government. Furthermore, in some Anglo-Saxon countries, e.g. Canada, New Zealand and the United

Kingdom, monetary authorities are trying to achieve monetary stability by an inflation target.[18] Finally, countries in Central and Eastern Europe, such as Hungary, Poland and the Czech republic, and in Latin America, Argentina, Chile and Mexico, are looking for a way to strengthen the position of their central bank in order to realize some degree of price stability.

Therefore now, following Rogoff (1985, pp. 1177—1180) we consider central bank independence as an institutional response to the time-consistency problem. Rogoff demonstrates that society can make itself better off by selecting an agent to head the central bank who is known to place a greater weight on inflation stabilization (relative to unemployment stabilization) than is embodied in the social loss function L_t. He also demonstrates that, in choosing among potential candidates, it is never optimal to choose an individual who is known to care 'too little' about unemployment.

Suppose, for example that in period t — 1 society selects an agent to head the central bank in period t. The reputation of this individual is such that it is known that if he is appointed to head the central bank, he will maximize the following objective function

$$I_t = \frac{(1+d_2)}{2} p_t^2 + \frac{\epsilon}{2} u_t^2 \qquad 0 < d_2 < \infty \tag{7.35}$$

When d_2 is strictly greater than zero, then this agent places a greater relative weight on inflation stabilization then society does. Hence following Eijffinger and Schaling (1993b, p. 5) we view the coefficient d_2 as a measure of the political independence of the central bank. The higher d_2 the more independent the central bank. Note that if $d_2 = 0$ equation (7.35) reduces to the social loss function (7.13) and we obtain the results under the fully discretionary regime of Section III.3.

Similarly, the case where $d_2 \to \infty$ is formally equivalent to the inflation targeting regime. More specific, setting $d_2 = \infty$ in equations (7.35) — (7.41) yields the results of Section IV.3. Hence, the case of central bank independence can be viewed as intermediate — as a 'balance' — between rules and discretion.

The algorithm for deriving the time—consistent equilibrium is exactly the same as in Section III.3.

Equations (7.36), (7.37) and (7.38) are the 'I' regime counterparts of equations (7.15), (7.16) and (7.17) respectively:

$$p_t^I = \frac{\varepsilon(1-\beta)}{(1+d_2)(1-\beta)^2+\varepsilon} \tilde{u} + \frac{\varepsilon}{(1+d_2)(1-\beta)^2+\varepsilon} E_{t-1} p_t^I$$

$$- \frac{\varepsilon}{(1+d_2)(1-\beta)^2+\varepsilon} \mu_t \tag{7.36}$$

$$E_{t-1}p_t^I = \frac{\varepsilon}{(1+d_2)(1-\beta)}\tilde{u} \tag{7.37}$$

$$w_t^I = [\frac{\varepsilon(1+d_2)^{-1} + (1-\beta)^2}{(1-\beta)}]\tilde{u} \tag{7.38}$$

where superscript I denotes the independent central bank regime. The more aggressive unions are (see Lemma 7.1), the more concerned society is about unemployment stabilization (larger ϵ) and the less 'conservative' the agent (smaller d_2), the higher nominal wage settings.

The resulting prive level, real wage and unemployment rate are

$$p_t^I = \frac{\varepsilon}{(1+d_2)(1-\beta)}\tilde{u} - \frac{\varepsilon}{(1+d_2)(1-\beta)^2 + \varepsilon}\mu_t \tag{7.39}$$

$$w_t^I - p_t^I = (1-\beta)\tilde{u} + \frac{\varepsilon}{(1+d_2)(1-\beta)^2 + \varepsilon}\mu_t \tag{7.40}$$

$$u_t^I = \tilde{u} - \frac{(1+d_2)(1-\beta)}{(1+d_2)(1-\beta)^2 + \varepsilon}\mu_t \tag{7.41}$$

A comparison of (7.17) and (7.38) shows that nominal wage claims under a fully discretionary regime and under an independent central bank regime are only identical if $d_2 = 0$. Since ex hypothesi $d_2 > 0$, $w_t^D > w_t^I$, i.e. nominal wage demands will be higher under the discretionary regime than under an independent central bank. This result confirms our intuition that credibly increasing the central banker's commitment to inflation stabilization reduces the discretionary rate of (wage) inflation.

Comparing (7.31) and (7.38) shows that nominal wage claims under a price level rule and under an independent central bank are identical if $d_2 \rightarrow \infty$. Since ex hypothesi, $d_2 < \infty$, $w_t^I > w_t^P$, i.e. nominal wage demands under an independent central bank will typically exceed wage demands under an inflation targeting regime.

Now we turn to a comparison of intermediate monetary targeting and central bank independence as institutional devices to overcome the time-consistency problem. A comparison of (7.27) and (7.38) shows that nominal wage claims under a nominal income rule and under an independent central bank are only equal if $d_2 = (\varepsilon - \beta(1-\beta))/\beta(1-\beta)$, hence $w^N_t > w^I_t$, i.e. nominal wage demands will be higher under a nominal income rule than under an independent central bank. We already know that $w_t^D > w_t^M > w_t^N$.[19]

Combining all information we have

$$w_t^P < w_t^I < w_t^N < w_t^M < w_t^D \text{ for } \frac{\varepsilon - (1-\beta)}{\beta(1-\beta)} < d_2 < \infty \quad (7.42)$$

In appendix A to this paper we show that wage setting depends on both *real* and *monetary* components:

$$w_t^A = (1-\beta)\tilde{u} + E_{t-1}p_t^A \quad (A7.3)$$

where superscript A stands for an arbitrary monetary regime. The first component of (A7.3) is invariant across monetary regimes. Note that equation (A7.3) is a slightly more general version of equation (7.5). From Lemma 7.1 it can be seen that this component is associated with the aggressiveness of the union.

The second term of (A7.3) does depend on the choice of monetary regime. From this component it can be seen that the lower the expected inflation rate the lower ceteris paribus nominal wage demands.

Combining (A7.3) with (7.42) we get

$$E_{t-1}p_t^P < E_{t-1}p_t^I < E_{t-1}p_t^N < E_{t-1}p_t^M < E_{t-1}p_t^D$$

for

$$\frac{\varepsilon - \beta(1-\beta)}{\beta(1-\beta)} < d_2 < \infty \quad (7.43)$$

Hence, if the weight on inflation stabilization relative to unemployment stabilization in the preferences of the agent who heads the central bank passes a lower boundary value the independent central bank regime outperforms intermediate monetary targeting regimes (nominal income rule, money supply rule) in tying down inflationary expectations. Note however, that this need not be the typical case. With a different value of d_2 it may well be the other way around.[20]

This completes the description of the results under an independent central bank. We now move on to compare the expected values of the loss functions of the union and society under the five alternative monetary regimes.

V EVALUATION OF MONETARY REGIMES

In this section we calculate the expected values of the loss functions of society under the five alternative monetary regimes. We show that society's optimal framework for monetary stability need not necessarily coincide with central bank independence. First, we evaluate monetary targeting and compare the performance of a money stock rule, a nominal income rule, a price level rule and the fully discretionary regime. Next we evaluate central bank independence. In examining social welfare we focus on supply shocks. The reason is that supply shocks are common to all regimes. A demand (velocity) shock influences social welfare only under a constant money supply rule.

V.1 Monetary Targeting

We are now prepared to evaluate monetary targeting regimes from the perspective of society. But to facilitate exposition in later sections, following Rogoff (1985), pp.1175—1176, we shall first develop a notation for evaluating the expected value of the central bank's loss function under any arbitrary monetary policy regime 'A', $E_{t-1}L_t^A$:

$$E_{t-1}L_t^A = \frac{1}{2}[\epsilon\ \tilde{u}^2] + \Pi^A + \Gamma^{A\,21} \tag{7.44}$$

where Π^A is the mean price level in period t.

$$\Gamma^A \equiv \frac{1}{2}E_{t-1}\ \{\epsilon[\frac{\mu_t}{1-\beta} + (p_t^A - E_{t-1}p_t^A)/(1-\beta)]^2 + (p_t^A - E_{t-1}p_t^A)^2\}$$

Again, the first component of $E_{t-1}L_t^A$, $\frac{1}{2}[\epsilon\ \tilde{u}^2]$ is nonstochastic and invariant across monetary regimes. It represents the deadweight loss due to the labour market distortion ($\tilde{u} > 0$ due to $d_4 > d_4^*$, see lemma 7.1). This loss cannot be reduced through monetary policy in a time-consistent rational expectations equilibrium. The second term, Π^A, depends on the mean inflation rate. This term is also nonstochastic but does depend on the choice of monetary policy regime.

The final term, Γ^A, represents the 'stabilization' component of the loss function. It measures how succesfully the central bank offsets disturbances to stabilize unemployment and inflation around their mean values.

By substituting the results relevant for the central bank ((7.18) and (7.20), (7.23) and (7.25), (7.28) and (7.30), (7.32) and (7.34)) into society's loss function (7.13) and taking expectations we obtain the M, N, P and D and regime counterparts of expression (7.44). Abstracting from the (common) deadweight loss, one gets

$$\Pi^M + \Gamma^M = \frac{\beta^2}{2\sigma_1^2}\tilde{u}^2 + \frac{1+\epsilon(\sigma_1-1)^2}{2\hat{\beta}^2}\sigma_\mu^2 + \frac{[\epsilon+(1-\beta)^2]}{2\hat{\beta}^2}\sigma_v^2 \tag{7.45}$$

where $\hat{\beta} \equiv \beta + \sigma_1(1-\beta)$

$$\Pi^N + \Gamma^N = \frac{\beta^2}{2}\,\tilde{u}^2 + \frac{1}{2}\sigma_\mu^2 \tag{7.46}$$

$$\Pi^P + \Gamma^P = \frac{\varepsilon}{2(1-\beta)^2}\,\sigma_\mu^2 \tag{7.47}$$

$$\Pi^D + \Gamma^D = \frac{\varepsilon^2}{2(1-\beta)^2}\,\tilde{u}^2 + \frac{\varepsilon}{2[(1-\beta)^2+\varepsilon]}\,\sigma_\mu^2 \tag{7.48}$$

As long as the union is cooperative ($d_4 = d_4^*$ and consequently $\tilde{u} = 0$) $\Pi^A = 0$, the choice of regime only depends on the stabilization component of the loss function.
It can then be shown that

$$\Gamma^D < \Gamma^N < \Gamma^M < \Gamma^P$$

for

$$\varepsilon > \frac{(1-\beta)^2}{(1-\beta)[2\sigma_1 - 1] + \beta}\,, \quad \sigma_v^2 = 0 \tag{7.49}$$

Hence the fully discretionary regime outperforms all intermediate targeting regimes in stabilizing supply shocks.

However, if the union becomes aggressive ($d_4 > d_4^*$ and $\tilde{u} > 0$) results differ significanly. In the absence of shocks society would prefer a price level rule to a nominal income rule, a money supply rule or the fully discretionary regime, because

$$\Pi^P < \Pi^N < \Pi^M < \Pi^D \quad \text{for} \quad \frac{\beta(1-\beta)}{\varepsilon} < \sigma_1 < 1 \tag{7.50}$$ [22]

As in Funke (1994, p. 336) the reason is, that under a price level rule the central bank varies the money supply in such a way that a strong union reaches its real wage target with zero price inflation, thereby avoiding the inflationary effect of higher nominal wage demands under a nominal income, a money supply rule or the fully discretionary regime.

From (7.49) and (7.50) it can be seen that a nominal income rule outperforms a constant money supply rule both in offsetting supply shocks ($\Gamma^N < \Gamma^M$) and in reducing the social loss associated with a high average inflation rate ($\Pi^N < \Pi^M$). Hence, obviously the central bank will never view a constant money supply rule as an optimal monetary arrangement.

From (7.49) it can be seen that the central bank's response to unanticipated supply shocks is best with discretion. This means that discretion gives the central bank the option of reacting optimally to domestic real shocks. On the other hand from (7.50) it can be seen that a nominal income rule outperforms the fully discretionary regime in bringing down the time-consistent average rate of wage inflation.

By choosing a nominal income rule the central bank reduces its *credibility* problem vis-à-vis the union but loses the option of reacting optimally to domestic real shocks, i.e. it loses *flexibility*. As shown by Lohmann (1992) and Alogoskoufis (1994), which of the two forces dominates depends on the relative strength of the two distortions, namely the inefficiency of the high natural rate of unemployment which produces the high inflation problem, and the inefficiency arising from pre-set nominal contacts that cannot take account of real shocks.

Subtracting (7.46) from (7.48) the per-period difference in welfare losses between the fully discretionary regime and a nominal income rule is given by,

$$E_{t-1}[L_t^D - L_t^N] = \frac{1}{2}\left[\frac{\epsilon^2 - \beta^2(1-\beta)^2}{(1-\beta)^2}\tilde{u}^2 - \frac{(1-\beta)^2}{(1-\beta)^2+\epsilon}\sigma_\mu^2\right] \tag{7.51}$$

A nominal income rule would dominate a fully discretionary regime if

$$\tilde{u} > \frac{(1-\beta)^2\,\sigma_\mu}{\sqrt{[(1-\beta)^2+\epsilon]}\,\sqrt{[\epsilon^2-\beta^2(1-\beta)^2]}} \tag{7.52}$$

To give a numerical example, with β being about 0.7, $\epsilon = 1$ and a standard deviation in productivity of the order of 0.02 — which according to Alogoskoufis (1994, p. 211) is not atypical — the inefficiency in the natural rate of unemployment must exceed about 0.18 percentage points to make implementing a nominal income rule worthwhile.[23]

The choice between a nominal income rule and price level (inflation rate) targeting also depends on the level of the natural rate of unemployment. Subtracting (7.47) from (7.46) the per-period difference in welfare losses between a nominal income rule and a price level rule is given by

$$E_{t-1}[L_t^N - L_t^P] = \frac{1}{2}\left[\beta^2\tilde{u}^2 + \frac{(1-\beta)^2-\epsilon}{(1-\beta)^2}\sigma_\mu^2\right] \tag{7.53}$$

Hence a price level rule dominates a nominal income rule if

$$\tilde{u} > \frac{\sqrt{[\epsilon-(1-\beta)^2]}\,\sigma_\mu}{(1-\beta)\beta} \tag{7.54}$$

Using the same parameter values ũ must exceed about 9.1 percentage points to make adoption of a price level rule worthwhile.

For intermediate values of ũ (0.18 < ũ < 9.1) it can be shown that a nominal income rule outperforms both the fully discretionary regime and a price level rule.

$$E_{t-1}L_t^D > E_{t-1}L_t^N < E_{t-1}L_t^P$$

for

$$\frac{(1-\beta)^2\sigma_\mu}{\sqrt{(1-\beta)^2+\epsilon]}\;\sqrt{[\epsilon^2-\beta^2(1-\beta)^2]}} < \tilde{u} < \frac{\sqrt{[\epsilon-(1-\beta)^2]}\;\sigma_\mu}{(1-\beta)\beta} \qquad (7.55)$$

From (7.52), (7.54) and (7.55) it can be seen that the optimal monetary regime from the perspective of the central bank (being concerned with social welfare) depends upon the level of the natural rate of unemployment.

By using Lemma 7.1 we can state the following. Loosely speaking, as the union becomes more aggressive the central bank moves from the fully discretionary regime to a nominal income rule. With an even higher weight placed on the real wage target, a nominal income rule in turn is dominated by an inflation targeting regime.

V.2 Central Bank Independence

In this section we evaluate central bank independence as an institutional device to overcome the time-consistency problem.

The expected loss for society at the end of t - 1 for period t ($E_{t-1} L_t^I$) under central bank independence is calculated by substituting the results under the I-regime (7.49) and (7.50) into society's loss function and taking expectations. Abstracting from the (regime-invariant) deadweight loss, one gets

$$\Pi^I + \Gamma^I = \frac{\varepsilon^2}{2[(1+d_2)(1-\beta)]^2}\,\tilde{u}^2 + \frac{\varepsilon[(1+d_2)^2\,(1-\beta)^2 + \varepsilon]}{2[(1+d_2)\,(1-\beta)^2 + \varepsilon]^2}\,\sigma_\mu^2 \qquad (7.56)$$

Comparing (7.56) with the expected losses for society under the M, N, P and D-regimes (7.45) - (7.48) reveals the following. Again as long as the union is cooperative ($d_4 = d_4^*$ and consequently $\tilde{u} = 0$) Π^A is 0, the choice of regime only depends on the stabilization component of the loss function. It can then be shown that

$$\Gamma^D < \Gamma^N < \Gamma^I < \Gamma^M < \Gamma^P$$

for

$$\varepsilon > \frac{(1-\beta)^2}{(1-\beta)\,[2\sigma_1 - 1] + \beta},$$

$$\frac{\varepsilon + (1-\beta)^2}{\varepsilon - (1-\beta)^2} < d_2 < r_2,\ \sigma_v^2 = 0^{24} \qquad (7.57)$$

Hence the independent central bank regime is intermediate between a nominal income rule and a money stock rule in stabilizing supply shocks.

Again, if the union becomes aggressive ($d_4 > d_4^*$ and $\tilde{u} > 0$) results differ significantly. In the absence of shocks society would prefer an independent central bank to a nominal income or a money stock rule, because

$$\Pi^P < \Pi^I < \Pi^N < \Pi^M < \Pi^D$$

for

$$\frac{\beta(1-\beta)}{\varepsilon} < \sigma_1 < 1 \text{ and } d_2 > \frac{\varepsilon - \beta(1-\beta)}{\beta(1-\beta)} \qquad (7.58)$$

From (7.57) it can be seen that the central bank's response to unanticipated supply shocks is better with a nominal income rule than when it is an independent agent. On the other hand from (7.58) it can be seen that the independent central bank regime outperforms a nominal income rule in bringing down the time-consistent average rate of wage inflation. By selecting an agent to head the central bank that is more inflation averse than society, society reduces its *credibility* problem vis-à-vis the union but loses the option of a better reaction to domestic real shocks, i.e. it loses *flexibility*.

As stated before, which of the two forces dominates depends on the relative strength of the two distortions. Subtracting (7.56) from (7.46) the per period difference in welfare losses between a nominal income rule and the independent central bank regime is given by,

$$E_{t-1}\,(L_t^N - L_t^I) = \tfrac{1}{2}\,\Big[\frac{\beta^2[(1+d_2)(1-\beta)]^2 - \varepsilon^2}{[(1+d_2)(1-\beta)]^2}\,\tilde{u}^2$$

$$- \frac{(1+d_2)(1-\beta)^2\,[\varepsilon(1+d_2) - 2\varepsilon - (1+d_2)(1-\beta)^2]}{[(1+d_2)(1-\beta)^2 + \varepsilon]^2}\,\sigma_\mu^2\Big] \qquad (7.59)$$

The independent central bank regime would dominate a nominal income rule if

$$\tilde{u} > \frac{(1+d_2)^{3/2}\,(1-\beta)^2\,\sqrt{[\varepsilon(1+d_2)-2\varepsilon-(1+d_2)(1-\beta)^2]}}{[(1+d_2)(1-\beta)^2+\varepsilon]\,\sqrt{\beta^2[(1+d_2)(1-\beta)]^2-\varepsilon^2}}\,\sigma_\mu \tag{7.60}$$

To give a numerical example, with d_2 being about 4 and the same parameter values as before, $\tilde{u}$ must exceed about 6.9 percentage points to make setting up an independent central bank worthwhile.

The choice between an independent central bank and price level (inflation rate) targeting also depends on the level of the natural rate of unemployment. Subtracting (7.47) from (7.56) the per—period difference in welfare losses between the independent central bank regime and a price level rule is given by

$$E_{t-1}\,(L_t^I - L_t^P)$$

$$= \frac{\varepsilon^2}{2}\left[\frac{1}{[(1+d_2)(1-\beta)]^2}\,\tilde{u}^2 - \frac{[2(1+d_2)(1-\beta)^2+\varepsilon-(1-\beta)^2]}{(1-\beta)^2[(1+d_2)(1-\beta)^2+\varepsilon]^2}\,\sigma_\mu^2\right] \tag{7.61}$$

Hence a price level rule dominates the independent central bank regime if

$$\tilde{u} > \frac{[(1+d_2)(1-\beta)]\,\sqrt{2(1+d_2)(1-\beta)^2+\varepsilon-(1-\beta)^2]}}{(1-\beta)\,[(1+d_2)(1-\beta)^2+\varepsilon]} \tag{7.62}$$

Using the same parameters values $\tilde{u}$ must exceed about 9.3 percentage points to make adoption of a price level rule worthwhile.

For intermediate values of $\tilde{u}$ $(6.9 < \tilde{u} < 9.3)$ it can be shown that the independent central bank regime outperforms both a nominal income rule and a price level rule.

$$E_{t-1}\,L_t^N > E_{t-1}\,L_t^I < E_{t-1}\,L_t^P$$

for

$$\frac{(1+d_2)^{3/2}(1-\beta)^2\,\sqrt{[\varepsilon(1+d_2)\;-\;2\varepsilon\;-\;(1+d_2)(1-\beta)^2]}}{[(1+d_2)(1-\beta)^2\;+\;\varepsilon]\,\sqrt{\beta^2[(1+d_2)(1-\beta)]^2\;-\;\varepsilon^2}}\,\sigma_\mu < \tilde{u}$$

$$< \frac{[(1+d_2)(1-\beta)]\sqrt{[2(1+d_2)(1-\beta)^2+\varepsilon-(1-\beta)^2]}}{(1-\beta)[(1+d_2)(1-\beta)^2+\varepsilon]}\sigma_\mu \qquad (7.63)$$

Combining (7.63) with (7.52), (7.54) and (7.55) we obtain Table 7.2

Table 7.2 Society's optimal monetary regime

$\tilde{u}$	$0 < \tilde{u} < \tilde{u}_1$	$\tilde{u}_1 < \tilde{u} < \tilde{u}_2$	$\tilde{u}_2 < \tilde{u} < \tilde{u}_3$	$\tilde{u}_3 < \tilde{u}$
Optimal Regime	D	N	I	P

where

$$\tilde{u}_1 \equiv \frac{(1-\beta)^2\sigma_\mu}{\sqrt{[(1-\beta)^2+\varepsilon]}\sqrt{[\varepsilon^2-\beta^2(1-\beta)^2]}}$$

$$\tilde{u}_2 \equiv \frac{(1+d_2)^{3/2}(1-\beta)^2\sqrt{[\varepsilon(1+d_2)-2\varepsilon-(1+d_2)(1-\beta)^2]}\ \sigma_\mu}{[(1+d_2)(1-\beta)^2+\varepsilon]\sqrt{\beta^2[(1+d_2)(1-\beta)]^2-\varepsilon^2}}$$

$$\tilde{u}_3 \equiv \frac{[(1+d_2)(1-\beta)]\sqrt{[2(1+d_2)(1-\beta)^2+\varepsilon-(1-\beta)^2]}\,\sigma_\mu}{(1-\beta)[(1+d_2)(1-\beta)^2+\varepsilon]}$$

From this table it can be seen that society's optimal framework for monetary stability need not necessarily coincide with central bank independence. By using Lemma 7.1 we can state the following. Loosely speaking as the union becomes more aggressive society moves from the fully discretionary regime to a nominal income rule. With a higher weight on the real wage target a nominal income rule is dominated by the independent central bank regime. With an even higher weight placed on the real wage target, the independent central bank regime in turn, is dominated by an inflation targeting regime.

This concludes the comparison of monetary regimes. We now move on to an investigation of the factors influencing the optimal degree of central bank independence. This is the subject of Section VI.

VI THE OPTIMAL DEGREE OF CENTRAL BANK INDEPENDENCE

In this section we show that the optimal degree of central bank independence is contingent on the labour market regime. More specific we show that the more aggressive the union the higher the optimal degree of central bank independence.

VI.1 The Rogoff Theorem

First we reproduce Rogoff's (1985) proof that for society it is optimal to select an agent to head the independent central bank who places a large, but finite, weight on inflation. The optimal degree of central bank independence d_2^* is defined as that value of d_2 that minimizes the expected value of the loss function of society $E_{t-1} L_t^I$.

Abstracting from the (regime-invariant) deadweight loss the expected value of the social loss function under regime 'I' is

$$\Pi^I + \Gamma^I = \frac{\varepsilon^2}{2[(1+d_2)(1-\beta)]^2}\tilde{u}^2 + \frac{\varepsilon[(1+d_2)^2(1-\beta)^2 + \varepsilon]}{2[(1+d_2)(1-\beta)^2 + \varepsilon]^2}\sigma_\mu^2 \quad (7.56)$$

To solve for the value of d_2 that minimizes $E_{t-1} L_t^I$, differentiate (7.56) with respect to d_2

$$\frac{\partial E_{t-1} L_t^I}{\partial d_2} = \frac{\partial \Pi^I}{\partial d_2} + \frac{\partial \Gamma^I}{\partial d_2} \quad (7.64)$$

$$\frac{\partial \Gamma^I}{\partial d_2} = \frac{\varepsilon^2(1-\beta)^2 d_2\, \sigma_\mu^2}{[(1+d_2)(1-\beta)^2 + \varepsilon]^3} \quad (7.65)$$

$$\frac{\partial \Pi^I}{\partial d_2} = \frac{-\varepsilon^2 \tilde{u}^2}{(1+d_2)^3(1-\beta)^2} \quad (7.66)$$

We are now ready to prove:

Proposition 7.1: For $\tilde{u} > 0$, $0 < d_2^* < \infty$.

Proof: note that $d_2 > -1$ by assumption. Thus by inspection of (7.66), $\partial\Pi^I/\partial d_2$ is strictly negative. Note also, by inspection of (7.65), that $\partial\Gamma^I/\partial d_2$ is strictly negative for $-[\varepsilon + (1-\beta)^2]/(1-\beta)^2 < d_2 < 0$, zero when $d_2 =$

0 and positive for $d_2 > 0$.

Therefore, $\partial E_{t-1} L_t^I/\partial d_2$ is strictly negative for $d_2 \leq 0$. $\partial E_{t-1} L_t^I/\partial d_2$ must change from negative to positive at some sufficienlty large value of d_2, since as d_2 approaches positive infinity, $\partial \Gamma^I/\partial d_2$ converges to zero at rate d_2^{-2}, whereas $\partial \Pi^I/\partial d_2$ converges to zero at rate d_2^{-3}. Therefore, $d_2^* < \infty$.[25]

Q.E.D.

VI.2 Wage Formation and the Optimal Degree of Central Bank Independence

Proposition (7.1) is Rogoff's theorem. In his analysis the labour market distortion is exogenous. In the present analysis this is no longer the case. Hence, the following can be seen as an extension of the Rogoff theorem.

First, using a graphical method we develop an alternative way of determining the optimal degree of central bank independence. Next, we show how this result is conditioned on the supply side effect of inflation.

By setting (7.1) equal to zero we obtain the first-order condition for a minimum of $E_{t-1} L_t^I$

$$0 = \frac{\partial \Pi^I}{\partial d_2} + \frac{\partial \Gamma^I}{\partial d_2} \tag{7.67}$$

Substituting (7.65) and (7.66) into (7.67) yields

$$\frac{-\varepsilon^2 \tilde{u}^2}{(1-\beta)^2(1+d_2)^3} + \frac{\varepsilon^2(1-\beta)^2 d_2 \sigma_\mu^2}{[(1+d_2)(1-\beta)^2+\varepsilon]^3} = 0 \tag{7.68}$$

Equation (7.68) determines d_2^* as an implicit function of ε, $\tilde{u}$, σ_μ^2 and β. A solution for d_2^* always exists and is unique.

To see this we adapt a graphical method used by Cukierman (1992, pp. 170-172) in the context of a dynamic game.

Rewrite (7.68) as

$$d_2 = \frac{[(1+d_2)(1-\beta)^2+\varepsilon]^3 \tilde{u}^2}{\sigma_\mu^2(1-\beta)^4(1+d_2)^3} \equiv F(d_2) \tag{7.69}$$

Note that the function $F(d_2)$ on the right-hand side of equation (7.69) is monotonically decreasing in d_2 that

$$F(0) = \frac{[(1-\beta)^2+\varepsilon]^3\tilde{u}^2}{\sigma_\mu^2(1-\beta)^4}, \quad \lim_{d_2\to\infty} F(d_2) = \frac{(1-\beta)^2\tilde{u}^2}{\sigma_\mu^2}$$

and

$$\frac{(1-\beta)^2\tilde{u}^2}{\sigma_\mu^2} < F(d_2) < \frac{[(1-\beta)^2+\varepsilon]^3\tilde{u}^2}{\sigma_\mu^2(1-\beta)^4}$$

(These statements are demonstrated in appendix D to this chapter).

We are now ready to prove:

Proposition 7.2:

$$\frac{(1-\beta)^2\tilde{u}^2}{\sigma_\mu^2} < d_2^* < \frac{[(1-\beta)^2+\varepsilon]^3\tilde{u}^2}{\sigma_\mu^2(1-\beta)^4}$$

Proof: the left-hand side of (7.69) is a 45-degree straight line through the origin. Since $F(0) = [(1-\beta)^2+\varepsilon]^3\tilde{u}^2/\sigma_\mu^2(1-\beta)^4$ and $\partial F/\partial d_2 < 0$ these two functions must intersect at one and only on point. Moreover, since $\tilde{u}^2(1-\beta)/\sigma^2_\mu < F(d_2) < [(1-\beta)^2 + \varepsilon]^3\tilde{u}^2/\sigma^2_\mu(1-\beta)^4$, the intersection occurs at a value of d_2 that is bounded between $(1-\beta)^2\tilde{u}^2/\sigma_\mu^2$ and $[(1-\beta)^2+\varepsilon]^3\tilde{u}^2/\sigma^2_\mu(1-\beta)^4$

Q.E.D.

Figure 7.3 illustrates the argument graphically. Clearly a solution for d_2 exists and is unique.

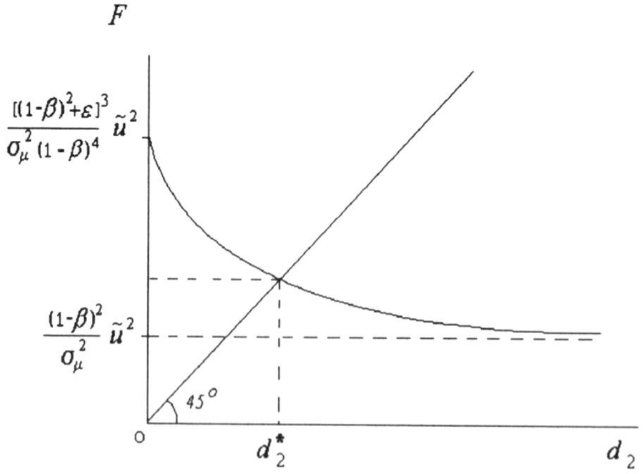

Figure 7.3 *The optimal degree of central bank independence*

We are now ready to prove:

Proposition 7.3: The more aggressive the union (the higher d_4) the higher the optimal degree of central bank independence.

Proof: from Appendix D, $\partial F / \partial d_4 > 0$, this implies that when d_4 goes up, the curve $F(d_2)$ in Figure 7.3 shifts upward. As a consequence the equilibrium value of d_2 increases.

The intuition behind this result is the following. If the union becomes more aggressive ceteris paribus nominal wage settlements go up.[26] The higher nominal wage settlements tend to have inflationary consequences. However, if society wants maximum social welfare it will choose an agent to head the central banking institution who will not accommodate these demands. This means that by putting the 'monetary screws' upon wage pressures inflation is stopped before it can emerge. This completes the section on the optimal degree of central bank independence.

VII CONCLUDING REMARKS

In many European countries large unions figure prominently in the wage formation process. This paper has investigated the interdependence of the choice of domestic monetary regime and the wage formation process.[27] Unlike in papers by Barro and Gordon (1983a, 1983b), Canzoneri (1985) and Lohmann (1992), the private sector here has an active strategic role.

The main implication of this is that the labour market distortion, which is assumed exogenous in the existing literature in this paper, depends on the aggressiveness of the union. As shown in Lemma 7.1, if the trade union becomes more aggressive the natural rate of unemployment is pushed upwards. The implications of this mechanism are twofold.

First, as shown in Section V society's optimal framework for monetary stability — being contingent on the level of the natural rate of unemployment — also depends on the aggressiveness of the union. Loosely speaking as the union becomes more aggressive society moves from the fully discretionary regime (which is first best in terms of *flexibility*) via GNP targeting and the independent central bank regime towards inflation targeting (which is first best in terms of *credibility*).

This means that in general it need not be optimal for society to have an independent central bank. Secondly, as shown in Proposition 7.3, if society's optimal framework for monetary stability does coincide with central bank independence, the more aggressive the union the higher the optimal degree of central bank independence. This means that society's optimal central banking institution is contingent on the labour market regime.

APPENDIX A7: MACROECONOMIC OUTCOMES UNDER ANY ARBITRARY INTERMEDIATE MONETARY TARGETING REGIME

In this appendix we develop a notation for deriving the macroeconomic results, i.e. the nominal wage, the price level, the real wage and the unemployment rate under an arbitrary intermediate monetary target. The results in Section IV can then be viewed as special cases of the more general results derived below.

A7.1 Macroeconomic Results

By equating the aggregate supply curve (7.7) and the aggregate demand curve (7.21) we get the following equation in the price level.

$$p_t^A = \frac{1}{\hat{\beta}}\left[\beta E_{t-1} p_t^A + \sigma_1 (1-\beta) m_t^A + \beta(1-\beta)\tilde{u} + (1-\beta)v_t - \mu_t\right] \quad (A7.1)$$

where $\hat{\beta} \equiv \beta + \sigma_1(1-\beta)$ and superscript A stands for an arbitrary monetary targeting regime, A = M, N, P. Taking expectations conditional on information at the end of t — 1 of (A7.1) yields

$$E_{t-1}p_t^A = \frac{\beta}{\sigma_1}\tilde{u} + E_{t-1}m_t^A \tag{A7.2}$$

In Section III.2 we showed that $\tilde{\ell} \equiv -\tilde{u}$. Substituting the latter in (7.5) and adding superscripts we get

$$w_t^A = (1-\beta)\tilde{u} + E_{t-1}p_t^A \tag{A7.3}$$

It is interesting to see that wage setting has both *real* and *monetary* components. The first component is invariant across monetary targeting regimes. From Lemma 7.1 it can be seen that this component is associated with the aggressiveness of the union.

The second term does depend on the choice of monetary targeting regime. From this component it can be seen that the lower the expected inflation — i.e. the more credible the monetary target — the lower ceteris paribus nominal wage demands.

Subtracting (A7.2) from (A7.1) we obtain the following expression for unanticipated inflation.

$$p_t^A - E_{t-1}p_t^A = \frac{1}{\hat{\beta}}(\sigma_1(1-\beta)(m_t^A - E_{t-1}m_t^A) + (1-\beta)v_t - \mu_t) \tag{A7.4}$$

Substituting the latter expression into (7.8) yields the solution for unemployment

$$u_t^A = \tilde{u} - \frac{1}{1-\beta}(p_t^A - E_{t-1}p_t^A + \mu_t) \tag{A7.5}$$

Now we turn to the determination of the real wage. Subtracting p_t^A from both sides of (A7.3) yields

$$w_t^A - p_t^A = (1-\beta)\tilde{u} - (p_t^A - E_{t-1}p_t^A) \tag{A7.6}$$

Finally, subtracting (A7.6) from (A7.3) we get an expression for the price level

$$p_t^A = w_t^A - (w_t^A - p_t^A) \tag{A7.7}$$

where the first term on the right hand side is known from (A7.3), whilst the second term follows from (A7.6).

A7.2 Money Stock Rule and Nominal Income Rule (A = M, N)

In case of a money stock rule $m_t^M = E_{t-1}m_t^M = 0$. It is then straightforward to derive the results of Section IV.1. First, compute unanticipated inflation from (A7.4) and then proceed along the lines suggested above.

Targeting nominal income ($y_t + p_t$) at c, where c = 0 implies the following rule for the evolution of the money supply[28]

$$m_t^N = d_3\, p_t^N - \frac{1}{\sigma_1} v_t \qquad \text{(A7.8)}$$

where $d_3 \equiv \sigma_1 - 1/1$

Hence, under a nominal income rule the central bank accommodates changes in the price level. It can be easily seen that $\partial d_3/\partial \sigma_1 = 1/\sigma^2_1 > 0$.

Hence, the greater the price elasticity of aggregate demand (or equivalently the more effective monetary policy relative to fiscal policy)[29] the higher the degree of monetary accommodation. Taking expectations of (A7.8) yields

$$E_{t-1}m_t^N = d_3\, E_{t-1}p_t^N \qquad \text{(A7.9)}$$

Subtracting (A7.9) from (A7.8), substituting the result in (A7.4) and rearranging we obtain an expression for unanticipated inflation. The results of Section IV.2 can then easily be derived.

A7.3 Price Level (Inflation Rate) Targeting (A = P)

The case of price level targeting is analytically the simplest. Ex hypothesi the central bank credibly commits to a zero inflation rate. Hence $p_t^P = E_{t-1}p_t^P = 0$. By using (A7.3), (A7.5) and (A7.6) the results for the nominal wage, the real wage and the unemployment rate as presented in Section IV.3 can then be obtained without difficulty.

APPENDIX B7: EXPECTED LOSS OF THE UNION UNDER ALTERNATIVE MONETARY REGIMES

In this appendix we calculate the expected values of the loss functions of the union under the five alternative regimes i.e. the fully discretionary regime, a constant money supply rule, a nominal income rule, a price level rule, and central bank independence.

In examining union welfare we focus on supply shocks. The reason is that supply shocks are common to all regimes. A demand (velocity) shock influences social welfare only under a constant money supply rule. We show that the choice of the optimal regime depends upon the aggressiveness of the union.

The expected loss of the union at the end of t—1 for period t ($E_{t-1} W_t^A$) under the four alternative regimes is calculated by substituting the results under each regime, ((7.8) and (7.9), (7.24) and (7.25), (7.29) and (7.30), (7.33) and (7.34), (7.40) and (7.41)) into the union's loss function (2.4) and taking expectations. One obtains:

$$E_{t-1}W_t^M = H + \frac{d_4 + (\sigma_1 - 1)^2}{2\hat{\beta}^2}\sigma_\mu^2 + \frac{1 + d_4(1-\beta)^2}{2\hat{\beta}^2}\sigma_v^2 \quad (B7.1)$$

$$E_{t-1}W_t^N = H + \frac{d_4}{2}\sigma_\mu^2 \quad (B7.2)$$

$$E_{t-1}W_t^P = H + \frac{1}{2(1-\beta)^2}\sigma_\mu^2 \quad (B7.3)$$

$$E_{t-1}W_t^D = H + \frac{(1-\beta)^2 + d_4\epsilon^2}{2[(1-\beta)^2 + \epsilon]^2}\sigma_\mu^2 \quad (B7.4)$$

$$E_{t-1} W_t^I = H + \frac{(1+d_2)^2 (1-\beta)^2 + d_4 \varepsilon^2}{2[(1+d_2)(1-\beta)^2 + \varepsilon]^2}\sigma_\mu^2 \quad (B7.5)$$

where

$$H \equiv \frac{1}{2}[d_4\tau^2 + \ell^{*2}] + \tilde{u}\,[\frac{(d_4(1-\beta)^2 + 1)}{2}\tilde{u} + \ell^* - d_4\tau(1-\beta)]$$

The first component of $E_{t-1}W_t^A$, i.e. H, is non-stochastic and invariant across monetary regimes. It represents the deadweight loss due to the union's preferences (τ, ℓ^*) and due to the labour market distortion ($\tilde{u} > 0$ due to $d_4 > d_4^*$, see Lemma 7.1). This loss cannot be reduced through monetary policy in a time-consistent rational expectations equilibrium.

The stochastic terms depend on the choice of monetary policy regime and represent the 'stabilization' component of the loss function. They measure how successfully employment and real wages are stabilized around their mean values.

(B7.1) describes the expected loss of the union under a constant money rule, (B7.2) the expected loss of the union under a nominal income rule, (B7.3) the expected loss of the union under a price level rule, (B7.4) the expected loss of the union under the fully discretionary regime and (B7.5) under central bank independence.

Comparing (B7.1), (B7.2), (B7.3) (B7.4) and (B7.5), reveals that - as in Funke (1994, p.335)[30] - the preferred regime on part of the union depends only on the size of the shocks. In the absence of shocks ($\sigma_\mu^2 = \sigma_v^2 = 0$), the loss of the union is identical under all five regimes. When demand shocks are large, a nominal income rule or a price rule is preferable to the union.

In the case of supply shocks, subtracting (B7.2) from (B7.4) the per-period difference in welfare losses between the fully discretionary regime and a nominal income rule is given by,

$$E_{t-1}[W_t^D - W_t^N] = \frac{(1-\beta)^2}{2}\left[\frac{1 - d_4(1-\beta)^2 - 2d_4\epsilon}{[(1-\beta)^2 + \epsilon]^2}\right]\sigma_\mu^2 \tag{B7.6}$$

The fully discretionary regime would dominate a nominal income rule if,

$$d_4 > \frac{1}{(1-\beta)^2 + 2\epsilon} \tag{B7.7}$$

To give a numerical example, with β being about 0.7 and $\varepsilon = 1$ the weight assigned to real wage stabilization relative to employment stabilization in the preferences of the union must exceed about 0.5 to make abandoning a nominal income rule worthwhile.

The choice between the discretionary regime and price level (inflation rate) targeting also depends on how much weight d_4 is placed on the real wage target.

Subtracting (B7.3) from (B7.4) the per-period difference in welfare losses between discretion and an inflation target is given by

$$E_{t-1}[W_t^D - W_t^P] = \frac{\epsilon}{2}\left[\frac{d_4(1-\beta)^2\epsilon - 2(1-\beta)^2 - \epsilon}{(1-\beta)^2[(1-\beta)^2 + \epsilon]^2}\right]\sigma_\mu^2 \tag{B7.8}$$

Hence a price level rule dominates the fully discretionary regime if

$$d_4 > \frac{2(1-\beta)^2\epsilon^{-1} + 1}{(1-\beta)^2} \tag{B7.9}$$

Using the same parameter values d_4 must exceed about 13.2 to make adoption of a price level rule worthwhile. For intermediate values of d_4 ($0.5 < d_4 < 13.2$) it can be shown that the discretionary regime outperforms both a nominal income rule and a price level rule.

$$E_{t-1}W_t^N > E_{t-1}W_t^D < E_{t-1}E\ W_t^P$$

for

$$\frac{1}{(1-\beta)^2 + 2\epsilon} < d_4 < \frac{1 + 2\epsilon^{-1}(1-\beta)^2}{(1-\beta)^2} \tag{B7.10}$$

Subtracting (B7.5) from (B7.4) the per-period difference in welfare losses between the fully discretionary regime and the independent central bank regime is given by

$$E_{t-1}[W_t^D - W_t^I] = \frac{\varepsilon d_2 (1-\beta)^2}{2}$$

$$[\frac{(d_4\varepsilon - 1)\ [2(1-\beta)^2 + d_2(1-\beta)^2 + 2\varepsilon] - \varepsilon d_2}{[(1-\beta)^2 + \varepsilon]^2\ [(1+d_2)\ (1-\beta)^2 + \varepsilon]^2}]\ \sigma_\mu^2 \tag{B7.11}$$

an independent central bank dominates the fully discretionary regime if

$$d_4 > \frac{1 + \varepsilon^{-1}(1-\beta)^2}{(1-\beta)^2 + 2\varepsilon(2 + d_2)^{-1}} \tag{B7.12}$$

To give a numerical example, with the same parameter values as before (β being about 0.7 and $\epsilon = 1$) the weight assigned to real wage stabilization relative to employment stabilization in the preferences of the union must exceed about 2.6 to make abandoning the discretionary regime worthwhile.

The choice between an independent central bank and prive level (inflation) targeting also depends on how much weight is placed on the real wage target.

Subtracting (B7.3) from (B7.5) the per-period difference in welfare losses between the independent central bank regime and an inflation target is given by

$$E_{t-1}[W_t^I - W_t^P] = \frac{1}{2}\ [\frac{\varepsilon[d_4\varepsilon(1-\beta)^2 - 2(1+d_2)(1-\beta)^2 - \varepsilon]}{(1-\beta)^2[(1+d_2)(1-\beta)^2 + \varepsilon]^2}]\ \sigma_\mu^2 \tag{B7.13}$$

Hence a price level rule dominates an independent central bank if

$$d_4 > \frac{1 + 2(1 + d_2)\varepsilon^{-1}(1 - \beta)^2}{(1 - \beta)^2} \tag{B7.14}$$

Using the same parameter values d_4 must exceed about 21.1 to make adoption of a price level rule worthwhile. For intermediate values of d_4 (2.6 < d_4 < 21.1) it can be shown that having an independent central bank outperforms both the fully discretionary regime and a price level rule.

$$E_{t-1} W_t^D > E_{t-1} W_t^I < E_{t-1} W_t^P$$

for

$$\frac{1 + \varepsilon^{-1}(1 - \beta)^2}{(1 - \beta)^2 + 2\varepsilon(2 + d_2)^{-1}} < d_4 < \frac{1 + 2(1 + d_2)\varepsilon^{-1}(1 - \beta)^2}{(1 - \beta)^2} \tag{B7.15}$$

From (B7.7), (B7.9), (B7.10), (B7.12), (B7.14) and (B7.15) it can be seen that the optimal monetary regime from the perspective of the union depends upon how much weight is placed on the real wage target.

Loosely speaking as the union becomes more aggressive it moves from a nominal income rule to the fully discretionary regime. With a higher weight placed on the real wage target, the discretionary regime in turn is dominated by having an independent central bank. However, the latter regime becomes inferior to an inflation targeting regime if aggressiveness increases even further. This state of affairs is summarized in Table B7.1.

Table B7.1 The union's optimal monetary regime

d_4	$d_4 < d_{41}$	$d_{41} < d_4 < d_{42}$	$d_{42} < d_4 < d_{43}$	$d_4 > d_{43}$
Optimal Regime	N	D	I	P

where

$$d_{41} \equiv \frac{1}{(1 - \beta)^2 + 2\epsilon}, \quad d_{42} \equiv \frac{1 + \varepsilon^{-1}(1 - \beta)^2}{(1 - \beta)^2 + 2\varepsilon(2 + d_2)^{-1}}$$

and

$$d_{43} \equiv \frac{1 + 2(1 + d_2)\varepsilon^{-1}(1 - \beta)^2}{(1 - \beta)^2}$$

The intuition behind this result is straightforward. If the union becomes more aggressive it is more interested in purchasing power stabilization than in employment stabilization. Thus as the union becomes more aggressive it also becomes more inflation averse. The latter preferences are reflected in the choice of its optimal monetary regime.

APPENDIX C7: THE DERIVATION OF THE EXPECTED VALUE OF SOCIETY'S LOSS FUNCTION UNDER ANY ARBITRARY MONETARY POLICY REGIME

In this appendix following Rogoff (1985), pp. 1175—1176 we develop a notation for evaluating the expected value of society's loss function under any arbitrary monetary policy regime 'A', $E_{t-1} L_t^A$ (equation (7.44) of the text). Unemployment under regime A is given by

$$u_t^A = \tilde{u} - \frac{1}{1-\beta}(p_t^A - E_{t-1}p_t^A + \mu_t) \tag{C7.1}$$

Squaring and taking expectations yields

$$E_{t-1}(u_t^A)^2 = \tilde{u}^2 + E_{t-1}[\frac{\mu_t}{1-\beta} + \frac{1}{1-\beta}(p_t^A - E_{t-1}p_t^A)]^2 \tag{C7.2}$$

The price level under regime A can be expanded as

$$p_t^A = \tilde{p}_t^A + (p_t^A - E_{t-1}p_t^A) \tag{C7.3}$$

where $\tilde{p}_t^A$ is the mean (expected) price level in period t. Squaring and taking expectations in turn yields

$$E_{t-1}(p_t^A)^2 = (\tilde{p}_t^A)^2 + E_{t-1}(p_t^A - E_{t-1}p_t^A)^2 \tag{C7.4}$$

The expected value of society's loss function under regime A is

$$E_{t-1}L_t^A = \frac{1}{2}E_{t-1}(p_t^A)^2 + \frac{\varepsilon}{2}E_{t-1}(u_t^A)^2 \tag{C7.5}$$

Substituting (C7.2) and (C7.4) into (C7.5) one obtains equation (7.44) of the text.

APPENDIX D7: DERIVATION OF THE PROPERTIES OF THE FUNCTION $F(d_2)$ IN EQUATION (7.68)

1 Demonstration that $\partial F/\partial d_2 < 0$. The first derivative of F with respect to d_2 is given by

$$\frac{\partial F}{\partial d_2} = \frac{-3\tilde{u}^2\varepsilon[(1+d_2)(-\beta)^2+\varepsilon]^2}{\sigma_\mu^2(1-\beta)^4(1+d_2)^4} \tag{D7.1}$$

which is negative.

2 Demonstration that $\partial^2 F/\partial d_2^2 > 0$. The second derivative of F with respect to d_2 is given by

$$\frac{\partial^2 F}{\partial d_2^2} = \frac{6\tilde{u}^2\varepsilon\Gamma[\Gamma-\varepsilon]}{(1-\beta)^4(1+d_2)^5\sigma_\mu^2} \tag{D7.2}$$

where $\Gamma \equiv (1+d_2)(1-\beta)^2 + 2\varepsilon$, (D7.2) is positive.

3 Demonstration that $F(0) = [(1-\beta)^2+\varepsilon]^3\tilde{u}^2/(1-\beta)^4$. This can be shown by direct examination of the right-hand side of (7.69) at $d_2 = 0$.

4 Demonstration that $\tilde{u}^2(1-\beta)^2/\sigma_\mu^2 < F(d_2) < [(1-\beta)^2+\varepsilon]^3\tilde{u}^2/\sigma_\mu^2(1-\beta)^4$ Since $F(0) = [(1-\beta)^2+\varepsilon]^3\tilde{u}^2/\sigma_\mu^2(1-\beta)^4$, $\lim_{d_2\to\infty} F(d_2) = \tilde{u}^2(1-\beta)^2/\sigma_\mu^2$ and $\partial F/\partial d_2 < 0$, $F(d_2)$ must be bounded between $\tilde{u}^2(1-\beta)^2/\sigma_\mu^2$ and $F(0)$.

5 Demonstration that $\partial F/\partial d_4 > 0$. We can expand this derivative as $\partial F/\partial\tilde{u} \cdot \partial\tilde{u}/\partial d_4$. The first term is given by

$$\frac{\partial F}{\partial \tilde{u}} = \frac{2[(1+d_2)(1-\beta)^2+\varepsilon]^3}{\sigma_\mu^2(1-\beta)^4(1+d_2)^3}\tilde{u} \tag{D7.3}$$

whilst the second term is known from Section II.3

$$\frac{\partial \tilde{u}}{\partial d_4} = \frac{(1-\beta)[\tau + (1-\beta)\ell^*]}{[d_4(1-\beta)^2 + 1]^2} \tag{7.10}$$

Since both (D7.3) and (7.10) are positive the product $\partial F / \partial d_4$ is always positive.

NOTES

1. For instance see Issing (1993).
2. Funke shows that the optimal framework for monetary stability depends on the wage negotiation behaviour of the union, and, vice versa, that the wage formation process is influenced by the choice of the nominal anchor. However, Funke's modelling of the labour market is rudimentary using real output as a proxy for employment. Moreover, his ranking of monetary regimes is correct only under the assumption that supply shocks are zero.
3. In Chapter 4 we only address deviations of unemployment, i.e. we analyze the more simple case where $d_4 = 0$.
4. Actual output and employment will equal their natural rates when all expectations are fulfilled. Hence, the natural rate of employment equals $\tilde{\ell}$ and the natural rate of output is $\beta\tilde{\ell}$.
5. Price-level targeting and inflation-rate targeting are equivalent here, since p_{t-1} is known at the time the central bank commits itself to achieving a target for $p_t - p_{t-1}$. Once monetary control errors are taken into account it becomes important to make the distinction between a *zero inflation target* and a *target of price stability*. See Fischer (1994a, pp. 33-34).
6. For a review of some important concepts of game theory see Blackburn and Christensen (1989).
7. Following the terminology of Tinbergen (1966, p. 40) and Theil (1968, pp. 97-98) at this point the preferences of the union and the central bank are *consistent*. As emphasized by Englander (1990, pp. 20-21) the existence of *inconsistent* preferences is a necessary condition for the emergence of an inflationary bias. This will be shown in Section III.3.
8. $\tilde{u} \equiv \ell^s - \ell$. Upon normalizing ℓ^s at zero we get $\tilde{u} \equiv -\tilde{\ell}$.
9. According to Friedman (1994, p. 104) in the United States the Federal Reserve System first began to incorporate explicit money growth targets in its policymaking process in 1970, and since 1975 the Fed has been required under law to set such targets and to report regularly to Congress on its success or failure in meeting them. Since then the practical importance of money growth targets in U.S. monetary policy making has varied over time. As is well known the targets were especially important during the period of disinflationary monetary policy in 1979-1982.
10. For the derivation of the macro-economic results under any arbitrary monetary targeting regime see appendix A to this chapter.
11. $\frac{\partial[\beta\sigma_1^{-1}]}{\partial\sigma_1} = \frac{-\beta}{\sigma_1^2} < 0$
12. With β being about 0.7 and $\varepsilon = 1$. σ_1 must exceed 0.21 for this inequality to be

satisfied.

13. According to Issing (1994, p. 138) the main objections against GNP targeting - particularly from those implementing monetary policy - are the following. Movements in GNP are subject to a variety of influences. This means that at best central banks can only try and control such a variable over a period far in excess of a year. Consequently, it is likewise impossible to set targets for a manageable period and to use these to illustrate one's commitment to price stability. Another drawback of GNP targeting is that data about GNP are available only with a long lag.
14. As pointed out by Mullins (1994, p. 11) because of the long time lags between monetary policy actions and the impact on inflation, one has to be wary of policy induced amplification of cycles from inflation rate targeting. For empirical evidence on this danger see Judd and Motley (1991).
15. In Chapter 2 inflation targeting is parametrized within an optimal contract framework.
16. The rule is $m_t = 1/\sigma_1 (y_t - v_t)$ where y_t is determined by equation (7.7).
17. This result sheds some doubt on Freedman's (1994, p. 26) claim that inflation targets allow for a form of partial stabilization of output fluctuations.
18. For a recent discussion about the independence of the Bank of England and the associated inflation targeting framework see CEPR (1993).
19. See section IV.2.
20. For instance if $\frac{\sigma_1 \varepsilon - \beta(1-\beta)}{\beta(1-\beta)} < d_2 < \infty$ we get $E_{t-1}p_t^P < E_{t-1}p_t^N < E_{t-1}p_t^I < E_{t-1}p_t^M < E_{t-1}p_t^D$.
21. We derive equation (7.44) in appendix C7.
22. $\sigma_1 > \frac{\beta(1-\beta)}{\epsilon}$ if $\epsilon > \frac{\beta(1-\beta)}{\sigma_1}$. Since $\frac{\beta(1-\beta)}{\sigma_1} > \frac{(1-\beta)^2}{(1-\beta)[2\sigma_1 - 1] + \beta}$ the inequality of (7.49) also holds.
23. Remember from Table 7.1 that the natural rate of unemployment is considered to be inefficiently high if $\tilde{u} > u^*$. Where u^* is the central bank's unemployment target. Hence the extent of the inefficiency can be expressed in percentage points as $\tilde{u} - u^*$. Having normalized u^* at zero this inefficiency simplifies to $\tilde{u}$.
24. r_2 is the larger (positive) root of the polynomial $[\varepsilon - 2A(1-\beta)^2]d_2^2 + 2[\varepsilon - 2A(1-\beta)^2 - 2A\varepsilon]d_2 + [\varepsilon - 2A\{(1-\beta)^2 + 2\varepsilon\} - (2A-1)(1-\beta)^{-2}\varepsilon^2]$ which arises from the comparison of Γ^I and Γ^M. The reduced form parameter $A \equiv 1 + \varepsilon(\sigma_1 - 1)^2/2\hat{\beta}^2$. Using the same parameter values as before ($\beta = .7$, $\sigma_1 = .5$, $\varepsilon = 1$) $r_2 = 6.44$.
25. As pointed out by Rogoff (1985, p. 1178) it is extremely difficult to write down a closed form solution for d_2^*.
26. See equation (A7.3).
27. See also Carter and Maddock (1987), Tabellini (1988b) and Akhand (1992).
28. It is obtained by adding p_t on both sides of (7.21), setting $(y_t + p_t) = 0$ and rearranging terms.
29. For a discusion in which σ_1 is a reduced form parameter from an explicit IS - LM model, see Chapter 5.
30. Funke does not include central bank independence in his analysis.

8. Summary and Concluding Remarks

The proper conduct of macroeconomic stabilization policy poses a number of interesting questions. An important and time-honoured issue, particularly relevant for monetary policy, is the rules versus discretion debate. This debate has continued to echo through the history of central banking. In particular, it underlies the theoretical rationale for central bank independence.

Chapter 2 of this book surveys the rules versus discretion debate both from historical and analytical perspectives. We show that there are two major theoretical issues in the controversy. That is, those who favour rules have employed two kinds of arguments in order to demonstrate the undesirability of discretion in monetary policy.

The first argument, originating in the writings of Friedman, is that policymakers not bound by a rule would be tempted into *excess activism*, destabilizing rather than stabilizing the economy.

The second argument dates back to the introduction to the notion of *dynamic inconsistency* which importantly changed the debate. In game-theoretic models the inflationary bias of monetary policy made the case for a monetary rule. Alternatively the dynamic inconsistency problem may be overcome by setting up independent central banks. Granting more or less independence to the central bank is a way to organize institutions that decide on, and implement monetary policy.

The question that is addressed in Part I of the book (Chapters 3, 4, and 5) is whether the structure of these institutions matters for the choice of policy and economic performance.

In Chapter 3 we quantify central bank independence using a number of legal attributes from central bank laws. Twelve industrial countries are examined: Australia, Belgium, Canada, France, Germany, Italy, Japan, the Netherlands, the United Kingdom, the United States, Sweden and Switzerland. First we compare the measures (indices) of central bank independence as presented in the literature. After a critical examination of the existing indices we construct a new index of central bank independence, called the Eijffinger-Schaling (ES) index. According to this index, for example, central banks in which the only or main objective of monetary policy (as specified in the law) is price stability are classified as being more independent than central banks with a number of objectives in addition to price stability, or banks in whose law price stability is not mentioned as an objective at all.

According to the ES index the Deutsche Bundesbank, De Nederlandsche Bank and the Schweizerische Nationalbank turn out to be the most independent central banks. Intermediate institutions are the central banks of Belgium, France, Italy, Japan, the United Kingdom, the United States and Sweden. The Reserve Bank of Australia and the Bank of Canada are the least independent central banks.

In Chapter 3 central banks in which the only policy goal (as specified in the law) is price stability are classified as being more independent than central banks with a number of objectives in addition to price stability. Therefore in Chapter 4 following Kenneth Rogoff we define central bank independence as the strength of the 'conservative bias' of the central bank as embodied in the law. Hence we follow the *legislative* approach to price stability.

In this Chapter on the basis of a slightly modified version of the Rogoff model, we derive several propositions concerning the relationship between central bank independence and (the variance of) inflation and output growth. These propositions are tested for the same set of countries for the post-Bretton-Woods period (1972-1991). In testing the model we use the indices of central bank independence discussed in Chapter 3.

The main conclusions of this Chapter are the following. First of all, both our model and estimation results give further support to the well-known inverse relationship between the degree of central bank independence and the level of inflation found in the literature. However, it should be emphasized that these results are particularly sensitive to the numerical values of indices. Secondly, we find no empirical evidence that the more independent the central bank is, the lower the variability of inflation. Thirdly, no relationship can be found between central bank independence and the level of real output growth. Our interpretation of this outcome is that the attainment and maintenance of low inflation by an independent central bank is not accompanied by large costs or benefits in terms of sustainable economic growth. The absence of a long-run trade off between inflation and growth implies that the establishment of central bank independence is a free lunch. Fourthly and finally, our estimation results reject clearly a positive relation between independence and the variability of real output growth. An independent central bank does not lead to more variable economic growth in the short run. In other words, inflation-averse central banks do not bear the costs of triggering recessions nor do politically sensitive central banks reap the benefits of avoiding them.

For a closed economy the inflationary bias of governments may be explained by two arguments. The first argument, the employment motive for monetary expansion, is based on the assumption that political forces in democratic societies may be tempted to trade price stability for temporary decreases in unemployment. This argument underlies the models of Chapters 4, 6, and 7.

The second argument, the revenue motive for monetary expansion, focuses on the risk of the government exploiting the central bank's capacity to create seigniorage to finance expenditure that the goverment is unwilling to finance out of current or future taxation. Hence constraints on the amount of credit that the government can receive from the central bank have traditionally been considered an essential component of independence.

Chapter 5 analyses central bank independence in the coordination of monetary and fiscal policies. We show that greater economic independence of the central bank - i.e. lower monetary accommodation of government budget deficits - reduces inflation persistence. Thus lower inflation persistence may not only be caused by the *exchange-rate regime* - as shown by recent empirical research - but also by the way monetary and fiscal policy are coordinated, i.e. by the *domestic monetary regime.* Also our result can be viewed as a dynamic extension of the inverse relationship between central bank independence and the level of inflation.

As pointed out in Chapter 2, the dynamic inconsistency literature does not dispute the possibility of stabilizing activist feedback policy. The model of Chapter 4, being a slightly modified version of the Rogoff model, is a fine example of a model in which - dynamic inconsistency issues notwithstanding - there is an important role for activist stabilization policy. Rogoff demonstrates that society can make itself better off by selecting an agent to head the central bank who is known to place a greater weight on inflation stabilization (has a stronger 'conservative bias') than is embodied in the social loss function. However, because the central bank has private information about productivity shocks, it also pays for society to have the central bank partly accommodate these shocks before they pass on to inflation and unemployment. Hence, determining the optimal degree of central bank independence involves trading off the *credibility* gains associated with lower average inflation versus loss of *flexibility* due to a distorted response to output shocks.

In part II of the book (Chapters 6 and 7) we investigate how central banks and monetary regimes themselves change and develop in response to individual and collective beliefs, preferences and strategies. Both chapters are extensions of Chapter 4; the central or workhorse model of the book. In this part using a graphical method we develop a new way of determining the optimal degree of central bank independence. Unlike the existing literature, we are able to express the upper and lower bounds of the interval containing this degree in terms of the structural parameters of the model. Also we show how the optimal degree of central bank independence is conditioned on the extensions investigated in these chapters.

Chapter 6 extends Chapter 4 to allow for an inflation sensitive natural rate of growth. Hence, we integrate the longer-term relationship between inflation and growth into the literature on central bank independence. As the evidence points strongly to a predominantly inverse long-term relationship we assume that the supply-side effect of inflation is negative. We find that this effect reduces the inflationary bias of discretionary monetary policy and mitigates society's credibility problem. As society's optimal framework for monetary stability depends on the balance between credibility and flexibility we show that the higher the supply side effect of inflation, the *lower* the optimal degree of central bank independence. Hence the inflation growth nexus weakens the case for central bank independence.

In Chapter 7 we combine the model of Chapter 4 with labour union behaviour along the lines of New-Keynesian bargaining theories of unemployment. This is in order to integrate the study of monetary institu-tions with that of labour market institutions. The result is that the natural rate of unemployment becomes endogenous. We characterize wage setting in a totally unionized economy under a constant money supply rule, GNP targeting, full commitment to a simple zero inflation rule, a discretionary regime and an independent central bank. The wage formation strategy of the union can be either cooperative or aggressive. We show that the natural rate of unemployment becomes proportional to the aggression of the union. Since the natural rate of unemployment corresponds with the labour market distortion, we find that the more aggressive the union the higher the inflationary bias of discretionary monetary policy and the bigger society's credibility problem. With society's optimal framework for monetary stability depending on the balance between credibility and flexibility, we show that the more aggressive the union the *higher* the optimal degree of central bank independence.

With society's optimal central banking institution being contingent on the labour market regime, this Chapter stresses the recent insight that independence should be viewed as a preventive rather than a remedial device. Once high inflation has been allowed to develop, central bank independence alone does not suffice to extirpate it.

References

Akhand, H. (1992): 'Policy Credibility and Inflation in a Wage-Setting Game', *Canadian Journal of Economics*, XXV, No. 2, May, pp. 407-418.

Akhtar, M. and Howe H. (1991): 'The Political and Institutional Independence of U.S. Monetary Policy, *Banca Nazionale del Lavoro Quarterly Review*, No. 179, September, pp. 343-389.

Alesina, A. (1988): 'Macroeconomics and Politics', *NBER Macroeconomic Annual*, Cambridge.

Alesina, A. (1989): 'Politics and Business Cycles in Industrial Democracies', *Economic Policy*, No 8, April, pp. 55-98.

Alesina, A. and Grilli, V. (1992): 'The European Central Bank: Reshaping Monetary Politics in Europe', in Canzoneri, M. Grilli, V. and Masson, P. (eds): *'Establishing a Central Bank: Issues in Europe and Lessons form the United States'*, Cambridge University Press and CEPR.

Alesina, A. and Summers, L. (1993): 'Central Bank Independence and Macroeconomic Performance: Some Comparative Evidence', *Journal of Money, Credit, and Banking*, Vol. 25, No. 2, May, pp. 151-162.

Alesina, A. and Tabellini G. (1987): 'Rules and Discretion with Non-Coordinated Monetary and Fiscal Policies', *Economic Inquiry*, 25, pp. 619-630.

Alogoskoufis, G. (1992): 'Monetary Accommodation, Exchange Rate Regimes and Inflation Persistence', *The Economic Journal*, 102, May, pp. 461-480.

Alogoskoufis, S. (1994): 'On Inflation, Unemployment and the Optimal Exchange Rate Regime', in F. van der Ploeg (ed), *Handbook of International Macroeconomics*, Oxford, pp. 192-223.

Alogoskoufis, G. and Smith, R. (1991): 'The Phillips Curve, The Persistence of Inflation, and the Lucas Critique: Evidence from Exchange-Rate Regimes', *American Economic Review*, Vol. 81, No. 5, December.

Andersen, L. and Jordan, J. (1968): 'Monetary and Fiscal Actions: A Test of Their Relative Importance in Economic Stabilization', *Federal Reserve Bank of St. Louis Review*, November, pp. 11-24.

Ando, A. and Modigliani, F. (1965): 'The Relative Stability of Monetary Velocity and the Investment Multiplier', *American Economic Review*,

September, pp. 693-728.

Argy, V. (1988): 'A Post-War History of the Rules vs Discretion Debate', *Banca Nazionale del Lavoro Quarterly Review*, No. 165, June, pp. 147-177.

Aufricht, H. (1961): '*Central Banking Legislation*', The International Monetary Fund, Washington, D.C.

Aufricht, H. (1967): '*Central Banking Legislation*', Volume II: Europe, The International Monetary Fund, Washington D.C..

Backus, D. and Driffill, J. (1985): 'Inflation and Reputation', *American Economic Review*, 75, pp. 530-538.

Bade, R. and Parkin, M. (1988):'Central Bank Laws and Monetary Policy', Working Paper Department of Economics University of Western Ontario, October.

Barro, R. (1974): 'Are Government Bonds Net Wealth?', *Journal of Political Economy*, 82, pp. 1094-1117.

Barro, R. and Gordon D. (1983a): 'Rules, Discretion and Reputation in a Model of Monetary Policy', *Journal of Monetary Economics,* 12, pp. 101-122.

Barro, R. and Gordon D. (1983b): 'A Positive Theory of Monetary Policy in a Natural Rate Model', *Journal of Political Economy*, 91, pp. 589-610.

Bartlett, M. (1962): '*An Introduction to Stochastic Processes*', Cambridge.

Batten, D., Blackwell, M., Kim, I., Nocera, S. and Ozeki, Y. (1990), 'The Conduct of Monetary Policy in the Major Industrial Countries Instruments and Operating Procedures', *IMF Occasional Paper*, No. 70, July.

Bean, C. (1983): 'Targeting Nominal Income: An Appraisal', *The Economic Journal*, 93, pp. 806-819.

Berck, P. and Sydsaeter, K. (1991): '*Economists' Mathematical Manual*', Springer-Verlag.

Blackburn, K. and Christensen M. (1989): 'Monetary Policy and Policy Credibility: Theories and Evidence', *Journal of Economic Literature*, XXVII, pp. 1-45.

Blanchard, O. and Fischer S. (1989): '*Lectures on Macroeconomics*', MIT Press, Cambridge MA.

Blanchard, O. and Summers, L. (1986): 'Hysteresis and the European Unemployment Problem', in S. Fischer (ed), *NBER Macroeconomics Annual*, Cambridge.

Blinder, A. and Solow, R. (1974): 'Analytical Foundations of Fiscal Policy', in *The Economics of Public Finance*, Brookings Institution, Washington.

Blunden, G. (1990): 'The Role of the Central Bank', *The Julian Hodge Bank Annual Lecture*, Given at The University of Wales College of Cardiff, 14 February.

Bordo, M. and Schwartz, A. (1984): *A Retrospective on the Classical Gold Standard*, 1821-1931, Chicago.

Bouvier, J. (1988): 'The Banque de France and the State from 1850 to the present day', in: Toniolo G, (ed), *Central Banks' Independence in Historical Perspective*, Berlin/New York.

Brainard, W. (1967): 'Uncertainty and the Effectiveness of Policy', *American Economic Review, Papers and Proceedings*, 57, pp. 411-425.

Bresciani-Turoni, C. (1953): *The Economics of Hyperinflation*, London.

Brown, A. (1955): '*The Great Inflation, 1939-1951*', London.

Buiter, W. (1988): 'Death, Birth, Productivity Growth and Debt Neutrality', *The Economic Journal*, Vol. 98, pp. 279-293.

Cagan, P. (1956): 'The Monetary Dynamics of Hyperinflation', in M. Friedman (ed), *Studies in the Quantity Theory of Money*, Chicago.

Calvo, G. (1983): 'Staggered Prices in a Utility Maximizing Framework', *Journal of Monetary Economics*, 12, pp. 383-98.

Cairncross, A. (1988): 'The Bank of England: Relationships with the Government, the Civil Service, and Parliament', in Toniolo, G. (ed), *Central Banks' Independence in Historical Perspective*, Berlin/New York.

Canzoneri, M. (1985): 'Monetary Policy Games and the Role of Private Information', *American Economic Review*, 75, pp. 1056-1070.

Canzoneri, M. and Henderson D. (1991): *Monetary Policy in Interdependent Economies A Game-Theoretic Approach*, Cambridge.

Capie, F., Goodhart, C. and Schnadt, N. (1994): 'The Development of Central Banking', Monograph Prepared for the Tercentenary of the Bank of England Central Banking Symposium, 9 June.

Cargill (1989): *Central Bank Independence and Regulatory Responsibilities: The Bank of Japan and the Federal Reserve*, Salomon Brothers Center for the Study of Financial Institutions, Monograph Series in Finance and Economics.

Carlin, D. and Soskice, W. (1990): *Macroeconomics and the Wage Bargain*, Oxford.

Carlson, J. (1988): 'Rules vs Discretion: Making a Monetary Rule Operational', *Economic Review Federal Reserve Bank of Cleveland*, 24, No. 3, pp. 2-13.

Carter, M. and Maddock, R. (1987): 'Inflation the Invisible Foot of Macroeconomics', *The Economic Record*, June, pp. 120-128.

Centre for Economic Policy Research (1993): '*Independent and Accoun-*

table A New Mandate for the Bank of England', A Report of an Independent Panel Chaired by Eric Roll, October.

Chow, G. (1975): *Analysis and Control of Dynamical Systems*, New York.

Chowdhury, A. (1991): 'The Relationship between the Inflation Rate and its Variability: The Issues Reconsidered', *Applied Economics*, 23, pp. 993-1003.

Christ, C. (1967): 'A Short-Run Aggregate Demand-Model of the Interdependence of Monetary and Fiscal Policies with Keynesian and Classical Interest Elasticities', *American Economic Review*, Vol 57, May, pp. 434-443.

Christ, C. (1968): 'A Simple Macroeconomic Model with a Government Budget Restraint', *Journal of Political Economy*, Vol 76, pp. 53-67.

Commission of the European Communities (1989): 'One Market, One Money - An Evaluation of the Potential Benefits and Costs of Forming an Economic and Monetary Union', *European Economy*, No. 44, October.

Committee of Governors of the Central Banks of the Member States of the European Economic Community, (1991): *Draft Statute of the European System of Central Banks and of the European Central Bank*, April.

Corbo, V. and Rojas P. (1992): 'Latin America's Economic Growth', Paper presented at the IV Villa Mondragone International Economic Seminar, June 30 to July 2.

Cottarelli, C. (1993): 'Limiting Central Bank Credit to the Government Theory and Practice,' *IMF Occasional Paper*, No. 110, December.

Crockett, A. (1994): 'Rules versus Discretion in Monetary Policy', in Beaufort Wijnholds J.A.H. de, Eijffinger S. and Hoogduin L. (eds), *A Framework for Monetary Stability*, Kluwer Academic Publishers, Dordrecht, pp. 165-184.

Cuddy, D. (1974): *Quantitative Methods in Economics*, Rotterdam.

Cukierman, A. (1986): 'Central Bank Behavior and Credibility: Some Recent Theoretical Developments', *Federal Reserve Bank of St. Louis Review*, 68, May, pp. 5-17.

Cukierman, A. (1992): *Central Bank Strategy, Credibility and Independence Theory and Evidence*, MIT Press, Cambridge MA.

Cukierman, A. (1993): 'Central Bank Independence, Political Influence and Macroeconomic Performance: A Survey of Recent Developments,' *Cuadernos de Economía*, 30, No. 91, Diciembre, pp. 271-291.

Cukierman, A. (1994): 'Commitment through Delegation, Political Influence and Central Bank Independence' in Beaufort Wijnholds,

J.A.H. de, Eijffinger, S., and Hoogduin, L., (eds), *A Framework for Monetary Stability*, Kluwer Academic Publishers, Dordrecht, pp. 55-74.

Cukierman, A., Kalaitzidakis, P., Summers, L. and Webb S. (1993): 'Central Bank Independence, Growth, Investment and Real Rates', *Carnegie-Rochester Conference Series on Public Policy*, 39, pp. 95-140.

Cukierman, A. and Meltzer, A. (1986): 'A Theory of Ambiguity, Credibility, and Inflation under Discretion and Asymmetric Information', *Econometrica*, 54, pp. 1099-1128.

Cukierman, A., Webb S. and Neyapti, B. (1992): 'Measuring the Independence of Central Banks and its Effect on Policy Outcomes', *The World Bank Economic Review*, 6, pp. 353-398.

Debelle, G. and Fischer, S. (1994): 'How Independent Should A Central Bank Be?', Mimeo, MIT, April.

Eijffinger, S. (1986): *Over de beheersbaarheid van de geldhoeveelheid* (On the Controllability of the Money Supply) [Dutch], Amsterdam.

Eijffinger, S. (1991): 'The Convergence of Monetary Policy - Germany and France as an Example', Research Memorandum Department of Economics Tilburg University, No. 467, January.

Eijffinger, S. (1992): 'Convergence of Monetary Policies in Europe-Concepts, Targets and Instruments', in K. Gretschmann (ed.), *Economic and Monetary Union: Implications for National Policy Makers*, Martinus Nijhoff Publishers, Dordrecht/Boston/London, pp. 125-149.

Eijffinger, S. (1994): 'A Framework for Monetary Stability - General Report' in: Beaufort Wijnholds J.A.H. de, Eijffinger S. and Hoogduin L. (eds), *A Framework for Monetary Stability*, Kluwer Academic Publishers, Dordrecht, pp. 309-330.

Eijffinger, S. and Gerards J. (1990): *Financiële markten en monetair beleid- ervaringen in zeven landen* (Financial Markets and Monetary Policy - Experience in Seven Countries) [Dutch], Amsterdam.

Eijffinger, S. and de Haan, J. (1994): 'De Politieke Economie van Centrale Bank Onafhankelijkheid', *Rotterdamse Monetaire Studies*, Jaargang 13, No. 2.

Eijffinger, S. and van Keulen, M. (1994): 'Central Bank Independence in Another Eleven Countries', Discussion Paper CentER for Economic Research, No. 9494, November.

Eijffinger, S. and van Rixtel, A. (1992): 'The Japanese Financial System and Monetary Policy: a Descriptive Review', *Japan and the World Economy*, No. 4, pp. 291-309.

Eijffinger, S., van Rooij M. and Schaling, E. (1994): 'Central Bank Independence: A Paneldata Approach', Discussion Paper CentER for

Economic Research, No. 9493, November.

Eijffinger, S. and Schaling, E. (1992a): 'Central Bank Independence: Criteria and Indices', Research Memorandum Department of Economics Tilburg University, No. 548, March.

Eijffinger, S. and Schaling E. (1992b): 'Central Bank Independence: Searching for the Philosopher's Stone', Discussion Paper CentER for Economic Research, No. 9251, December.

Eijffinger, S. and Schaling E. (1993a): 'Central Bank Independence in Twelve Industrial Countries', *Banca Nazionale del Lavoro Quarterly Review*, No. 184, March, pp. 1-41.

Eijffinger, S. and Schaling, E. (1993b): 'Central Bank Independence: Theory and Evidence', Discussion Paper CentER for Economic Research, No. 9325, May.

Eijffinger, S. and Schaling, E. (1993c): 'Central Bank Independence: Searching for the Philosophers' Stone', in Fair, D.E. and Raymond, R.J. (eds.), *The New Europe: Evolving Economic and Financial Systems in East and West*, Kluwer Academic Publishers, Dordrecht, pp. 263-279.

Eijffinger, S. and Schaling, E. (1994): 'Central Bank Independence: Criteria and Indices', *Kredit und Kapital*, Vol. 27, Beihefte 13, pp. 185-217.

Eijffinger, S. and Schaling, E. (1995): 'The Ultimate Determinants of Central Bank Independence', Paper presented at the CentER Conference Positive Political Economy: Theory and Evidence, Tilburg, January, 23-24.

Eizenga, W. (1983): 'The Independence of the Federal Reserve System and of the Netherlands Bank: a Comparative Analysis, *SUERF Papers on Monetary Policy and Financial Systems*, No. 41a.

Eizenga, W. (1987): 'The Independence of the Deutsche Bundesbank and the Nederlandsche Bank with Regard to Monetary Policy A Comparative Study', *SUERF Papers on Monetary Policy and Financial Systems*, No. 2.

Eizenga, W. (1990): 'The Banque de France and Monetary Policy', *SUERF Papers on Monetary Policy and Financial Systems*, No. 8.

Eizenga, W. (1991): 'The Bank of England and Monetary Policy', *SUERF Papers on Monetary Policy and Financial Systems*, No. 10.

Englander, A. (1990): 'Optimal Monetary Policy Design: Rules versus Discretion Again', Research Paper Federal Reserve Bank of New York, August.

Ewijk, C. van (1991): *On the Dynamics of Growth and Debt*, Clarendon Press, Oxford.

Fair, D. (1979): 'The Independence of Central Banks', *The Banker*,

October, pp. 31-41.

Fair, D. (1980): Relationships Between Central Banks and Governments in the Determination of Monetary Policy', *SUERF Working Paper.*

Federal Reserve Bank of Kansas City (1990): 'Central Banking Issues in Emerging Market-Oriented Economies', *Federal Reserve Bank of Kansas City Symposium Series*, Kansas City.

Federal Reserve Bulletin, Federal Reserve Board, Washington D.C. (1977), December.

Ferguson, B. and Gupta, K. (1981): 'On the Dynamics of Inflation and Unemployment in a Quantity Theory Framework', *Economica*, 181, No. 46, pp. 51-59.

Fischer, S. (1977a): 'Wage Indexation and Macroeconomic Stability', *Carnegie Rochester Conference Series on Public Policy*, 5, pp. 107-147.

Fischer, S. (1977b): 'Long-Term Contracts, Rational Expectations, and the Optimal Money Supply Rule', *Journal of Political Economy*, 85, pp. 191-205.

Fischer, S. (1990): 'Rules versus Discretion in Monetary Policy', in *Handbook of Monetary Economics*, Amsterdam, pp. 1156-1184.

Fischer, S. (1991): 'Growth, Macroeconomics and Development', *NBER Macroeconomic Annual*, pp. 329-379.

Fischer, S. (1992): 'Growth: the Role of Macroeconomic Factors.', Paper presented at the IV Villa Mondragone International Economic Seminar, June 30 to July 2.

Fischer, S. (1993): 'The Role of Macroeconomic Factors in Growth', *Journal of Monetary Economics*, 32, No. 3, December, pp. 485-512.

Fischer, S. (1994a): 'The Costs and Benefits of Disinflation', in Beaufort Wijnholds, J.A.H. de, Eijffinger, S. and Hoogduin L. (eds), *A Framework for Monetary Stability*, Kluwer Academic Publishers, Dordrecht, pp. 31-42.

Fischer, S. (1994b): 'Modern Central Banking', Monograph Prepared for the Tercentenary of the Bank of England Central Banking Symposium, 9 June.

Fisher, I. (1945): *100 % Money*, City Printing Company, New Haven.

Fisher, I. (1973): 'A Statistical Relation between Unemployment and Price Changes', *International Labour Review*, 13, June 1926, pp. 785-792. Reprinted as 'I Discovered the Phillips Curve', *Journal of Political Economy*, 81, March April, pp. 496-502

Flanders, J. (1990): 'Rules versus Rules under the Gold Standard Peel's Act (The Bank Act of 1844), the Cunliffe Committee and the Bank of England', Working Paper Tel-Aviv University, No. 18-90, August.

Flood, R. and Isard, P. (1989): 'Monetary Policy Strategies', *IMF Staff*

Papers, 36, No. 3, September.
Freedman, J. (1994): 'Formal Targets for Inflation Reduction: The Canadian Experience' in: Beaufort Wijnholds, J.A.H. de, Eijffinger, S. and Hoogduin, L. (eds) *A Framework for Monetary Stability,* Kluwer Academic Publishers, Dordrecht, pp. 17-29.
Friedman, B. (1994): 'Intermediate Targets versus Information Variables as Operating Guides for Monetary Policy in: Beaufort Wijnholds, J.A.H. de, Eijffinger, S. and Hoogduin, L.(eds), *A Framework for Monetary Stability*, Kluwer Academic Publishers, Dordrecht, pp. 109-133.
Friedman, M. (1948): 'A Monetary and Fiscal Framework for Economic Stability', Reprinted in *Essays in Positive Economics.*
Friedman, M. (1953): 'The Effects of a Full-Employment Policy on Economic Stability; A Formal Analysis', in *Essays in Positive Economics*, Chicago University Press, Chicago.
Friedman, M. (1959): '*A Program for Monetary Stability*', Fordham University Press, New York.
Friedman. M. (1968): 'The Role of Monetary Policy', *The American Economic Review*, 68, March, pp. 1-17.
Friedman, M. (1969): 'The Lag in Effect of Monetary Policy', in M. Friedman, *The Optimum Quantity of Money*, Aldine, Chicago.
Friedman, M. and Meiselman, D. (1963): 'The Relative Stability of Monetary Velocity and the Investment Multiplier in the United States 1897-1958', in *Stabilization Policies*, Englewood Cliffs.
Friedman, M. and Schwartz, A. (1963): '*A Monetary History of the United States*, 187-1960', Princeton University Press, Princeton.
Funke, N. (1994) 'Centralized Wage Setting under Alternative Monetary Policy Rules', *De Economist*, 142, No. 3, August, pp. 327-339.
Gandolfo, G. (1983): '*Economic Dynamics: Methods and Models*', Amsterdam.
Goodhart, C. (1993): 'Central Bank Independence', LSE Financial Markets Group Special Paper Series, November.
Goodhart, C. (1994): 'Game Theory for Central Bankers: A Report to the Governor of the Bank of England', *Journal of Economic Literature*, XXXII, March.
Grauwe, P. de, and Papademos, L. (1990): *The European Monetary System in the 1990s*, Harlow.
Gray, J. (1976): 'Wage Indexation: A Macroeconomic Approach', *Journal of Monetary Economics*, 2, pp. 221-235.
Grier, K. and Tullock, G. (1989): 'An Empirical Analysis of Cross-national Economic Growth, 1951-1980, *Journal of Monetary Economics*, 24, September, pp. 259-276.

Grilli, V., Masciandaro, D. and Tabellini, G. (1991): 'Political and Monetary Institutions and Public Financial Policies in the Industrial Countries', *Economic Policy*, Vol. 6, No. 13, October, pp. 342-392.

Grimes, A. (1991): 'The Effects of Inflation on Growth: Some International Evidence.', *Weltwirtschaftliches Archiv*, 127, Heft 4, pp. 631-644.

Haan, J. de and Sturm, J. (1992): 'The Case for Central Bank Independence' *Banca Nazionale del Lavoro Quarterly Review*, Vol. 45, No. 182, September, pp. 305-327.

Havrilesky, T. (1987): 'A Partisanship Theory of Fiscal and Monetary Regimes', *Journal of Money, Credit and Banking*, 19, pp. 308-325.

Hetzel, R. (1985): 'The Rules versus Discretion Debate over Monetary Policy in the 1920s', *Economic Review Federal Reserve Bank of Richmond*, November-December, pp. 3-14.

Hetzel, R. (1990): 'Independence in Historical Perspective: a Review Essay', *Journal of Monetary Economics*, Vol 25, January, pp. 165-176.

Hibbs, D. (1977): 'Political Parties and Macroeconomic Policy', *The American Political Science Review*, 71, December, pp. 1467-1487.

Holmes, J. and Smyth, D. (1970): 'The Relation between Unemployment and Excess Demand for Labour: An Examination of the Theory of the Phillips Curve', *Economica*, August, pp. 311-315.

Hume, D. (1875): 'Political Discourses', 1752a, in *Essays, Moral, Political and Literary*, London.

Hume, D. (1955): 'Of Money', 1752b, Reprinted in his '*Writings on Economics*'. Rotwein, E. (ed), Madison.

Humphrey, T. (1985): 'The Early History of the Phillips Curve', *Economic Review Federal Reserve Bank of Richmond*, September/October, pp. 17-24.

Humprey, T. (1988): 'Rival Notions of Money', *Economic Review Federal Reserve Bank of Richmond*, September-October, pp. 3-9.

Issing, O. (1993): 'Central Bank Independence and Monetary Stability', Institute of Economic Affairs, Occasional Paper, No. 89.

Issing, O. (1994): 'Monetary Policy Strategy in the EMU' in: Beaufort Wijnholds, J.A.H. de, Eijffinger, S. and Hoogduin, L. (eds), *A Framework for Monetary Stability*, Kluwer Academic Publishers, Dordrecht, pp. 135-152.

Jarrett, J. and Selody, J. (1982): 'The Productivity-Inflation Nexus in Canada 1963-1979.', *Review of Economics and Statistics*, 64, August, pp. 361-367.

Jong De, A. (1960): *De wetgeving nopens de Nederlandsche Bank 1814-1958*, Den Haag.

Jong, F. de and Ploeg, F. van der (1993): 'Seigniorage, Taxes, Government Debt and the EMS', CentER Discussion Paper, No. 9134, February.

Judd, J. and Motley B. (1991): 'Nominal Feedback Rules for Monetary Policy', *Federal Reserve Bank of San Francisco Economic Review,* Summer, pp. 3-17.

Keller, R. and Revier, C. (1981): 'The Hazards of a Monetarist Rule Extended', *Southern Economic Journal*, 47, No. 3, January, pp. 824-830.

Keuzenkamp, H. (1991): 'A Precursor to Muth: Tinbergen's 1932 Model of Rational Expectations', *The Economic Journal*, 101, No. 408, September, pp. 1245-1253.

Klein, L. and Goldberger, A. (1955): *An Econometric Model of the United States 1929-1952*, Amsterdam.

Klein, M. and Neumann, M. (1990): 'Seigniorage What Is It And Who Gets It?', *Weltwirtschaftliches Archiv*, Band 126, Heft 2, pp. 205-21.

Koch, H. (1983): *L'histoire de la Banque de France et de la monnaie sous la quartieme Republique*, Paris.

Kormendi, R. and Meguire, P. (1985): 'Macroeconomic Determinants of Growth: Cross-Country Evidence', *Journal of Monetary Economics*, 16, September, pp. 141-163.

Krooss, H. and P. Samuelson, (1969):'*Documentary History of Banking and Currency in the USA*', Vol. 4, New York.

Kreps, D. and Wilson, R. (1982a): 'Sequential Equilibrium', *Econometrica*, Vol. 50, pp. 863-894.

Kreps, D. and Wilson, R. (1982b): 'Reputation and Imperfect Information', *Journal of Economic Theory*, Vol. 27, pp. 352-379.

Kretzmer, P. (1992): 'Monetary vs. Fiscal Policy: New Evidence on an Old Debate', *Economic Review Federal Reserve Bank of Kansas City*, Vol. 77, No 2, Second Quarter, pp. 21-30.

Kydland, F. and Prescott, E. (1977): 'Rules Rather than Discretion: The Inconsistency of Optimal Plans', *Journal of Political Economy*, 85, No. 3, June, pp. 473-492.

Lerner, A. (1944): *The Economics of Control*, New York.

Levine, P. and Pearlman, J. (1994): 'Labour Market Structure, Conservative Bankers and the Feasibility of Monetary Union', Discussion Paper Centre for Economic Policy Research, No. 903, February.

Levine, R. and Renelt, D. (1992): 'A Sensitivity Analysis of Cross-Country Growth Regressions', *American Economic Review*, 82, No. 4, September, pp. 942-963.

Lindbeck, A. and Snower D. (1986): 'Wage Setting, Unemployment and Insider-Outsider Relations', *American Economic Review*, Papers and

Proceedings, 76, pp. 235-239.

Lippi, F. and Swank, O. (1994): 'On the Optimal Degree of Central Bank Independence: Trading Off Credibility versus Flexibility', Working Paper Erasmus University Rotterdam, May.

Lipsey, R. (1960): 'The Relationship Between Unemployment and the Rate of Change of Money Wages in the UK 1861-1957: A Further Analysis', *Economica*, 27, pp. 1-31.

Lohmann, S. (1990): 'Monetary Policy Strategies - A Correction', *IMF Staff Papers*, 37, No. 2, June.

Lohmann, S. (1992): 'Optimal Commitment in Monetary Policy, *American Economic Review*, 82, pp. 273-286.

Long De, J. and Summers, L. (1992): 'Macroeconomic Policy and Long-Run Growth', *Economic Review Federal Reserve Bank of Kansas City*, 77, pp. 5-29.

Lucas, R. (1973): 'Some International Evidence on Output-Inflation Trade-Offs', *American Economic Review*, 63, pp. 326-334.

Lucas, R. (1973): 'Some International Evidence on Output-Inflation Trade-Offs', *American Economic Review*, Vol. 63, pp. 326-334.

Lucas, R. (1976): 'Econometric Policy Evaluation: A Critique', *Carnegie Rochester Conference Series on Public Policy*, 1, pp. 19-46.

Mascaro, A. and Meltzer A. (1983): 'Long- and Short-Term Interest Rates in a Risky World', *Journal of Monetary Economics*, 12, pp. 485-518.

Masciandaro, D. and Tabellini, G., (1988): 'Fiscal Deficits and Monetary Institutions: a Comparative Analysis', in H. Cheng (ed), *Challenges to Monetary Policy in the Pacific Basin Countries*, Amsterdam.

Mayer, T. (1990) (ed): '*The Political Economy of American Monetary Policy*', Cambridge.

McCallum, B. (1987): 'The Case for Rules in the Conduct of Monetary Policy: A Concrete Example', *Economic Review Federal Reserve Bank of Richmond*, September/October, pp. 10-18.

McMillin, D. and Smyth, D.: 'A Multivariate Time Series Analysis of the Aggregate Production Function', *Empirical Economics* (forthcoming).

Miller, P. (1983): 'Higher Deficit Policies Lead to Higher Inflation', *Quarterly Review Federal Reserve Bank of Minneapolis*, 7, pp. 8-19.

Minford, P. (1993): 'Time-Inconsistency, Democracy and Optimal Contingent Rules', Discussion Paper Centre for Economic Policy Research, No. 767, February.

Mishkin, F. (1992): *The Economics of Money, Banking, and Financial Markets*, New York.

Mullins, D. (1994), 'Keynote Speech by the Vice Chairman of the

Federal Reserve Board: A Framework for Monetary Stability - A Policy Maker's Perspective' in: Beaufort Wijnholds, de J.A.H., Eijffinger, S. and Hoogduin, L. (eds) *A Framework for Monetary Stability*, 1993, Kluwer Academic Publishers, Dordrecht, pp. 5-15.

Mundell, R. (1963): 'Inflation and Real Interest', *Journal of Political Economy*, 71, pp. 280-283.

Muth, J. (1961): 'Rational Expectations and the Theory of Price Movements', *Econometrica*, 29, pp. 315-335.

Nardozzi, G. (1988): 'A Central Bank between the Government and the Credit System: The Bank of Italy after World War II', in Toniolo, G. (ed), *Central Banks' Independence in Historical Perspective*, Berlin/New York.

Neumann, M. (1991): 'Precommitment by Central Bank Independence', *Open Economies Review*, 2, pp. 95-112.

Persson, T. and Tabellini, G. (1990): '*Macroeconomic Policy, Credibility and Politics*', Harwood Academic Publishers, London.

Persson, T. and Tabellini, G. (1993): 'Designing Institutions for Monetary Stability', *Carnegie-Rochester Conference Series on Public Policy*, 39, pp. 53-84.

Phelps, E. (1968): 'Money-wage Dynamics and Labour Market Equilibrium', *Journal of Political Economy*, 76, August, pp. 678-711.

Phillips, A. (1954): 'Stabilisation Policies in a Closed Economy', *The Economic Journal*, 64, pp. 290-323.

Phillips, A. (1957): 'Stabilisation Policies and the Time Form of Lagged Responses', *The Economic Journal*, 67, pp. 265-277.

Phillips, A. (1958): 'The Relation Between Unemployment and the Rate of Change of Money Wage Rates in the United Kingdom, 1861-1957', *Economica*, 25, pp. 283-299.

Ploeg, F. van der (1991): 'Unanticipated Inflation and Government Finance: The Case for an Independent Common Central Bank', CentER Discussion Paper, No. 9115, April.

Poole, W. (1970): 'Optimal Choice of Monetary Policy Instruments in a Simple Stochastic Macro Model', *Quarterly Journal of Economics*, 84, pp. 197-216.

Radcliffe Report (1959): *The Committee on the Working of the Monetary System: Report*, Cmnd. 827, HMSO: London.

Raith, M. (1993): 'Fiscal Flexibility and the Optimal Degree of Central Bank Independence', Discussion Paper Universität Bielefeld No. 278, September.

Rich, G. (1989): 'Central Bank Autonomy: A Swiss Perspective', Paper Presented at the Seminar on Central Bank Experiences, Santiago Chile, March 31.

Rogoff, K. (1985): 'The Optimal Degree of Commitment to an Intermediate Monetary Target', *Quarterly Journal of Economics*, 100, pp. 1169-1190.

Rudebusch, G. and Wilcox, D. (1994) 'Productivity and Inflation: Evidence and Interpretations', Mimeo, Federal Reserve Board, Washington DC, April.

Samuelson, P. and Solow, R. (1960): 'Analytical Aspects of Anti-inflation Policy', *American Economic Review*, May, pp. 177-194.

Sargent, T. (1973): 'Rational Expectations, the Real Rate of Interest, and the Natural Rate of Unemployment', *Brookings Papers on Economic Activity*, No. 2, pp. 429-480.

Sargent, T. and Wallace, N. (1975): 'Rational Expectations, the Optimal Monetary Instrument, and the Optimal Money Supply Rule', *Journal of Political Economy*, Vol. 83, pp. 241-254.

Sargent, T. and Wallace, N. (1984): 'Some Unpleasant Monetarist Arithmetic' in Griffiths, B. and Wood, G. (eds), *Monetarism in the UK*, London pp. 42-60, reprinted from *Federal Reserve Bank of Minneapolis Quarterly Review* (1981), Vol. 5, Fall, pp. 1-17.

Schaling, E. (1993), 'On the Economic Independence of the Central Bank and the Persistence of Inflation, Discussion Paper CentER for Economic Research, No. 9336, June.

Schaling, E. and Smyth, D. (1994): 'The Effects of Inflation on Growth and Fluctuations in Dynamic Macroeconomic Models', Discussion Paper CentER for Economic Research, No. 9439, May.

Shigehara, K. (1992): 'Causes of Declining Growth in Industrialized Countries', in *Policies for Long-run Economic Growth in Industrialized Countries*, Kansas City: Federal Reserve Bank of Kansas, pp. 15-39.

Sijben, J. (1990): 'Geloofwaardigheid en monetaire politiek', *Rotterdamse Monetaire Studies*, No. 38.

Sijben, J. (1992): 'Monetary Policy in a Game Theoretic Framework', *Jahrbücher fur Nationalökonomie und Statistik*, Bd. 210, No. 3-4, pp. 233-253.

Sijben, J. (1994): 'Regels versus activisme in de monetaire politiek opnieuw bezien' (Dutch), Working Paper Tilburg University.

Skanland, H. (1984): *The Central Bank and Political Authorities in Some Industrial Countries*, Oslo.

Simons, H. (1948): *Economic Policy for a Free Society*, Chicago.

Simons, H. (1936): 'Rules versus Authorities in Monetary Policy', *Journal of Political Economy*, Vol. 44, No. 1, pp. 1-30.

Smyth, D. (1992): 'Inflation and the Growth Rate in the United States' Natural Output', *Applied Economics*, 24, pp. 567-570.

Smyth, D. (1993): 'Energy Prices and the Aggregate Production Function', *Energy Economics*, 15, April, pp. 105-110.

Smyth, D. (1994a): 'Inflation and Growth', *Journal of Macroeconomics*, 16, Spring, pp. 261-270.

Smyth, D. (1994b): 'The Supply Side Effects of Inflation in the United States: Evidence from Multifactor Productivity', Working Paper Louisiana State University.

Smyth, D. (1994c): 'Inflation and Total Factor Productivity in Germany', Working Paper Louisiana State Univerisity.

Smyth, D. (1994d): 'The Phillips' Curve', Mimeo, forthcoming as Chapter 11 in Smyth, D.: *Macroeconomics*, West Publishers.

Stanners, W. (1993): 'Is Low Inflation an Important Condition for High Growth?', *Cambridge Journal of Economics*, 17, March, pp. 79-107.

Stevenson, A., Muscatelli, V. and Gregory, M. (1988): '*Macroeconomic Theory and Stabilisation Policy*', Oxford.

Stock, J. and Watson M. (1988): 'Variable Trends in Economic Time Series', *Journal of Economic Perspectives*, 2, pp. 147-174.

Sultan, P. (1957): *Labor Economics*, New York.

Suzuki, Y. (1987): *The Japanese Financial System*, Oxford.

Swinburne, M. and Castello-Branco, M. (1991): 'Central Bank Independence: Issues and Experience', IMF Working Paper, No. 58.

Tabellini, G. (1988a): 'Monetary and Fiscal Policy Coordination with a High Public Debt', in Giavazzi, F. and Spaventa, L. (eds), *High Public Debt: The Italian Experience*, Cambridge.

Tabellini, G. (1988b): 'Centralized Wage Setting and Monetary Policy in a Reputational Equilibrium', *Journal of Money, Credit and Banking*, Vol. 20, No. 1, February, pp. 102-118.

Taylor, J. (1982): 'Macroeconomic Tradeoffs in an International Economy with Rational Expectations', in Hildenbrand, W. (ed), *Advances in Economic Theory*, Cambridge, pp. 235-252.

Taylor, J. (1985): 'What would Nominal GNP Targeting do to the Business Cycle' in *Carnegie-Rochester Conference Series on Public Policy*, Vol. 22, pp. 61-84.

Theil, H. (1968): *Optimal Decision Rules for Government and Industry*, Second Edition, Amsterdam.

Thornton, H. (1939): *An Enquiry into the Nature and Effects of the Paper Credit of Great Britain*, 1802, Edited with an introduction by F. A. von Hayek, New York.

Tinbergen, J. (1932): 'Ein Problem der Dynamik', *Zeitschrift fur Nationalokonomie*, III. Bd, 2.H., pp. 169-184.

Tinbergen, J. (1951): *Businnes Cycles in the United Kingdom, 1870-1914*, Amsterdam.

Tinbergen, J. (1959): *An Economic Policy for 1936*. reprinted in his 'Selected Papers', Klaassen, L., Koyck, L. and Witteveen, J. (eds), Amsterdam.

Tinbergen, J. (1966): *On the Theory of Economic Policy*, Fourth Edition, Amsterdam.

Tobin, J. (1965): 'Money and Economic Growth', *Econometrica*, 33, pp. 671-684.

Tobin, J. (1983): 'Monetary Policy: Rules Targets, and Shocks', *Journal of Money, Credit, and Banking*, pp. 506-518.

Tobin, J. (1990): 'On the Theory of Macroeconomic Policy', *De Economist*, 138, No. 1, pp. 1-14.

Turnovsky, S.J. (1977): *Macroeconomic Analysis and Stabilisation Policy*, Cambridge.

Ungerer, H. (1990): 'The EMS, 1979-1990, Policies-Evolution-Outlook', *Konjunkturpolitik*, 36, Heft 6, pp. 329-362.

Walsh, C. (1993): 'Optimal Contracts for Independent Central Bankers: Private Information, Performance Measures and Reappointment', Working Paper 93-02, Federal Reserve Bank of San Francisco, May.

Wheelock, D. (1992): 'Monetary Policy in the Great Depression: What the Fed Did, and Why', *Federal Reserve Bank of St. Louis Review*, March/April, pp. 3-28.

White, L. (1984): *Free Banking in Britain*, Cambridge University Press.

Wilson, J. (1952): 'The Commonwealth Bank of Australia' in Sayers, R.S (ed.), *Banking in the British Commonwealth*, Oxford, pp. 39-99.

Wilson, J. (1962): 'France', in Sayers, R.S. (ed.), *Banking in Western Europe*, Oxford, pp. 1-52.

Index